Navigating Terrains of War

Methodology and History in Anthropology

General Editor: David Parkin, Director of the Institute of Social and Cultural Anthropology, University of Oxford

Volume 1
Marcel Mauss: A Centenary Tribute
Edited by Wendy James and N.J. Allen

Volume 2
Franz Baerman Steiner: Selected Writings
Volume I: Taboo, Truth and Religion. Franz B. Steiner
Edited by Jeremy Adler and Richard Fardon

Volume 3
Franz Baerman Steiner. Selected Writings
Volume II: Orientalism, Value, and Civilisation. Franz B. Steiner
Edited by Jeremy Adler and Richard Fardon

Volume 4
The Problem of Context
Edited by Roy Dilley

Volume 5
Religion in English Everyday Life
By Timothy Jenkins

Volume 6
Hunting the Gatherers: Ethnographic Collectors, Agents and Agency in Melanesia, 1870s–1930s
Edited by Michael O'Hanlon and Robert L. Welsch

Volume 7
Anthropologists in a Wider World: Essays on Field Research
Edited by Paul Dresch, Wendy James and David Parkin

Volume 8
Categories and Classifications: Maussian Reflections on the Social
By N.J. Allen

Volume 9
Louis Dumont and Hierarchical Opposition
By Robert Parkin

Volume 10
Categories of Self: Louis Dumont's Theory of the Individual
By André Celtel

Volume 11
Existential Anthropology: Events, Exigencies and Effects
By Michael Jackson

Volume 12
An Introduction to Two Theories of Social Anthropology: Descent Groups and Marriage Alliance. Louis Dumont
Edited and Translated by Robert Parkin

Volume 13
Navigating Terrains of War: Youth and Soldiering in Guinea-Bissau
By Henrik Vigh

NAVIGATING TERRAINS OF WAR

Youth and Soldiering in Guinea-Bissau

Henrik Vigh

Berghahn Books
New York • Oxford

First published in 2006 by
Berghahn Books
www.berghahnbooks.com

©2006, 2007 Henrik Vigh
Paperback edition reprinted in 2007

All rights reserved. Except for the quotation of short passages for the purposes of criticism and review, no part of this book may be reproduced in any form or by any means, electronic or mechanical, including photocopying, recording, or any information storage and retrieval system now known or to be invented, without written permission of the publisher.

Library of Congress Cataloging-in-Publication Data

Vigh, Henrik, 1969-
Navigating terrains of war : youth and soldiering in Guinea-Bissau / Henrik Vigh.
p. cm. – (Methodology and history in anthropology ; v. 13)
Includes bibliographical references and index.
ISBN 1-84545-148-1 – ISBN 1-84545-149-X (pbk.)
1. Children and war—Guinea-Bissau. 2. Child soldiers—Guinea-Bissau.
3. Urban youth—Guinea-Bissau. 4. Veterans—Social networks—Guindea-Bissau.
5. War and Society—Guinea-Bissau. 6. Social status—Guinea-Bissau. I. Title.
II Series.
HQ784.W3V54 2006
306.6'40835096657049—dc22 2006040110

British Library Cataloguing in Publication Data

A catalogue record for this book is available from the British Library

Printed in United States on acid-free paper

ISBN 1-84545-148-1 hardback
ISBN 1-84545-149-X paperback

For I.E. Vigh

CONTENTS

Acknowledgements	ix
PART I INTRODUCTION	
1. Mbuli the Victorious: The Micro-history of an Aguenta	3
2. Perspectives and Positions	10
PART II THE AGUENTAS	
3. Becoming Aguentas	39
4. Wars without Enemies	64
PART III SOCIAL NAVIGATION	
5. The Social Moratorium of Youth	89
6. Dubriagem and Social Navigation: Constructing Social Trajectories through War	117
PART IV ON SHIFTING GROUND	
7. Inhabiting Unstable Terrains: The Everyday of Decline and Conflict	143
8. From Negritude to Ineptitude: On Horizons and Broken Imaginaries	173
PART V IN APPEASEMENT?	
9. Recategorising Men as Children: Bottom-up Reconciliation	219
10. Closure	234
Bibliography	241
Index	253

ACKNOWLEDGEMENTS

Contrary to much other research, doing anthropology is not a solitary, isolated endeavour. It builds on encounters and dialogue, and in this respect the book belongs as much to others as to myself. Among these, special recognition must go to Laura Gilliam, Susan R. Whyte and Michael Jackson. Their tireless aid, critique and support have been inestimable. I furthermore address my thanks to Sally Anderson, Jens Guldager, Turf Böcker Jakobsen, Peter Hansen, Henrik Rønsbo, Oleg Koefoed, Kåre Jansbøl and the Bandim war group, who have all contributed to the dissertation through judicious comments and constructive criticism. I also owe much gratitude to the warm friendship of Fransisco Jorge Da Costa, Quintino Có, Nita Nielsen, Vladimir Cá and Tio Bubacar Baldé, who made the fieldwork enjoyable and the ethnography rich. Finally I wish to thank the Department of Anthropology, University of Copenhagen, Peter Åby, the staff at Projecto Saúde Bandim, the Council for Development Research (RUF) and the Social Scientific Research Council (SSF) for financial and institutional support.

PART I

INTRODUCTION

Chapter 1

MBULI THE VICTORIOUS

THE MICRO-HISTORY OF
AN AGUENTA

As Brigadier Asumané Mané lost his life, Mbuli regained his social status. In his uniform, leaning against the small wall surrounding Nti's house, he was aglow with pride. Almost boastful in posture, his bearing symbolised the transformation from despondent loser to astute, triumphant young man. Mbuli was answering questions about what had really happened during the last few weeks of fighting and political uncertainty: who was allied with whom, how such and such person had fared and, not least, what had happened to the ex-Brigadier.

When I first met Mbuli he was sitting in the yard, behind his uncle's house, drinking palm wine with friends. It had been late in the morning and yet Mbuli was already in such a state that I remember wanting to leave rather than hang around trying to extract data from the stream of drunken drivel. As the months passed things had not improved, and, after an incident involving Mbuli, too much alcohol, a gun and a taxi-driver, I had written him off as a safe, let alone useful, informant. That is, until I saw him here. Becoming victorious was a radical transformation, a complete metamorphosis of social being.

This book is about urban youth caught in the conflict and turmoil of the small West African country of Guinea-Bissau.[1] Or, rather, it is about the Aguentas, a militia of young men recruited during the civil war from 1998 to 1999 and their attempt at securing a tolerable life for themselves within the difficult social and political situation in Guinea-Bissau. Contrary to most academic work on war or political strife it is thus not about what in Creole is called *homi garandis*, big men, but rather about the 'small men' that do the actual fighting (see Bayart 1993, Peters and Richards 1998). It is about youth trying to survive and forge a future in the space of political quarrels and conflicts – a topic within which Mbuli constitutes an exceptionally good example.

Though the complex life of Mbuli cannot be reduced to type or generality, his way of creating a path through the movement of Guinean society is representative of the majority of my informants' attempts at steering their lives through the decline and conflict they found themselves part of. Thus, it is not Mbuli's complex life, which is representative of my other informants' lives but his attempts at navigating in and through Guinean society within the last couple of years of turmoil and conflict.

Mbuli as Aguenta

Mbuli had left Bissau just prior to the start of war in 1998. As he got tired of hanging around waiting for opportunities that did not materialise because of economic decline and the meagreness of social possibilities, he left for Cacheu, hoping to be able to make a living through fishing.[2] Catching fish was, however, hard and tiresome work that generated little more than was needed to survive and so, as news of the war reached him, he packed up and went back to Bissau in June 1998, entering the city by crossing the front line of what was now a civil war between government forces and the Junta Militar. Mbuli first went home to see his family, but as the fighting flared up again he packed his things, went to the headquarters of the *Governo* forces and, preferring to fight for his *parente*, kinsman,[3] President Nino Vieira, he enrolled as a soldier in the government forces. In this manner Mbuli came to be an Aguenta, a militiaman on the government side of the war fighting to protect the democratically elected president.

The war went well for neither Mbuli nor the Aguentas. The misery he endured and the trauma of warfare, witnessing many of his friends and colleagues die on the battlefield and spending months on end at the front, turned out to be in vain as the *Governo* side lost the war on 7 May 1999. Mbuli, however, did not suffer the ultimate defeat personally as he was in Senegal at the time, being trained as a 'presidential escort'. Yet he returned to Bissau a loser and went and presented himself to the victorious Junta Militar, no longer as a proud combatant but as a scared Aguenta bereft of the power base that had granted him his short-lived status and prospects. Mbuli was questioned and sent home, not to hear from the Junta again, but to bear the brunt of an abundance of abuse from the people in his neighbourhood, as the defeat transformed the Aguentas into legitimate targets for bantering and abuse in the aftermath of the war.

Post-war Problems and Possibilities

This is when I first encountered Mbuli. Being without a job and not having the possibility of getting one – employment being difficult to find for youth in general and impossible for Aguentas – being called an array of foul names whenever he ventured outside the safe confines of his uncle's house and courtyard, and constantly nervous of being persecuted by the Junta soldiers, his life was, as he euphemistically phrased it, 'not sweet'.[4] And it seemed only to be getting worse as Mbuli, despite not having any money or an apparent income, was more or less constantly drunk and incoherent.

However, with the first post-war election and the inauguration of the new government of Kumba Yala things began to improve for Mbuli. First of all, Kumba Yala's electoral victory over the Junta Militar's candidate Malam Bacai Sanha was a symbolic victory as it showed that the Junta did not have popular backing – which as opposing entities in war was of importance to the Aguentas. Secondly, it entailed the Junta suffering a relative loss of control over the political scene in Guinea-Bissau. And, thirdly, and even more importantly, the specific constitution of Yala's government proved a stroke of good luck for Mbuli as it meant that he, via his uncle's network, suddenly acquired a contact with a high-ranking government official.[5] Yala's victory thus granted Mbuli a point of entry into a patrimonial network opening a space of possibility for him in relation to improving his life chances (Dahrendorf 1979). And this space of possibility was soon to be put to good use as his training as a presidential escort during the war combined with his patrimonial connection meant that he was able to secure himself a job as a guard for a newly appointed top politician. In other words, as the Junta were pushed further and further backstage within the political scenario in the country, Mbuli seemed to be finding his feet, gaining an income and a new perspective on his life and possibilities.

However, the Junta were not about to give their political control over the state apparatus away willingly and therefore sought to maintain a central, though withdrawn, position of power. Although Kumba Yala had won the presidential election by beating Malam Bacai Sanha, Asumané Mané had put himself in place as the country's *éminence grise*. Stepping down as Chief of Staff, leaving the position to General Verissimo Correia Seabre, he established himself as a relatively detached co-president, claiming to function merely as a watchdog for democracy but in effect controlling both the military and the state apparatus from behind the scenes.

Mbuli Remobilised

As Mbuli's life situation was getting better, the political situation of the country was thus rapidly deteriorating. Despite the victory of Kumba Yala, the country's army continued to make it clear that they intended to play a part in the country's politics. Furthermore, the new government of Mr Yala was making no political or social advances, seemingly being more interested in consumption than in reconstruction.[6] Bissau was going from bad to worse, with the water supply being weekly at best, electricity all but non-existent and the price of rice constantly rising, while people had less and less money to buy it with. 'Luz ka tem, iagu ka tem, arroz sta carro' (no light, no water, and expensive rice) was the apt chorus of the popular rap song of the period.

The downward social and economic spiral entailed a general dissatisfaction with the government, who were living in luxury while the general population were becoming increasingly impoverished; and, as the state of affairs deteriorated even further, the government came under increasing pressure from the Junta Militar, who were dissatisfied with the course of events, as well as from the opposition parties who demonstrated against Yala's government, yelling that he had 'cerebral diarrhoea',[7] as they marched through town on 15 October 2000. As time passed, the problems and conflicts of interest between the Junta Militar and the government of President Kumba Yala were to augment in scale until, by the end of November, a full-blown conflict seemed unavoidable.

Following a direct provocation and undermining of the authority of the retired Brigadier Mané by Kumba Yala and the new Chief of Staff General Verissimo Correia Seabre, the discord between the government and the Junta Militar led to renewed fighting in Bissau.[8] On the national holiday for the armed forces in November 2000, Kumba Yala promoted a number of, primarily Balanta,[9] officers while passing over the Junta Militar's supporters within the army and navy. The response from Asumané Mané was swift. Denouncing the promotions as unjust, false and non-transparent,[10] he relieved Verissimo Correia Seabre of his position and subsequently reinstated himself as Brigadier General, thus seeking to regain control over the armed forces. On 20 November the Junta Militar issued the following press statement:

> The Supreme Commando of the Junta Militar informs the population in general and especially the inhabitants of Bissau of the events that resulted in the meeting of the Military Chiefs today and on whose resolution the decision for this social communication has been taken.
> 1. The problem in question will naturally be resolved purely within the military so there is no cause for alarm.

2. With the deepest serenity we guarantee the population that the situation in Bissau and in our country will maintain in perfect calm. (*Diario de Bissau* 20 November 2000 [my translation])

Of course, calm did not prevail and the following night fighting broke out between the Junta Militar and troops loyal to the government as Mané's men tried to take control of the presidency but were beaten back by the Presidential Guard. Eight days later, the conflict ended with the execution of Asumané Mané in Quinhamel, some 30 kilometres outside Bissau. Asumané Mané was clubbed to death. The tragic irony behind his extremely violent death was his *medicinhos*, that is, his magic charms, which were seen as protecting him from being killed by 'conventional' methods ranging from knives to bazookas.[11] The next day a picture of Asumané's corpse was on the front page of the newspaper *Diario de Bissau*, the image of his broken, disjointed body being paraded through town by the newspaper boys.

It was the day after this that I met Mbuli again, proud as can be, outside Nti's house. As I approached him I asked how he had been; his answer was: 'Good. But they should not have killed the *homi garandi* [big man], they should not, they should have let him go, so that he could go to Gambia. Like Nino they should have let him go.' Asumané Mané was the very symbol of what had brought torment to Mbuli's life. He was the head of the Junta Militar and thus emblematic of the force responsible for the initial failure of his tactics and shrinking of his social possibilities, resulting in Mbuli having to live an everyday life of utmost uncertainty and fear. Yet the remark reveals an empathy towards one's 'enemy' in war that I would come to know as typical not just of my Aguenta interlocutors, but of most of the people I was to speak to about conflict and warfare in Guinea-Bissau.

Mbuli's story directs our attention to the general social position from which my informants moved towards becoming Aguentas, namely that of youth. It directs our attention to the ethnic undertones of their mobilisation and to the importance of having contacts within the patrimonial networks that have colonised the state structures, towards the rapid social and political change within Guinean society resulting in a permanent state of instability, towards the difficult interwar period the Aguentas went through, and, finally, as seen in the last quote, towards a peculiarly compassionate construction of the Other within Guinean conflict – all general aspects of the lives of the Aguentas, which will be investigated further in the course of this book. But, most of all, Mbuli's history is a good example of how youth seek to navigate war as event, and the networks that open up towards them in the process of factional conflict, as they try to make the best of political turmoil in order to enhance their life chances

Yet in his success – in bettering his life situation, getting a job, an income and opening up the space of possibilities that relative financial security and wealth provide – Mbuli's history is in fact atypical of the Aguentas. In Mbuli's case the defeat of the government side of the war was a temporary tragedy; in the case of my other informants it has been a pervasive one, spoiling not only their plotted life trajectories but also the very networks they depend upon to manage in the immediate social environment and to prosper in the future. As with Mbuli, the lives of my other informants provide good examples of attempted social navigation (Vigh 2003): that is, of the way they take a bearing of the changes within their socio-political environment and seek to make the best of emergent social possibilities in order to direct their lives in an advantageous direction.[12] But, for most, the navigation went wrong.

Notes

1. The republic of Guinea-Bissau is one of West Africa's smaller countries, covering an area of about 36,125 square kilometres. The majority of the coastal area of the country consists of deltas and mangrove swamps, whereas the interior of the country is either cultivated or wooded savannah. There are approximately 1.2 million inhabitants in the country, of which roughly a quarter live in the capital Bissau. Over twenty different languages exist in Guinea-Bissau, with Portuguese Creole being the lingua franca and Portuguese the official language, though spoken only by 10 per cent of the population (Einarsdóttir 2000: 7). 30 per cent of the population are said to be Muslim, 5 per cent are Christian and 65 per cent are animist (Forrest 1992: 131), although there are elements of animism intertwined with the two world religions, and most non-Muslims, by counter-identification, see themselves as Christians.
2. Cacheu is the name of one of the country's major cities as well as the most northern of the country's nine administrative regions.
3. *Parente* in Creole refers to someone of the same ethnic affiliation. Preferring to fight for ones *parente* thus indicates an ethnic orientation within the process of mobilisation. However, as we shall see in Chapter 3 this does not necessarily indicate the existence of inter-ethnic fear or hatred.
4. The Creole word *sabi* has a wide breadth in meaning and connotes anything from, for example, the sweetness of honey to the efficiency of rhetoric and the sharpness of knives.
5. The government of Kumba Yala saw the reincorporation of a number of ex-*Governo* supporters, among whom Baciro Dabo, President Nino's chief of security, and Malai Sané, the ex-Minister of Social Communication, are the most prominent (*Diario de Bissau* 21 November 2000; *Diario de Noticias* 18 November 2001).

6. Leading to problems between the government and the IMF (International Monetary Fund), Kumba Yala's government spent one and a half million dollars on 'travel expenses' in eight months, with eighteen billion FCFA (Franc Communauté Financière d'Afrique), approximately 30 million dollars, unaccounted for by the end of the year 2000 (*Diario de Bissau* 18 October 2000; 9 November 2000).
7. *Panga barriga di cabeza*
8. Verissimo Correia Seabre was formerly a high-ranking officer within the *Junta Militar*.
9. His own ethnic group.
10. *Banobero* 29 November 2000.
11. The belief in *medicinho* cuts across cultures and religions in both Guinea-Bissau and West Africa in general, and although different rituals are used in their production they all serve the same function and are of roughly the same appearance in Bissau. One can thus have *medicinho* as protection against any type of accident, disease, bad luck, curse or other natural or supernatural act of aggression, as well as to enhance one luck or powers. It is common for soldiers to have *medicinho* against weapons such as knives, guns, shrapnel and so on, with the cost of the magical protection being related to the destructive potential of the weapon in question.
12. I use the normally unspecific word 'socio-political' throughout the book. The reason for this is, as we shall see, that the classical political science distinction between the sphere of politics and that of civil society is directly misleading in the current context (see Chabal and Daloz 1999) – just as its dominance is, I would contend, highly exaggerated in many other parts of the world. Social ties and obligations are not detached from political ones in Bissau.

Chapter 2

PERSPECTIVES AND POSITIONS

I began to climb the wheel like a squirrel; but I would hardly get the boat started to port before I would see new dangers on that side, and away I would spin to the other; only to find perils accumulating starboard, and be crazy to get to port again. Then came the leadsman's sepulchral cry:

'D-e-e-p four!'

Deep four in a bottomless crossing! The terror of it took my breath away.

'M-a-r-k three! M-a-r-k three! Quarter-less-three! Half twain!'

This was frightful! I seized the bell-ropes and stopped the engines.

'Quarter twain! Quarter twain! *Mark Twain!*'

I was helpless. I did not know what in the world to do. I was quaking from my head to foot, and I could have hung my hat on my eyes, they stuck out so far.

'Quarter less twain! Nine-and-a-half!'

(*Life on the Mississippi*, Mark Twain 1963: 70)

As in the above description, my informants navigate dangerous waters. Senses, memory and intellect stretched to the utmost they are trying to draw the right trajectories through the stormy waters of predicted and unpredictable societal turmoil. As shown in the case of Mbuli, they navigate an unstable political landscape where the shifts, tows and underlying dangers require strategy and tactics to be constantly tuned to the movement of the immediate socio-political environment as well as to its future unfolding. Yet unlike Mark Twain, my informants really did run aground, suffering the panic and distress of navigation gone wrong, the process so acutely communicated in the above passage.

My main analytical aim within this book is to propose a perspective of youth in war through a theory of social navigation: that is, through attentiveness to the way in which agents seek to draw and actualise their life trajectories in order to increase their social possibilities and life chances in a shifting and volatile social environment.[1] As shown in the case of Mbuli the general perspective is not on politics or warfare in itself, or on the Clausewitzian link between them,[2] but rather on the socially situated rationales that lead people in and out of warfare. My focus is thus on how and why a group of agents deliberately engage in warfare: on the social position, perspectives and praxis of a group of urban, West African youth as they seek to survive – socially and physically – in a terrain of conflict and war (Abdullah 1997; Bangura 1997; Utas 2003; Vigh 2003). It is not a 'blood and guts monograph', a retailing of suffering and the horrors of warfare. Rather, it is centred on the social predicaments and possibilities that underlie my informants' engagement with conflict. I shall thus examine the pragmatics of warfare (cf. Whyte 1997) from the perspective of a small group of urban youth that served in the Aguenta militia in Guinea-Bissau during the civil war from 1998 to 1999.

The Perspective

In other words, contrary to many other ethnographies on the subject of conflict or warfare, this book is not centred on how a community, faction or other group of agents seek to impose their political will on others by engaging in political violence or on how agents resort to war in order to attain autonomy, but rather on how a group of agents seek to survive as well as possible when caught in a situation of societal and political instability (see Richards 1996; de Boeck and Honwana 2000). Its focus is not primarily on the construction and realisation of a political order but on the construction and realisation of social being. It is about the project of social becoming, set in a terrain of conflict and war.[3]

Theoretically the perspective takes its point of departure in the interplay between social perspectives, actions and forces, which, inspired particularly by the work of Pierre Bourdieu, has come to characterise a large part of the social sciences in the last few decades. Creating a constructive dialogue between such seemingly irreconcilable theoretical positions as phenomenology and structuralism, the Bourdieuesque perspective has allowed us to see the dialectic between individual agency and social forces (Bourdieu 1989, 1992), gaining in the process a richness of analytical insight and possibilities. Focusing on how a group of agents seek to move within a complex set of societal structures and confinements, my work clearly owes a great deal to Bourdieu. Yet, in trying to make sense of the actions of agents within a socio-political environment that is in itself in motion, we need to go further than the concepts of 'field' and 'habitus' can take us.

Terrains and Environments

As my attention is on a group of youth and their efforts to live their lives in an unstable socio-political environment characterised by a constant process of fluctuation rather than slow sedimentation, I prefer to use the concept of social 'terrain' or 'environment' rather than 'field'. To avoid mixed metaphors the two concepts will frequently be interchanged; yet, as confusing as this might be, the point is to create a picture of social forces as surrounding or uneven matter rather than stable and hardened surface and as matter in constant becoming rather than solidified being. 'For its inhabitants, journeying along their respective ways of life, the world itself *has no surface*' Ingold states (2000: 241), echoing a similar point made by Jackson explaining that we move *in* our world not *on* it (Jackson 1998: 204). Where the concept of social environment lets us analytically approach the fact that our social worlds are understood from within, the concept of terrain points our attention towards a continuously unfolding topography. Taken together, the two concepts succeed in referring to the social forces surrounding our lives as being at times a non-transparent social topography, at other times fluid and in continual movement and at yet other times volatile and explosive. The use of terrain or environment, in other words, takes on the quality of the different elements underlying the predicament of living in Guinea-Bissau, where one has to constantly assess and reinterpret the character, dangers and possibilities of the shifting social matter – having certainty only of the frailty of socio-political orders. The point, then, is to confer an image of a socio-political environment that is non-transparent and in motion rather than transparent, solid and stable.

Social Navigation

Despite its fluidity and volatility, the Guinean social terrain has, however, never completely dissolved. It should thus be emphasised that not all things social are adrift and fluid in Bissau. The country has not seen the type of warfare that draws whole generations of youth into war and my focus, within this book, is specifically on mobilisation and war engagement as socio-political praxis. Entering the military in Bissau is most often a willed choice rather than a forced decision,[4] and choosing to navigate the terrain of war is primarily a question of evaluating the movement of the social environment, one's own possibilities for moving through it, and its effect on ones planned and actual movement. It is this evaluation and praxis I have termed 'social navigation', serving as an analytical optic able to illuminate the way agents guide their lives through troublesome social and political circumstances, that is, to illuminate 'governance and adjustment between self and other rather than the maintenance of a fixed line' (Jackson 1998: 18). Rather than navigating concrete environments or cognitive maps (see Gell 1993; Ingold 2000: Chapter 13) I am concerned with the way my interlocutors navigate networks and events as they move within fluctuating social structures.

Generally, the concept of navigation seems to occur in relation to descriptions of praxis in unstable places. As such, Honwana (2000: 77), Johnson-Hanks (2002: 878) and Mertz (2002: 265) all refer to navigation in relation to contexts of social change.[5] Yet social navigation is, I hold, an applicable analytical concept not only in relation to the Aguentas or situations of rapid change. It is a useful concept in relation to social praxis in general. Though it becomes increasingly noticeable in turbulent social and political circumstances, it does not stem from them. We all navigate, but the intensity of our navigational efforts depends on the speed and volatility of social change (see Evans and Furlong 1997; Virilio 2001). However, the element my informants seek to navigate is not only unstable or changing, it is dangerously so, requiring that the agent must be attentive towards both the immediate and the future social configurations and possibilities in order to secure his safety. As the initial quote from Mark Twain so hauntingly shows, in dangerous waters one navigates simultaneously around underlying perils and through oncoming waves as well as towards a distant point in or beyond the spatio-temporal horizon, whilst, importantly, at all times being also forcibly moved by the current.

The concept of navigation thereby adds to our customary understanding of social action in two main areas. First of all, it enables us to see how agents simultaneously navigate the immediate and the imagined. We concurrently plot trajectories, plan strategy and actually move towards a telos[6] a distant goal in or beyond the horizon, and we do so both in relation to our current position and possibilities in a given social environment and in relation to our imagined future position and possibilities of movement. Secondly, whereas we normally conceptualise agents positioning themselves and acting within relatively demarcated and stable social fields, navigation is able to describe praxis in which social change is taken into consideration. It affords an analysis of praxis that is able to encompass the way in which agents act not only in relation to each other, or in relation to larger social forces, but in relation to the complex interaction between agents, terrain and events, thereby making it possible to encompass social flux and instability, and the way they influence and become ingrained in action, in our understanding of a specific praxis. In other words, when navigating we are aware that we might be repositioned by shifting terrains and circumstances. As we seek to move within a turbulent and unstable socio-political environment we are at the same time being moved by currents, shifts and tides, requiring that we constantly have to attune our action and trajectory to the movement of the environment we move through. Social navigation may thus involve detours, unwilling displacement, losing our way and, not least, redrawing trajectories and tactics. Social navigation in this perspective is the tactical movement of agents within a moving element. It is motion within motion.

Between Agency and Social Forces

Though navigation emphasises movement, it must be stressed that we are not free to move entirely as we want. Anyone who has ever sailed will testify to the idiocy of trying to navigate with indifference to the forces of the environment, and the concept of social navigation is thus not another metaphor for agency,[7] but rather designates the interface between agency and social forces, focusing our attention on the inseparability of act and environment (Ingold 2000: Chapter 13), knowledge and praxis (Scott 1998: Chapter 9), and – not least – agency and social forces.

Theoretically, the idea of social navigation is inspired by praxis theory and the concept of 'life chances' as developed in the work of the German political sociologist Ralf Dahrendorf (1979, 1988). Dahrendorf's use of the concept of 'life chances' builds on the Weberian idea of 'social options', designating the realm of possibility open to the individual through his position within society. Or, as Dahrendorf chooses to describe Weber's use of the concept, it is 'the notion of chance to indicate opportunities provided by social structure' (Dahrendorf 1979: 29). Life chances are, in Dahrendorf's perspective, constituted by social options and ties:[8] that is, the relationship between social possibilities and social allegiances and bonds (1979: 28, 30).[9] 'Options' are the choices people in a given situation have available to them and ties – or 'ligatures' – are the social bonds or attachments in which these choices emerge and are embedded. When these are combined in an analytical perspective, they grant us a possibility to investigate situated action. Much as with the focus of this book, Dahrendorf's concept thus both includes a focus on the social anchoring of persons and acts and on social change, perspectives and horizons. Yet, contrary to

Dahrendorf, I shall not restrict myself to the theory and typology of societies and politics but show how my informants actually seek to live their lives in relation to their social embeddedness, their social horizons and the context of instability, conflict and warfare.

The Empirical Setting

The empirical foundation for the book is sixteen months of fieldwork done in Bissau, the capital of the small West African country of Guinea-Bissau, between January 2000 and November 2003.

I arrived in Guinea-Bissau just after the first parliamentary election following the civil war, and spent the first nine months of my fieldwork in the suburb (*bairro*) of Bandim. My first impression of Bissau was to inform my future work. As the flight crew announced that we would be landing shortly, I watched for the city. The landscape visible to us from above seemed anything but urban being a massive delta with finely drawn blue lines of rivers cutting their way through the green terrain. The plane landed, seemingly, in the middle of the bush. Yet, as we made our way out of the aeroplane, through customs and towards town, Bissau opened up in front of us in a pungent mix of moist heat, dilapidation, garbage and mango trees. On a first encounter, the lushness of the vegetation and warmth of the city's inhabitants, combined with the mould-ornamented decay and still visible destruction, place Bissau, absurdly, on the interface between rot and renewal, gloom and brightness.

Bandim

Bandim, the place I was to live in during the first part of my fieldwork, is to a large degree characterised by the same duality. The first aspect of life that one notices in Bandim is the poverty. Yet it is a general context of poverty inhabited by mild, humorous and, not least, resilient people constantly inviting one to partake in their meal, of which they normally only have one a day. As such, one spends a great deal of time in Bissau cursing the misery and hardness of societal mis-dynamics, but an equal amount of time struck by the flexibility of these same social dynamics and the kindness of the city's inhabitants.

Guinea-Bissau is, as is much of West Africa,[10] an ethnically mixed country, and all of the country's ethnic groups are represented within the capital. Yet Bandim is a predominantly Papel area,[11] consisting of a sprawling network of mud brick houses separated by red dirt roads. It is a wonderful place: a neighbourhood that during the day is alive with roaming packs of children searching for something to play with, tease or investigate, with adolescents playing football on the bumpy, makeshift football pitch, and adults chatting, cooking or sleeping in the shade of mango trees or verandas. During the evening, Bandim is confined to darkness but is audibly alight, with groups of youth chatting at corners at an adequate distance from the ears of parents and siblings for flirting to be possible, women gathered in peer groups, and the occasional party with people getting drunk on cashew wine and women singing in the finest high-pitched voices.

Praça

I enjoyed living in Bandim; however, after my wife and children moved back north, luckily just before the outbreak of fighting in November 2000, the place became a constant reminder of their absence. With the house too big and the social relations somehow missing their foundation I decided to move into a friend's house in town.

Praça, which is the Portuguese-derived name for the inner part of Bissau city, consists, unlike Bandim, of Portuguese-style brick houses and (what used to be) asphalt roads. The oldest part, called Bissau Veillo, is located around the harbour and is a pretty but decaying colonial Portuguese neighbourhood, with pastel-coloured houses, narrow streets and alluring, shady balconies. Around Bissau Veillo, government institutions, foreign companies and 'indigenous' Portuguese or Lebanese grocery stores occupy a primarily commercial area of two-storey town houses, and around this area stands an inner city residential area formerly populated by the Portuguese or Cape Verdean elite but redistributed to the privileged within the liberation party after independence.

One of these houses belonged to Facho's family, and was the place I was to spend the rest of my time in Bissau. Within this two-storey building on a small side street in the inner part of Bissau city lived the family of five, along with some tenants. As luck would have it there was a spare room, next to Facho's, which I was able to rent. Not that I moved far from a physical point of view, there being only a couple of kilometres between my new room and my old house, but there are notable differences between Bandim and Praça, and on a social scale the two areas are far more than only a couple of kilometres apart.

Despite looking as if it has not been repaired or renovated since colonial days, the inner city is seen as smart. Regardless of the broken water pipes and eternal mud puddles, the rubbish dumps and the multitude of vultures and mangy dogs, it is a trendy place to live, with a handful of cafes, bars, shops and restaurants nearby. However, the commercial area apart, inner city Bissau does not, despite its 'trendy' character, differ greatly from Bandim in its people or their activities. They constitute, in general, a more varied group than the Bandim residents, and are better off. Yet their daily routines and praxis are all but identical, and Praça seems to house as many Aguentas, my primary group of informants, as Bandim does.

Networks Rather than Locations

As it would turn out, my exact location was to be of minor importance in relation to my research focus on the Aguentas. Similar for both Bandim and Praça is the way people go about their day. As urban spaces, the neighbourhoods are continuously traversed by a myriad of outsiders, insiders, visitors, intruders and wanderers. Equally, my informants would traverse through the many urban demarcations, as they would move in and out of different areas, groups and communities, following social relations and networks based on kin, friendship, politics or business.

One of the primary characteristics of the Bissauian urban landscape (besides the dilapidation and poverty) are the groups of young people that dot the city. The vast majority of young people in Bissau are unemployed and economically marginal and thus dependent on the goodwill of a parent, aunt or uncle to feed and shelter them.[12] Being dependants in this manner equally means that they are not able to establish their own household and acquire their own space. So, it is common for groups of peers, no matter what generational category they belong to, to organise themselves in informal social institutions called *mandjuandades* or *collegasons* (cf. Gable 2000).[13] Most young people, not having a place of their own, organise themselves socially in these *collegasons* by appropriating bits of public space and transforming them into meeting-places. In this manner all young people seem to have a *collegason*, a peer group consisting of local friends of roughly the same age, which meets at the same place every day, where they often spend most of their day. These *collegasons* of youth – of boys and girls, men and women – form an important part of the urban landscape and young people walk between *collegasons* as they move through the streets visiting friends, romantic acquaintances and relatives from other areas.

Although sexually mixed, men and women will often sit a bit apart within their *collegasons*. Thus, women sit in groups braiding hair, chatting or doing chores, while groups of men hang out, not tending to have any activities but just chatting, discussing the people passing by, sports, women and politics. While this book is squarely centred on the lives of young men, as I have not met any women Aguentas,[14] the presence of women within *collegasons* has nonetheless made a significant contribution to my understanding of Guinean society and the lives of youth in Bissau in general. Despite their absence within my narrow focus on the Aguentas, the voices and lives of many of my female friends and acquaintances form an important backdrop to the analysis.

Rhizomatic Fieldwork

Because of the centrality of *collegasons* researching young males in Bissau offers a myriad of ready-made social networks. It offers a large, spread out, decentralised, rhizomatic network that youth orient themselves towards in relation to their social life:[15] that is, in relation to parties, romance and friendship. A rhizomatic structure, as a counterpart to hierarchical arborescent structures, is an interconnected set of horizontal and vertical – rather than merely vertical – orderings. In the words of Deleuze and Guattari: 'Form rhizomes and roots, never plant! Don't sow, forage! Be neither a One nor a Many, but multiplicities! Form a line, never a point! ... A rhizome doesn't begin and doesn't end, but is always in the middle, between things, interbeing, *intermezzo* (Deleuze and Guattari 2002: 24–25).

What is important in the current context is that the concept implies decentralisation rather than localisation, and that it points our attention to the interconnectivity of horizontal and vertical structures rather than their separateness.[16] Although being part of one primary *collegason*, each youth will also have contact with a number of others, with one point of a local network always being connected to a multitude of external ones. In this perspective, no matter what one's age, most people 'hang out' not only with their local peer groups but also, occasionally, with the *collegasons* associated with friends, girlfriends or family.

Analytically localising my fieldwork in a suburb such as Bandim or Praça would be a representation of my fieldwork that would be in tune with the traditionally localised ethnographic praxis, but it would be a misrepresentation of my actual field practice. I spent most my time in Bissau sitting on walls, worn and broken chairs, or just *djunguto*, squatting, hanging out with my informants as they spent time with their peer group, and moving between them. The primary 'place' of my fieldwork was, in other words, more closely related to the meeting-places of different *collegasons*, and the relation between my informants and different *collegasons*, than to a specific neighbourhood or other traditional urban-geographical demarcations.

The Informants

Not being a localised group or community, my informants do not conform to the traditional anthropological object of study. Losing the war and subsequently being disbanded, the Aguentas constituted a short-lived military group, different from the type of historically deep and spatio-temporally demarcated (or at least represented as such) groups which are traditionally in focus within anthropology. The Aguentas have neither a common territory nor a common mythology or set of traditions to set them apart from the rest of Guinean society. Furthermore, having been disbanded after the war, they currently do not even constitute a defined military unit. Yet they do share a number of defining characteristics in relation to the rest of Guinean society, such as their social positions as primarily Papel, primarily animist-Catholic, and not least their status as youth. But what specifically defines the Aguentas is that they have the same conflict position and history, which means that they can be seen as constituting a 'community of experience',[17] sharing specific ordeals, praxis, perspectives and positions within a given terrain and thus sharing certain points or spheres of reference. Their specific history of losing the war has created an experiential bond, a commonality of experience, which differentiates them from the rest of the Guinean society and enables them to imagine each other's lives as related and similar to their own (see Mannheim 1952; Anderson 1993).[18]

It was the Aguentas' ascribed social position through the experience of losing the war that initiated my interest in them in the first place, as their social and political position seemed to provide an advantageous site for illuminating reconciliation processes after the civil war. As a stigmatised group of youth, my expectation was that the Aguentas would be able to grant me an insight into the process of social reintegration after a period of upheaval and fragmentation. Indeed, although my focus on reconciliation was diverted by a period of conflict and war, this social relation based on the shared experience of conflict and defeat proved ethnographically rich as my informants are able to enter into and inhabit a mutual discursive and social space despite not necessarily sharing location, strata or culture.

A community of experience, in this perspective, exists due to a specific point of reference resulting from shared history and position rather than necessarily shared language, ethnicity or ideology. Suffering similar ordeals creates a space of commonality (see Werbner 1991). War evidently leads to a (relative) polarisation of the conflicting social categories, but it also works on a more subtle level generating social formations and bonds as people find themselves sharing the ordeals of flight, refuge, combat or post-war difficulties, generating communities of experience that are as enduring as they are profound – a fact which can be demonstrated in the annual veterans' marches around the world.[19] In this perspective the Aguentas share a common social position, predicament and history.[20]

Although there are no institutionalised forums bringing them together, my informants do actually meet and interact with each other on the basis of their identity as Aguentas. All of my informants interact with friends whom they have served with in the Aguentas, meeting coincidentally or visiting each other, mainly debating what happened to this or that person and catching up on news related to their side of the war. In other words, despite not having a formalised relationship or place to meet, my informants still seek each other's company and, although there might not be an explicit network of Aguentas, the visibility and durability of the feeling of community between the Aguentas are tangible when, for example, being guided in and out of the rhizomatic networks of *collegasons*.[21]

Urbanised Aguentas

In order to properly position my informants within the Guinean context, I ought to specify that my focus is on urban Aguentas, and thus on urban youth. Although there are obvious similarities between the urban and the rural arising from their shared social predicament and history there are definitely also differences.[22] It must, in other words, be specified that my informants represent a subgroup within the Aguentas since they, as urban youth from the capital Bissau, do not do justice to the diversity of the militia. The empirical focus of this book is as such quite restricted, as I am working with a subgroup of a subgroup. I shall, however, throughout the analysis, take into account the general make-up of the Bissauian social context and make use of a variety of ethnographic and demographic knowledge so as to properly contextualise my key interlocutors. As the book is focused on urbanised youth and specifically on those who chose to join the Aguenta militia, I shall be portraying the social position, understandings and praxis of this narrow group of agents in relation to the larger social formations and processes of which they are a part.

Masking My Informants

Whereas much effort will be put into positioning the Aguentas within the general context of youth in Bissau, the specific details surrounding their lives are of less significance for my study. My informants do not present themselves as Aguentas and I do not want to be the one to do so for them by relaying the specificities of their lives and thus pointing them out against the social background of youth in Bissau. Moreover, Bissau is currently, although not at war, unstable in the extreme and, although my informants are not in direct danger from a specific political or military faction, divides can easily re-emerge and be re-actualised and hatred can remain smouldering. The details of my informants' lives have therefore been clouded. I have changed the names of those who wished to be anonymous, and omitted details that would lead to their identification. This is the price that must be paid when doing anthropology with marginalised groups in conflict situations and, although the richness of detail might be academically missed, its absence is an ethical must. I hope that my informants' voices will nonetheless speak out from the quotes spread throughout the book and their lives become visible in the social context and actions that I seek to portray.

Methods and Positions

The narrowness of my focus not only entails ethical reflections in relation to the presentation of my data. It is also itself the result of a number of ethical reflections related to the context of my fieldwork. Besides the evident need for some sort of demarcation the reason that my focus is one-sided, directed towards the losing presidential side of the war, is related to doing fieldwork in a context of conflict and instability, with as much attention being paid to my informants' safety as possible. Because of their misdeeds during the war, including rape, theft and violence, the Aguentas were disliked both during the war and after it.[23] Many of my informants therefore see themselves as occupying marginal and vulnerable social positions within Guinean society, as the Aguentas were harassed, beaten and murdered by opposing soldiers and civilians in the turmoil following the fall of the presidential side. Thus they continue to be in a generally vulnerable position and we need to make this vulnerability an important part of our methodological reflections while researching conflict and warfare.

Yet, when studying conflict and warfare, we need equally to be aware that we too will be positioned and politicised as we enter the field and that this will influence both our access to data and how our interlocutors are positioned, in turn, in light of their acquaintance with us. This can obviously be said to be so no matter what fieldwork we choose to do; yet in the above-mentioned situations the consequences have the potential to have a negative, at times life-threatening, impact on our interlocutors as the distinction between informant and informer becomes easily blurred. Because situations of conflict entail a polarisation of social identities and heightened awareness of newcomers and seekers of information, we must be aware that our motives for seeking specific knowledge are likely to be misinterpreted and related to the context of conflict we seek to investigate, rather than to our research objective. When it comes to our possible effect on the security and well-being of our informants, our methodological reflections become obligations. Methodologically, it is thus important that we remain alert to the fact that the difference between doing anthropology and prying is not always clear for others.

Researching people in vulnerable positions, such as the Aguentas, it therefore becomes important that we represent ourselves expediently so as to position ourselves and their collaboration positively. One way of crafting this representation, in relation to my informants in Bissau, was to control who I was seen talking to and what I was seen doing, making sure that my interlocutors felt at ease talking to me and did not doubt my motives. It would without doubt have been more difficult to get the depth of data that I wanted if I had been seen investigating the opposing side of the conflict as well. Being seen to pay an interest in the young Junta soldiers, the so-called Adjunta,[24] could very well have been an erosive factor in the relationship of trust that is so important to attain when doing qualitative research in such contexts. The narrowness of researching urban Aguentas within the context of the civil war in Bissau is thus both an ethical and a methodological choice.

The Force of the Ethnographic Method

Except for the fact that when researching conflict and warfare we need to seriously rethink the consequences of our methods – and the information the finished product will convey – the ethnographic method is exceptionally adept at scientifically engaging in such situations. As propagated political discourse and narrative are there for all to see and analyse, ethnographic research allows one to slip beneath the obvious or speculative. It enables us to go behind the thick, shiny surfaces of politicised discourse and analyse everyday political praxis instead. It allows us to gain the depth needed to achieve an insight into people's lives and thereby to properly contextualise their actions. Many renderings of political processes, journalistic or academic, seem to build on either speculation or politically communicated representations, which, though not necessarily poor or irrelevant, are often politicised and sloganised. Political discourse, especially surrounding conflicts, most often works through simplification, positioning actors and processes within a bipolar social environment, and is therefore not the right data needed to see the actual density and depth of social processes as people seek to live their lives in situations of conflict. Herein lies part of the strength of the ethnographic fieldwork and method as they enable us to simultaneously work within, beneath and between political representations and subjective horizons, to see beyond the stereotypes of the helpless, undifferentiated population, resistance hero and power-monger, victim and victimiser (Nordstrom and Robben 1995: 8). As ethnographic interviews allow us to elucidate points of view and social horizons, the reflexive socialisation of participant observation enables us to gain an understanding of social terrains and navigational praxis. In this manner, ethnography has the key to illuminating, although not necessarily solving, one of the key phenomena in the creation of spirals of violence, namely that of the social production of radical polarities of Otherness and relations of negative reciprocity.

From Violence to Conflict and Warfare

It is, obviously, working with relationships characterised by hostility that defines the anthropology of conflict. However, as conflict lurks beneath all social constellations and arrangements, researchers within the sub-field work in very different cultural and social settings. Given this diversity, we need a comprehensive and thorough positioning of our use of the concept of conflict and the related concepts of violence and warfare so as to be aware of the differences and similarities of our research and gain a better foundation for dialogue and comparison.

At its most basic violence is a relationship between agents whereby at least one of the parties experience a limitation of his/her agency that is interpreted as illegitimate (see Riches 1986; Taussig 1992; Krohn-Hansen 1994; Jackson 1998: 17). This relation between violence and limited agency becomes no clearer than in the Scandinavian languages where being controlled involuntarily by others is literally defined as 'being in someone's/something's violence'.[25] Using this perspective, violence goes beyond interpersonal violence, including the concepts of structural, cultural and symbolic violence (Galtung 1979, 1990; Bourdieu 1992; Jackson 2002). Common to all violence is thus an issue of agentive impairment constituted within the relationship between the aggressor and the victim. Yet definitions of victims and aggressors are often contested and upon ethnographic investigation most violence proves to be retaliatory or protective. This distinction is unfortunately often blurred because laypersons, journalists and researchers alike enter into the study of violence with a predefined normative polarisation of the conflict situation and too little time to gain a nuanced insight into the social context the violence is related to. Violent interaction will most often contain a mutual objectification or de-subjectification of the fighting parties (Jackson 2002); yet we often engage in the same process of constructing Others when we engage academically in the subject of violence defining victims and perpetrators and in the process framing our field of analysis normatively. This is, of course, not a process spurred by ill will but rather, as Bourdieu phrases it, by the fact that: 'It is infinitely easier to take up a position for or against an idea, a value, a person, an institution or a situation, than to analyse what it truly is, in all its complexity' (Bourdieu 1998: 23). Identifying the 'good' and the 'bad' means, however, that social scientists run the risk of becoming part of the problem rather than of its eventual solution and, although I do not advocate moral relativism, I believe that we are obliged to reflect on how we become morally engaged and how this engagement reflects on our work, so that we at least avoid contributing to the process of constructing radical Others.

Levels of Violence

If we are to focus more narrowly on interpersonal violence it can be differentiated from conflict and war by looking at the crystallisations of the agents involved in the antagonistic relationship. Thus, three social phenomena may be differentiated by the demarcation of the agents in dissension. 'Interpersonal violence' is defined as acts of aggression between identified, individual agents. 'Conflict' defines a relation of aggression between diffuse, changing or poorly identified agents, at least on one side of the antagonistic relationship. 'Warfare' can be seen as a radicalisation whereby the agents in conflict, as social categories, become defined and positioned as opponents.[26] It is a move, in other words, along levels of violence, from an antagonistic relationship between defined individuals, between opaque conflictual social categories, to violence between defined social categories (Vigh 2002).

The differentiation, however, leads us immediately to notice indeterminate concepts, such as low-intensity conflict, terror, random violence and social suffering. Concerning the latter, suffering is the experience and feeling of the victim centred on the one-sided consequences of the relationship that constitutes it. The currently popular concept of 'social suffering' has been used to define the experience of being the victim not of an individual but rather of social forces or institutions (Kleinman et al. 1997). Social suffering is, by this definition, 'the devastating injuries caused by social forces' (ibid.: ix) as individuals fall victim to symbolic or cultural violence.[27]

In considering 'random violence', our attention is pointed towards the ambivalence underlying 'randomness'. Normally the victim is, in such situations, not simply in the wrong place at the wrong time but more precisely belongs to the wrong social category in the wrong place at the wrong time, unwittingly representing a threat, an authority or an opponent. Random violence is, in other words, often only random from the victim's point of view.

Concerning the position of 'terror' and 'low-intensity conflict', it might be analytically useful to focus on the actual social relation in question instead of differentiating between acts of violence between social agents on the basis of statehood and convention, or between ideologically opposed and territorially bounded entities. We should start tuning our conceptual apparatus to changes within the dominant modes of warfare,[28] as war is increasingly within rather than between states (Lutz 1999: 614–15), which is of course exactly where terror and low-intensity conflict most often take place. Yet both categories are ambiguous as the agents in dissension are most often in flux, not clearly identifiable but constantly changing identities between civilians and guerrillas or terrorists. Low-intensity conflict is in this perspective characterised by unclearly defined agents of violence, and thus fits into the concept of conflict.

However, as the different concepts are often blurred by the fact that they overlap and coexist, it is important that we distinguish between them, because 'while conflicts are caused by structural conditions like the unequal access to resources, population shifts or external pressures, wars do not automatically result from them' (Schmidt and Schröder 2001: 4–5). In other words, although the different states on the continuum from violence to warfare often overlap and feed into each other, one does not necessarily evolve into the other. There is no pre-given process from peace through violence and conflict to war, nor is there a necessary drift into peace after warfare; rather, as wars die down, they most often seem to drift back into periods of conflict.[29] The focus of analysis is in this perspective not on how a group of agents move from peace to war but on how, in a social context of enduring instability, they move between the different states of conflict and warfare, a movement which can, unfortunately, be seen in quite a few West African countries.

Small Wars

In relation to West Africa the Aguentas, as a militia, are not as uncommon as we could wish them to be. In fact, as an irregularly recruited militia, having committed an array of human rights abuses, the Aguentas are almost iconic of the image of youth within African wars.

New Barbarism

As such, my informants enter into the irrationality that, seen from the outside, has become especially connected with West African wars.[30] Many of them are what we would normally place in the normative category of perpetrators, and the easiest way of writing this book would be to inscribe my informants into the already swelling subcategory of uncivilised African youth: of young men, driven by greed and an innate propensity for violent behaviour, taking what they need by way of the gun. That is, into what Richards has called the 'new barbarism' theory (Richards 1996). Yet, as Richards so clearly demonstrates, the vision of 'new barbarism' becomes impossible to sustain if we actually research the people supposed to embody the barbarity. Rather, it seems derived from the fleeting gaze of journalists on organised field trips to the battlefields or the safe outlook from ivory towers. It is, in other words, generated by either brief encounters or distant views.

In relation to the journalistic accounts of 'new barbarism', the catastrophic wars in West Africa have, however, become general, encompassing and enduring representations of the whole continent's troubles. Images of radical societal disorder and extreme acts of violence enter our world through the evening news and, as we follow the extraordinary images, we conclude that the people involved in these distant processes cannot be like us: that there must be something intrinsically wrong to make such starvation possible, something intrinsically potent about their sexuality to make such AIDS epidemics possible, something intrinsically violent about them to make such atrocities possible. Yet the essentialisation serves a point. By constructing the people caught up in the human-made disasters as radical Others, we are able to remove them from our social world, to externalise them to the point where we are no longer part of their world and their misery is no longer part of ours (see Daniel 1996). The outcome of the narrative of African barbarism is absolution. It leaves us guilt-free, ready to become richer as they become poorer and to enjoy our peace as they go about their violence.

Not Quite Detachable

With its epidemics, dilapidation, corruption and political instability, Guinea-Bissau fits easily into the mainstream representation of postcolonial African states. It epitomises 'Africa as usual'. Were we, however, to look more closely at the war in Guinea-Bissau between 1998 and 1999 and the following years of instability, it becomes obvious that, even though the civil war might have been fought within the borders of the small state's territory, it was an 'interventionist civil war' (Tin 1997) and thus regional not only in cause but also in relation to the combatants fighting within it. The war involved troops from Guinea-Bissau, Guinea Conakry and Senegal as well as MFDC forces.[31] Yet, as the war threatened to destabilise the sub-region, the non-regional parties involved in the conflict, diplomatically or militarily, equally came clearer into focus, with France supporting the former government and Portugal lobbying for the opposite side of the war, the Junta Militar, wishing to consolidate its presence in the lusophone country.

In this perspective, rather than merely being an expression of uncivilised Africa, the war in Guinea-Bissau points our attention to the global interconnectedness of African politics. Neither the war in Guinea-Bissau nor the acts and understandings of my informants can be confined to the local, and we need to start focusing on and, not least, communicating the interconnectedness between global economic interests and networks and the wars that we see in areas where exploitation (local, regional and global) is running wild, instead of attributing them to the areas themselves (see Richards 1996; Kaldor 1999; Duffield 2001). In Bayart's words:

> Some of the events which are often said to be evidence of its alleged de-linking from the world in fact serve most eloquently to demonstrate the opposite. Thus, some of Africa's bloodiest conflicts, often predictably interpreted as manifestations of its supposed primitiveness, cannot be separated from the ebbs and flows of the global economy and also from global cultural practice. (Bayart 2000: 240)

Accepting the global interconnectedness of present-day wars is, however, not easy as it contextualises rather than essentialises, making war the responsibility of us all rather than the pathology of the few.

Wars Old and New

Unfortunately, despite the work of Richards (1996), the perspective on war in the marginalised areas of the world as expressions of innate genetic, cultural, or societal pathologies or backwardness seems to be gaining in popularity as the gap grows between the richer and the poorer parts of the world, and as free-market liberalism has come to dominate the conceptual framework around which differences in wealth are explained. Many recent studies have thus been engaged in defining the distinction between former and current modes of warfare (of the civil war variant rather than the internationally led wars on, for example, Iraq and Serbia) through the conceptual dichotomy of 'old' and 'new' wars.[32]

Of direct relevance to this differentiation is the very negative view of the role of youth in so-called 'new' wars. With the change from inter-state warfare to civil wars, the combatants are no longer the only ones bearing the brunt of the violence.[33] Instead, there are now many more civilian casualties and losses caused by deregulated scenarios of war and irregular militias of youth, where the killing is supposedly centred around a mixture of greed, power and the resurgence of age-old cultural and ethnic hatred. The identification of this new type of war is in direct relation to Richards's earlier identification of the idea of 'new barbarism', which analyses Africa's small wars as 'apolitical events [that are] indistinguishable from banditry and crime' (1996: xiv). Instead of regulated interstate warfare, we see, within this mode of war – be it novel or barbaric – messy, untamed and chaotic wars, with the main agents of chaos being armed, irregular youth, who are mobilised as '[f]ormer administrative or intellectual elites ally with a motley collection of adventurers on the margins of society to mobilize the excluded and abandoned, alienated and insecure' (Kaldor 1999: 84).

The change from 'old' to 'new' wars inheres, however, not in the identity or social position of those involved, since youth, the marginalised, the poor and the unemployed have always formed the mainstay of cannon fodder, but rather in what the combatants are seen as fighting for (Kalyvas 2001: 101).[34] What is being proposed in the distinction is that modern wars, free of ideology, are being fought over naked power and economic gain (Kaldor 1999: 8; Berdal and Malone 2000; Collier 2000); or even, as Enzensberger would have us believe, over nothing at all: 'What gives today's civil wars a new and terrifying slant is the fact that they are waged without stakes on either side, that they are wars *about nothing at all* ... there is no longer any need to legitimise your actions. Violence has been freed from ideology' (1994: 30, emphasis in original).

Enzensberger clearly confuses the fact that he can see no meaning with the fact than none exists. The absurd idea of meaninglessness quickly loses its validity if we look at the social positions, terrains and rationales of the youth actually engaged in collective violence. Were Enzensberger thus to communicate with the people whose acts he seeks to account for, he might see these 'perpetrators' as more than driven by their '*autistic nature*' (ibid.: 20, 26) and thereby be able to contribute to the debate and not only to the analytical production of monsters. The meaning behind mch of the conflict engagement in today's small wars is, I hold, not necessarily located in ideological narrative but in praxis, in socially situated action. It is not *politically articulated* but *socially situated*, and the intellectual flaw behind the pairing of 'non-ideological' and 'meaningless' is that it fails to grasp that meaning does not only reside in discourse (Mbembe 2003: 4). The meaning behind many of the world's 'small wars' escapes the fleeting glance of journalists or the telescopic views of political scientists, as it is not necessarily written in policies, handed out in manifestos or articulated in ideologies. Through the course of this book, I hope to be able to show that the mobilisation of the Aguentas is meaningful and pragmatic, despite not necessarily being ideologically motivated or articulated.

Against Economism

Pragmatism should, however, not be confused with economism, which is an equally unfortunate tendency of the 'new war' proponents. We should, in other words, not see the meaning of these types of war in purely instrumentalist or economic terms. The simplistic underlying assumption that money is the name of the game for young combatants is unfortunate as it reduces complex social motivations to simple monetary logic. With reference to the acts of looting as explanations for organised violence and disorder Kalyvas states, in accordance with the above point of view, that: 'the linkages between looting and grievance are complex and fluid. Can we seriously reduce the 1992 Los Angeles riots to a phenomenon of "looting" even though much looting – among many other things – did take place?' (2002: 104).

What we need to make clear when focusing on the economic incentive, which becomes foregrounded by the focus on, for example, looting, is that rampant looting takes place in situations where the appropriation of resources is deemed relatively impossible by other means, which would seem – frighteningly – equally valid for areas of Los Angeles as for Guinea-Bissau. In other words, the economic incentive for youth in war ought not to point our attention towards new types of war and conflict but towards the societal states underlying them. If we are starting to see a general pattern in the actions of youth in war or violence, ought we not to look towards the underlying social processes that bring about these decisive changes?

Were we to look for meaning where Enzensberger sees none, the focus should, in other words, not be simply economistic. As Bourdieu has shown us, resources do not necessarily have to be monetary in essence. By opening up the concept of capital to the symbolic, Bourdieu demonstrates the complexity of conflicts of interest and the social embeddedness of strategic action (Bourdieu 1986, 1992).[35] I shall thus focus on the conflict engagement of my informants as expedient action but from a perspective of social possibilities rather than sheer resource appropriation. The view from within the naked rationality of monetary logic is narrow and instrumentalistic in the extreme, offering very few possibilities of analytically encompassing the complexity of social action, and, although economic gain and social possibilities are obviously related, they are most definitely not identical.

Situating Perspectives and Rationalities

The above point is not just a passing remark in the theoretical positioning of my analysis, but should rather be understood as the very point of departure of an anthropological investigation of conflict and warfare. The recourse to violence is a universal social possibility; it is a human modality rather than an individual or social pathology (cf. Jackson 1998: 5), and, instead of being confined to investigating certain societies or subjects as essentially violent, the theoretical implication of the above argument is that we open up the field of study to investigate why and how agents are motivated to violence (Cairns 1995: 122; Richards 1996), thus moving the analytical focus from essentialisation to actualisation. According to the psychologist Cairns, young people and children who become engaged in political conflict are no more introverted, uneducated or psychopathic than other youth, and will, most often, confine their violent behaviour to specific contexts (Cairns 1995: 123, 134).[36] We must therefore look at social positions and processes rather than types, essences or specific personalities and genetic, social or cultural traits. There is no specific type of agent that becomes a soldier, as, for example, the alpha male theory would have us believe,[37] and joining a military unit in the middle of bloody warfare is not the act of thrill seekers but the act of those whose space of possibilities is narrow or non-existent.

Both Cairns's and Bayart's work lead us towards analysing situated rationalities (Boudon in Bayart 1993), that is, towards illuminating 'the good reasons' that motivate our actions (Bayart 1993: 270). This is not to say that what is being proposed is a rational choice study, as the acts of the Aguentas do not lend themselves easily to the narrow idea of rationality within rational choice theory (cf. Boudon 1998: 822). Yet all actions, advantageous or not, are related to situated readings of terrains, horizons and possibilities (see Koselleck 2004). In other words, in order to make sense of my informants' motives and actions, I need to address what they see as their socially and politically manifest and imaginable terrain and their possibilities of movement within it: that is, to define the configuration of those social and political factors and processes which they see themselves as able or unable to navigate. In doing so I shall often return to the concept of horizon, which needs to be positioned in advance so as to avoid theoretical confusion.

Social Horizons

I use the concept of horizon throughout the book to indicate the spaces of possibilities and spheres of orientation that constantly arise in the interaction between agents in motion and the shifting social and political circumstances they seek to move within. New horizons arise either by movement of the agent or by the agent being moved by the social environment, both situations resulting in new points of orientation and spaces of possibilities. As social horizons are thus multiple and transient, accounting for the field of the politically possible and navigable may be easier said than done. Yet, if we look closer at the concept of the horizon, we see that it can be separated into a temporal and a spatial dimension (Koselleck 2004). Social horizons can thus be defined as 'the line behind which a new space of experience will open, but which cannot be seen yet' (Koselleck in Greverus 1996: 125); our horizon spatially distinguishes our terrain from the unknown with the imaginable being the saturated line of demarcation (see Crapanzano 2004).[38] However, in the above quote we are equally made aware of the temporal aspect of horizons; that is, that our horizons demarcate that which we have come to know from that which we might come to know,[39] with our current social terrain flowing into both the past and the future.

In relation to an analysis of action, the term horizon gains its value from being able to fuse points of view with terrains of action and thereby set the framework for our navigational possibilities and endeavours. As spatio-temporal demarcations (see Schutz and Luckmann 1995; Koselleck 2004), horizons thus position us according to where we have come from, illuminated by the retrospectively known, and where we see ourselves as going, illuminated by the prospectively possible. It is our position in a given configuration of social and political factors and processes that defines our horizon just as (apologies for the tautology) our horizons define, by demarcation, our social terrain. On a different subject, Schutz has commented that an agent acts from and on the part of his world, 'which arranges itself spatially and temporally around him as centre'. It is this spatio-temporal environment, fusing points of view and terrains of action, which I refer to as horizons.

Horizons depend on the possibilities of orientation we have from the specific point of view, as well as 'ways' of seeing, which are themselves historically and culturally constituted. Even if occupying relatively the same space and point of view, we may not necessarily be experiencing the same terrain or seeing the same topography, and so, in order to make sense of my informants' social navigation, I must analyse their position in their social environment so as to see what trajectories are open to them from their viewpoint. Yet I must also analyse their specific points of view, that is, the historically and culturally constituted mode by which they orient themselves and which informs their perception. It is a social construction of points of orientation and readings of social terrains which we are all constantly engaged in but which, because of the constantly shifting terrain and instability created by prolonged conflict, stands out all the more clearly in Guinea-Bissau.

Organisation of the Book

To accomplish this complex task the logic of this book is one of progressive contextualisation. If I wish to substantiate the claim that the Aguentas' engagement into war can be seen as social navigation, I need to gain knowledge of three different aspects of their social lives: the constitution of the primary social positions they act from; their understanding of the movement and 'unfoldings' of the social terrain; and their attempts to move within it. As with the quote from Mark Twain, which opened this chapter, social navigation directs our attention to the interaction between a navigator, the process of navigation, and the environment or terrain being navigated. The book is therefore divided into thematic sections, each of which contains a number of separate chapters that seek to illuminate these primary aspects of social navigation.

The first of the themes is thus focused on the constitution of the social navigators at the heart of my study, namely the Aguentas. It traces the Aguentas historically, illuminating how they came into existence as a militia, following them through the last couple of years of turbulence in Bissau and drawing attention to some of the primary conditions of youth in Bissau. It is directed towards the social becoming of the Aguentas in a context of decline, conflict and warfare.

In the second part of the book I explore my interlocutors' actual attempts at navigating the volatile and fluctuating environment that constitutes the Guinean social terrain. My intention is to illuminate the limitations and circumstances that characterise their social position and possibilities outside the context of warfare, as well as to examine how warfare influenced their life chances in an already difficult situation of decline and scarcity. The focus is on the possibilities and limitations of navigating terrains of conflict and decline, on the characteristics such terrains possess, and on how they influence the navigational endeavours of the agents.

In the third part of the book, I explore my interlocutors' ideas of the social environment they inhabit, see themselves as part of and seek to navigate, focusing on my interlocutors' interpretations and readings of the general movement of their society and on how they orient themselves in relation to what they see as its characteristics. Through focusing on social imaginaries, essentialisations and expectations of socio-political change, this segment of the analysis thus illuminates my interlocutors' understanding of their possibilities and limitations of action, which underlie their actual navigation.

In the fourth and final section, the focus is on appeasement and the social reintegration of the Aguentas in the post-war period up till today. I seek to bring together the different parts of the book in accounting for the specific process of reconciliation, as well as to illuminate the consequences of this process in relation to their eventual remobilisation. Ultimately, in closure, I draw us into the present and the immediate future of Guinea-Bissau and the lives of my informants.

Finally, it should be said, the book has a temporal structure, although a circular one. We shall, in this manner, follow my informants back in time to their mobilisation into the Aguentas in 1998, towards their present experiences in the current period of tension and uncertainty in Guinea-Bissau, and into their imagined futures, finishing with a return to their current position as they are engaged now, not in war but in a quest for social reintegration and new political affiliation.

First of all, however, in order to get an adequate understanding of the Aguentas, we need to go back in time. The general history of the Aguentas is closely tied to the general history of political turmoil and conflict in Guinea-Bissau, and my informants' attraction to a militia must be seen as constituted and shaped in a terrain which seems to be constantly shifting between political conflict and its radicalisation in coups and warfare. We need, in other words, to illuminate both the context in which the militia came into being and the way in which my informants chose to become Aguentas. Thus I shall now turn to the history leading to the constitution of the Aguentas, the history of my informants as Aguentas and the social positions from which they entered the Guinean civil war.

Notes

1. On the concept of 'life chances' see Dahrendorf (1979).
2. I discuss Clausewitz's work in greater detail in Chapter 5.
3. Focusing on the social, I prefer the concept of becoming to that of emergence. Despite the fact that both concepts refer to a process of constitution, the concept of becoming nonetheless has the advantage of indicating such a process with the entity in question being an active part of its constitution. Emergence refers more to a process that takes place around and without the active engagement of the entity in question.
4. Of course, there are social and economic pressures that have resulted in some areas of Bissau, and Guinea-Bissau in general, had larger percentages of inhabitants choosing to join one side of the war instead of the other, but becoming engaged in warfare in Bissau is a question of social position, perspectives, projects and process rather than force, and by far the largest part of the young men mobilised did so voluntarily.

5. Unfortunately, none of them elaborate on their use of the term.
6. I use the concept of telos rather than objective as it more adequately connects to the idea of navigational trajectories. The related concept of teleology refers to a process which has an anticipated goal as it is initiated. However, my use of the concept has extra emphasis on the anticipated, and I do not use the concept to refer to our lives as being imbued with directionality, but rather as lived along and containing multiple situational and intersecting trajectories which are constantly emerging, being discarded and adjusted to the terrain and our possibilities in it. A given telos is in other words constantly being readjusted during the process of navigation.
7. See Evans and Furlong (1997: 17–19)
8. Dahrendorf refers to these social ties as 'ligatures'.
9. Dahrendorf places the concept within a process of modernisation in which he sees the movement from *Gemeinschaft* to *Gesellschaft* as being equal to an increase in options and a decrease in ties, and yet modernisation is not seen as necessarily entailing an increase in life chances, as '[l]igatures without options are repressive, whereas options without bonds are meaningless' (Dahrendorf 1979: 31).
10. See Ajayi and Crowder (1971) and Crowder (1978).
11. The Papels (Papeis, Papelis) are seen as the original inhabitants of Bissau and the surrounding area. They are an ethnic group of West Atlantic Senegambian origin which constitutes 7 per cent of the current population (Lobban and Forrest 1988: Appendix C; http://www.countryreports.org/content/guineb.htm).
12. The process of decline and the burden of superfluous youth on urban households can be seen through comparing low-rank public worker salaries and the price of one bag of 50 kilos of rice. In the early 1980s a bag of rice is estimated to have cost 18 per cent of the monthly salary, in 1989 it would absorb 91 per cent, and in 1994 it superseded the minimum monthly salary (Lourenço-Lindell 2002: 71). In relation to this drastic fall in income and increase in prices, the burden of having extra mouths to feed becomes clearer.
13. *Mandjuandade* and *collegason* refer to roughly the same social institution or mode of arrangement, with the difference that *mandjuandade* refers to a traditional age group, whereas a *collegason* is the urban variant of an age group-cum-peer group arrangement. A *mandjuandade* thus connotes a social institution centred more strictly on age as an organising principle than does a *collegason*. Both words are used by my informants, with *mandjuandade* being used primarily by women to designate a tight-knit group of girlfriends and the more common word of *collegason* used to designate mixed groups.
14. There are women within the armed forces in Guinea-Bissau, as there were women involved in the civil war, and yet I have not heard of or met any female Aguentas. For an illumination of the lives of young women and conflict see Nordstrom (1999, 2001) and Utas (2003).
15. I use the concept of rhizomatic networks, rather than only social or political networks, as the latter often come to imply isolated and separate networks or systems whereas rhizomatic networks direct our attention towards interconnectivity and possibilities of movement.
16. See Malkki's article (1992) on the relation between arborescents, roots, social groups and social science, where she illuminates how the traditional anthropological idea of culture focuses on social groups as territorialised and growing out of the ground, rather than as interconnected becoming.
17. Experience in this perspective refers to shared experience as a mutual point of reference and common history rather than to a condition experienced subjectively as in an individual process of cognition.

18. Mannheim's theory of 'generations' (1952) bears a number of similarities to Anderson's idea of 'imagined communities' (1993) as both are directed towards explaining the constitutions of feelings of unity within 'abstract' communities.
19. Although such marches evidently have a forceful representational and symbolic dimension, this should not lead us to overlook the actual experience of *communitas* they are built upon and generate.
20. I do not see this sort of community construction as a rarity or oddity, but rather as an increasingly common crystallisation of relatedness in a world where communities are increasingly defined by social positions and networks rather than territorial anchoring and traditions: an aspect of the constitution of communities which is increasingly visible in 'new social movements'.
21. We should, furthermore, be aware of the fact that being an Aguenta is an ascribed identity directed at them from somewhere between teasing and stigmatisation, and is as such not one that is allowed to fade.
22. From a Papel point of view, the differences are noticeable. The Papels being matrilinear and avuncular-local, there is, first of all, a difference in the social position of youth related to the line of inheritance and the intergenerational dynamics. Whereas the urban Papels primarily follow a European code of law called *lei branku*, 'white law', the rural Papels primarily follow *lei preto*, 'black law'. Those following *lei preto* inherit through their mother's uncles, whereas the adherents of *lei branku* follow a patrilinear line of inheritance. Furthermore, the urban Aguentas have very little or no land, so most seek to make a living as wage earners and are thus harder struck in periods of crisis as they are dependent on money for mere subsistence. There are also differences between them in level of education and a range of other social and cultural indices.
23. Many of the Aguentas' human rights offences were committed under orders. The Aguentas are accused of carrying out assassinations and of having attacked anti-war demonstrations and civil assemblies, all of which was, allegedly, done under orders and the control of *Governo* or Senegalese officers. Although this does not excuse their actions it does show them as acting on military grounds rather than portraying them as intrinsically violent.
24. An amalgamation of *adirri Junta*, meaning to admire/support the Junta.
25. *At være i nogens vold.*
26. Henrik Rønsbo, personal communication.
27. Yet it seems to me that Kleinman et al. manage to pathologise both social structure and agency in the definition. In their perspective, anything that constrains one's agency becomes a violation, making social structure inherently coercive and agency inherently autonomous. Instead of seeing the social world as defined by social dynamics, it becomes the site of a hypothetical struggle between absolute subjects and colonising structures, making, for example, socialisation protrude as an act of violence. The concept of social suffering, by constructing the relation between agent and structure as innately negative, thus inheres the danger of leading us to overlook the fact that people invest their agency in social process, and that they might seek immediate subjugation in order to enhance their agentive potential in the long run.
28. It may also be useful to tune into changes within our general understanding of societal entities as concepts such as 'nation' and 'states' are increasingly able to be given the prefixes of 'trans' or 'post'.
29. Schmidt and Schröder define war as 'a state of confrontation in which the possibility of violence is always present and deemed legitimate by the perpetrating party' (2001: 4).
30. I am here thinking, of course, of the wars in Sierra Leone, Angola, Liberia, Casamance (i.e. the southern region of Senegal) and Côte d'Ivoire.

31. Mouvement des Forces Démocratique de Casamance, that is, the separatist forces in Casamance.
32. See for example, Enzensberger (1994), Kaldor (1999), Collier (2000), Duffield (2001) and Kalyvas (2001).
33. According to the UN, civilian casualties have 'climbed from 5 per cent of the war-related deaths at the turn of the century to more than 90 per cent in the 1990s' (Human Development Report 1998: 35).
34. Enzensberger refers to the same motley collection as mobs and marauding bands, connoting the same underlying idea of disorganised, entropic groups (1994: 17).
35. The fact that Bourdieu is seen by some to be economistic is puzzling. Where economists reduce complex social processes to capital, Bourdieu embeds capital (social, cultural symbolic or economic) within complex social processes. Where economists reduce capital to monetary value, Bourdieu unfolds the meaning of capital in relation to social worth and recognition (see Bourdieu 1986).
36. Cairns's study is primarily based on data from children and youth in Northern Ireland and can be applied here in so far as both situations tend to extremes of violence. However, the dominance of political ideology in Ireland does not find a parallel in Guinea-Bissau.
37. If we must talk of a predisposition to enter into warfare, I believe we would be better off doing so from an identity perspective, as we see lineages, clans and castes that are identified, and identify themselves, as being especially closely related to soldiering; however, this construction arises from membership in a specific social category rather a genetic inclination. Furthermore, the theory of alpha males, if not a random mutation, ought to collapse on itself as the alpha males must, by definition, be a diminishing genealogy as they bear the death toll of charging into warfare, whilst the world paradoxically is getting no more peaceful.
38. I do not refer to the concept of the imaginary in the sense of fantasy or fiction but rather as related to the Husserlian 'protention', as an induction built experience. The concept will be dealt with in detail in Chapter 8.
39. In a Schutzian perspective we can thus say that horizons encompass both 'the world within actual reach', 'the world within potential reach' and 'the world within attainable reach' (Schutz and Luckmann 1995: 37–41; Schutz 1996: 277). I shall not, however, be going into the specific details of the concept of horizon as developed by Schutz, as the above-mentioned Husserlian idea of protention (1964) and the temporal dimension of the social imaginary (Castoriadis 1997: 146–47) are more closely related to my explanatory aim.

PART II

THE AGUENTAS

Chapter 3

BECOMING AGUENTAS

'Here progress has already died,' Yvette said. She was cooking for Dario and the girls, with Rubin, having no money to contribute to the meal, waiting around to attend to eventual leftovers. 'These days, things only go from bad to worse,' she continued as she turned to the mortar to pound chillies, onion, stock cubes and lime into 'conserva' to go with the fish. 'If God helps us we will all go to Portugal, we will all go. We will be well there.' After her last sentence she looked up at me and smiled, keeping the pleasant prospect of mass migration hanging in the air: yet her smile also underlined the absurdity of the statement, Guinea-Bissau apparently being seen as too far gone to be salvaged, the process of decline and conflict as so massive that the only thing left to do is for its population to jump overboard – if only they could.

My main aim within this chapter is to illuminate the social becoming of the Aguentas in relation to the progressive decline that has come to characterise Guinean society. I shall, in relation to this endeavour, locate the war of 1998–1999 within a longer historical period, briefly sketching the last 500 years of Guinean history and the general context the war emerged from and in and ultimately bringing the reader back to the present. Having illuminated the becoming of the militia historically, I shall seek to position them socially, politically and militarily in order to further our understanding of the constitution of the militia and the reasons behind their mobilisation. First of all, however, I will turn my attention to the earlier history of Guinea-Bissau in order to supply the reader with a brief overview of the creation of the country, its demographic make-up and the context from which the Aguentas emerged.[1]

Five Hundred Years of Colonisation

Despite the fact that the Portuguese first made their presence felt in what now constitutes Guinea-Bissau in the year 1446, the last 500 years of Guinean history cannot solely or even primarily be seen as characterised by Portuguese colonisation.[2] As we look back into the historical data from the last half of the second millennium, we thus see three overlapping and interacting processes of invasion and colonisations of the area that now constitutes Guinea-Bissau, all of which implied processes of domination, enslavement and exploitation.

Historically the area now constituting Guinea-Bissau was originally inhabited by Senegambian ethnic groups that were to develop into the primary ethnic groups of the Balanta, the Beafata, the Budjugu, the Diolas,[3] the Nalu, the Papel and the Serer.[4] However, during the last 500 years, these groups have been increasingly marginalised by Mandinga,[5] Fula[6] and Portuguese invasions,[7] pushing the Senegambian groups towards the coastal mangrove swamps as they tried to protect themselves from war parties and slave raids (see Hawthorne 2001).[8] What was eventually to become a period of Portuguese colonisation, through the building of forts and trading posts in the river estuaries, thus overlapped with appropriations of the hinterland by the Mandinga kingdom of Gabu and by the Fula states of Futa Toro and Futa Jallon (see Mabogunje 1971).[9]

The Kingdom of Gabu

The Gabu kingdom, a tributary kingdom of the Mandinga kingdom of Mali, was initially to have a grave impact on the lives of the Senegambian people inhabiting the Guinean hinterland. The kingdom was founded in the thirteenth century by the Malian general Tiramakhan Traore, who settled, together with his soldiers, in the Casamance region of Senegal and the northern part of Guinea-Bissau. In the middle of the sixteenth century the kingdom was established as an autonomous entity and subsequently grew to be the strongest kingdom of the region, covering parts of what are currently Gambia, Senegal and Guinea-Bissau (Forrest 2003: 27–44).

The kingdom was initially an important part of the Malian trade of salt, gold and slaves with the Europeans. Selling slaves taken from the interior of the country or conquered through war, the Mandinga kingdom was influential in forging the current demographic picture of Guinea-Bissau, as the Mandinga land conquests and slave raids led to a migration of the Senegambians towards the coastal river estuaries (Lobban and Forrest 1988: 72; Forrest 2003: 39–42). In fact, the Gabu kingdom was so efficient that its activities resulted in a decimation of, primarily, the Diolas and Balantas. By the end of the sixteenth century, an estimated 50 per cent of all African slaves are supposed to have been supplied by the Gabu kingdom, further pushing many Senegambian groups into the coastal mangrove swamps and establishing what is now their tradition for wetland rice farming (Lobban and Forrest 1998: 71–74; Mark 1999; Hawthorne 2001: 14).

The Portuguese, who had by then settled on the coast, seem to have been fairly disengaged from the conflicts taking place in the hinterland. They were instead fortifying their trading posts and taking maximum advantage of the hinterland conflicts by being willing buyers of the prisoners of war, sold off as slaves to plantations in the Americas through the Cape Verdean-based slaving company Cachen Rios e Comércio da Guiné (see Blake 1942: section 1; Lobban and Forrest 1998: 36).[10] The Portuguese were not a dominant power in the interior of the country but seemed satisfied with playing a commercial rather than colonial role, consolidating their dominance only in the estuaries of the major rivers of the area, which were of strategic importance in the extraction of goods and slaves. Of prime importance for this control were the cities of Bolama, Bissau and Cacheu of which Bolama was the first capital of the country and Bissau the second, with Cacheu subsequently losing its influence and turning into a provincial town.

Futa Jallon and Futa Toro

Towards the end of the eighteenth century, the Gabu kingdom had lost its power and was coming under attack from the Fula states of Futa Jallon and Futa Torro, from what is now the neighbouring Guinea Conakry. The Fula and the Mandinga had long been competing for land and influence within the interior of the country, with the Fula being forced to assume a submissive position, but with the kingdom of Gabu losing power the Mandinga hegemony was coming under increasing pressure. The Fulas, who had first settled in the area as early as the twelfth and thirteenth centuries were now, towards the end of the eighteenth century,[11] starting to pose a real challenge to the Mandinga, as the state of Futa Jallon had risen to be an organised and structured regional counterweight to Gabu. The growth of the power of Futa Jallon and the decline of Gabu eventually resulted in an invasion by the Fulas and, by 1867, the kingdom of Gabu had surrendered to a 12,000-strong Fula army, consisting of earlier settled Fulas and the invading Fula forces from the south (Forrest 2003: 64–83).

Because of the conflicts between the Mandinga and the Fula the Portuguese were able to consolidate their presence on the coast in relative peace from the two dominant forces of the region (ibid.). Furthermore, they eventually managed to pacify the different ethnic groups of the region, subjugating the Guinean population by allying themselves with the dominant ethnic group of the later part of the period, namely the Fula. However, it was not until after the Conference in Berlin in 1886, that the Portuguese actually started a general 'pacification' campaign in order to gain control of the land outside their fortified towns and trading posts,[12] and not till 1915–1916 that we can actually talk about larger Portuguese-controlled areas,[13] even when we disregard numerous armed insurgencies all the way up till 1936. Thus Portugal was effectively in control of Guinean territory for only about thirty-five years, as it lost control of the north and south of the country during the ten-year liberation struggle and eventually granted Guinea-Bissau independence in 1974.

Furthermore, it would seem that the differentiation between the Portuguese as colonisers and the indigenous population as colonised, along with the clear racial differentiation within the divide, emerged primarily within the last century of Portuguese influence in Guinea (Mark 1999: 2002). Being Portuguese was formerly not a question of pigmentation. Rather, from the sixteenth to the nineteenth century, being Portuguese in West Africa referred to being 'Luso-African',[14] which 'represented a socially complex and geographically dispersed community' (Mark 1999: 174) stretching from Cape Verde to Senegal and Sierra Leone on the Guinean coast. Being Portuguese covered a number of cultural and religious and linguistic traits yet equally served as an important contrast to being a slave. It was a social identity rather than a racial one, and pigmentation seems not to have been emphasised as an essential trait of Portuguese identity until the nineteenth century, as it gradually, within the relatively short period of Portuguese hegemony, developed into a racially based definition of colonisers and colonised, authority and worth (ibid.: 188).

The Liberation War

The Portuguese were, in other words, neither a very efficient nor a long-lasting colonial force, and seem throughout the largest part of the described period to have emphasised a strategy of trade rather than focusing on acquisition of land, control of colonial subjects and the construction of sovereign space. Up till the end of the nineteenth century they were the lesser of the three dominant forces of the area, and yet they came, through a series of ruthless military campaigns, to gain control of Guinea-Bissau in the first part of the twentieth century, until the onset of the liberation war in the early 1960s.

The person who was to be the moving force in the Guinean move towards independence was Amilcar Cabral. Cabral created a Marxist liberation theory in which Portuguese hegemony was identified as being the regressive factor of Guinean history, responsible for having halted Guinean society in its precolonial historical trajectory (Cabral

1973: 40–44). Guinea-Bissau had always been the least developed of the Portuguese territories (Chabal 2002: 48), however, rather than merely testifying to the miserable state of the Portuguese *Guiné*, Cabral's identification of the illegitimacy of Portuguese rule was to be the ideological point of departure which, together with the racial inequality and general social oppression of colonial Portuguese Guinean society, was to lead to the onset of the liberation struggle in 1963 (Cabral 1980).

The party that was to be the dominant force behind these liberation efforts was the PAIGC.[15] Founded in 1956 the PAIGC was to gain international acclaim for its innovative and egalitarian political programmes and projects. Initially, Cabral had formed an independence party with another dominant liberation leader, Henri Labery, in 1954. However, differences of opinion between the role and intensity of the Guinean Cape Verdean unity and collaboration caused a split of the original party into the FLING and PAIGC.[16] Cabral, born in the Guinean town of Bafata with a Cape Verdean father and a Guinean mother, was a staunch defender of unity between the two countries. Labery, on the contrary, mistrusted the Cape Verdeans for the role they played in the colonial administration, where many served within the colonial administration, and for their participation in the slave trade along the Guinean coast (Lobban and Forrest 1988: 63, 97). However, from this split, it was Cabral who managed to secure popular support for the PAIGC, initially as a peaceful worker-based independence party that organised unions and civil protest, but after 1961 as an armed revolutionary party. In 1963 the party launched a ten-year armed liberation struggle against the Portuguese army and colonial system and the PAIGC were to establish themselves in the rural and forestry areas of the country. Relying on guerrilla tactics, they were within half a year fighting the Portuguese along two fronts and by 1965 the PAIGC was in control of half the country. Despite being backed by NATO and in possession of superior military technology and weaponry, the Portuguese were fighting an uphill battle, receiving local support only from parts of the Fula population.[17] As they increasingly lost control over the inner Fula-dominated areas of the country, their control was effectively reduced to the areas around the major cities and the coastal estuary, the areas in which they had fortified their interests in the early colonial days.

In the final stages of the war, the Portuguese succeeded in assassinating the charismatic leader of the liberation movement. Amilcar Cabral was shot and killed in Guinea Conakry through the combined efforts of the FLING, the Portuguese secret police (the PIDE)[18] and internal factional conflicts within the PAIGC. However, despite losing their leader, the PAIGC nonetheless succeeded in toppling Portuguese control over Guinea-Bissau, declaring independence on 24 September 1973 and being recognised as an independent country by the Portuguese state on 10 September 1974.

Thirty Years of Factional Struggle

Yet the Cabralian Marxist regime did not succeed in leading Guinea-Bissau forwards. Rather than being characterised by progress and prosperity the twenty-five years of official Cabralian Marxism led to growing poverty and, paradoxically, to a massive gap in wealth between the country's small elite and the general population. However, this very non-egalitarian and non-socialist distribution of wealth for a long time ran parallel with Cabral's ideology being institutionalised into the state apparatus and actively disseminated via the elementary school curriculum. Just as the social Darwinist ideology of the colonial system was taught in schools prior to independence, so was the Cabralian Marxist theory of progress taught within the educational system after independence, through the subject of *Formação Militante*.[19] However, due to the changing climate within the global political situation,[20] the constellation of beneficiaries and the scientific value of Marxism and historical materialism, the regime in Bissau was forced to start making the structural changes necessary for freeing market forces in the 1980s and early 1990s, in so far as they wished to boost the economy and continue to attract international aid (Aguilar and Stenman 1997, 2001; Forrest 2002).

From an educational perspective, this entailed abandoning the teaching of *Formação Militante*, which, in Bissau, was replaced, in 1991, with what was seen as a more up-to-date subject, *Educação Social*, tuned instead to progress and citizenship within a democracy. The change reflected a move from a one-party state to a multiparty democracy, and from a planned economy to an economic policy of free market forces. Yet, despite political changes and ideological shifts there was still a massive gap between the ideal and the real within Guinean politics. With the ideological shift, the subsequent structural adjustment programme, the entrance into ECOWAS,[21] the attempted implementation of free trade and the move towards democracy, Guinea-Bissau was supposed to be placed politically, economically and developmentally on the road to growth within a world of capitalist societies. Yet the neo-liberalist version of capitalist development which took over as Marxist ideology was discredited in the 1990s and which was propagated in its wake equally did not lead to progress.

The Coup in 1998

What we have seen is three major changes in historical understandings of the Guinean movement through time within the last thirty years, but with none of the historical trajectories and promising futures being proposed actually materialising. What emerged instead were increasing conflict and turmoil, warfare and, not least, a popular juxtaposing of politics to greed and ideologies to lies. As such, politics is currently seen by my interlocutors as a general oscillation between *sabi boca* and *suso barriga* (see Chapter 8), that is, between a 'sweet mouth' and a 'dirty belly', or, phrased differently, from political rhetoric and lies to corruption and consumption. Much to my amazement, my Guinean informants thus did not interpret the period of time since independence as characterised by positive social change but rather by decline and conflict. Equally, from an outsider's perspective, it seems fair to say that the political history of Guinea-Bissau since independence has been characterised by what can be called 'stable instability', that is, continuous political instability and conflict. Being caught in a seemingly incessant process of factionalist struggle,[22] the country falls into the common post-independence scenario of internal conflict invading the political stage as soon as the external enemies have been defeated (Chabal 2002). Factions are, as Mayer informs us, 'units of conflict activated on specific occasions rather than maintained by formal organization'. They are 'loosely ordered' and based more on 'transaction than issues of principle' (Mayer 1966: 116). Yet, contrary to other similar situations the political factions, primarily within the PAIGC and now within the multiparty 'democratic' Guinean political scene, seem not to institutionalise themselves into enduring political units, but rather to be caught in a flow of constantly changing political configurations and factions.

However, the violent potential of these power struggles and sociopolitical configurations had been more or less restrained, confined to minor outbreaks of fighting as a more persistent move from conflict to warfare was somehow avoided – that is, until the fighting commenced in 1998.

From Conflict to War

Early on Sunday 7 June 1998, the clatter of gunfire sounded over Bissau. On tuning into their radios, the city's inhabitants heard that the fighting would soon be over and the situation returned to normal. However, instead of returning to normal, the events of 7 June were to explode into full-scale warfare, calm not being restored, even temporarily, until fifty days later.

Having been in power since November 1980, the president, João Bernardo Vieira, popularly referred to as Nino, was no stranger to coup attempts. In fact, he seemed exceptionally adept at the art of surviving and controlling factional and political conflict. He had himself gained office in 1980 by overthrowing President Luis Cabral,[23] and prior to the coup in 1998, which was to be his downfall, he had survived three alleged coup attempts. In 1983, the current prime minister, Victor Saúde Maria, was dismissed and imprisoned, along with his alleged accomplices, for planning to topple the government; in 1986, Paulo Correia, a hero of the war of independence and the leading figure for a large part of the majority Balanta population, was arrested and executed, together with a handful of other prominent politicians, on charges of plotting to overthrow the government (Forrest 1992: 251);[24] and, in 1993, João Da Costa, an influential politician, along with the head of the paramilitary rapid Intervention Force and a dozen soldiers, were arrested on charges of being involved in a military coup.[25] Nino's uncanny ability to manoeuvre through a political terrain as factionally destabilised as the Guinean one gave him a reputation of possessing a special ability to see the plotting of coups despite their clandestine and covert character.

Despite the alleged coups, Nino managed to stay in power up till the first democratic, multiparty election in July 1994.[26] Furthermore, he succeeded in being re-elected into the presidential seat after the election, his party, the PAIGC gaining 62 out of 102 seats in the National Assembly, and Nino, as the party president, subsequently gaining another four years in power, or as it would turn out, nearly four more years (see also Lyon 1980; Forrest 1992, 2003: 222–32; Kovsted and Tarp 1999: 12; Rudebeck 2000: 2).

A Regional Point of Departure

The coup in 1998, led by the former Chief of Staff and long-term ally of President Nino, Asumané Mané, was initiated only a few months prior to the second multiparty election in the country's history. Yet the decisive factor for the instigation of the *coup d'état* seems to have had more to do with a question of regional arms sales than with the coming democratic elections.

The coup was a consequence of the dismissal of Brigadier Asumané Mané as Chief of Staff on 5 June 1998.[27] Half a year prior to the start of the war,[28] Asumané Mané had been suspended following accusations of arms sales from the Guinean armed forces to the MFDC rebel movement in Casamance, Senegal.[29] During their fight for independence, the MFDC have had close connections to Guinea-Bissau, as they have used the northern, Diola/Felupe-dominated areas of the country as a safe haven for tired soldiers recuperating from the war. However with the Guinean entry into the West African Monetary Union and the gradual alignment of President Vieira's politics with the French field of interest in West Africa, which favour the Senegalese side of the Casamance conflict, there was an increased focus on Guinea-Bissau's role in supporting the MFDC cause through sales of arms. As a consequence of the pressure from France and Senegal, Brigadier Mané was singled out to bear the blame for the apparent arms sales to the rebels, and a parliamentary investigation was launched on 27 February.[30] The report, which was due on Monday 8 June, was said to have been heavily influenced by the president, freeing him of blame while grossly incriminating Mr Mané. However, Mané, more soldier than politician, made sure the report was not presented on the set date, gathering a group of allied troops around him and launching his *coup d'état* the day before the parliamentary commission was to announce its conclusions (Kovsted and Tarp 1999: 11; Forrest 2002: 255–59).[31]

Early Stages of the War

Indicative of the regional character of the Guinean conflict, it did not take long before four different military forces participated in the war. The Guinean army was split in two, with the large majority of the soldiers opting to join Asumané Mané's side of the conflict. However, the few hundred men, mostly officers and the presidential guard, who did choose to stay on the presidential side of the conflict got the backing of an artillery battalion from Guinea Conakry consisting of 500 men, as well as 1300 Senegalese commandos within less than two days.

The speed of the arrival of foreign forces in Bissau bears witness to President Vieira's ability to foresee political movement, as well as to his national intelligence apparatus, as he must have had a premonition of Brigadier Mané's plans. President Nino seems, however, to have underestimated the reaction of the common soldier and the general Guinean population, as the influx of foreign troops appears to have been a turning point for those who had not yet taken sides in the conflict and had the effect of massively strengthening the popular support for the politico-military faction that now called itself the Junta Militar.[32] Equally, the rapid creation of the Junta Militar would seem to testify to a nearly undivided stand within the army on the question of illegal arms sales, or at least on the question of the evaluation of and retribution for the offence. While avoiding the question of responsibility for the sales of arms, it seems necessary to add that during the war, as well as after it, Asumané Mané was able to count on the help of the MFDC guerrillas, indicating that the relationship between the two parties was not a negative one.[33]

What we see when looking at the early stages of the war is thus a conflict between a politically elected government side backed by a relatively large number of high-ranking officers, a few loyal local troops and a large contingent of Senegalese and Conakrian military personnel, fighting against a Junta Militar backed by the large majority of the local military personnel as well as an unknown number of MFDC troops,[34] with the support of the population in general. So, despite their claimed political legitimacy, the government forces were not able to gain local support or make military advances, being constantly on the retreat. Within the next fifty days the Junta Militar had taken control over the majority of the country, leaving the government in control of the Prabis peninsula, the cities of Bafata and Gabu, the Bijagos islands, and a hemmed in area of Bissau,[35] with the front line drawn along the city's outer suburbs.[36] From a military perspective, the fifty days of fighting saw the commencement of heavy artillery shelling of the city and a heavy casualty toll among the Senegalese troops at the front line in Bissau.[37] However, despite the disadvantaged position of the government side, a truce was negotiated by the CPLC on 26 July 1998,[38] with an actual ceasefire being signed on 26 August in Praia, Cape Verde, coordinated jointly by CPLP and ECOWAS.[39]

The ceasefire was to last two and a half months, and seemed above all to provide the government side with a welcome opportunity to mobilise support in a situation where they were practically deprived of backing from existing Guinean military personnel and experiencing heavy casualties on the front line. Lacking support from the general population, the government turned instead to the large group of 'superfluous' young men within the country, and managed to mobilise a few thousand youths via promises and the allure of invitations into patrimonial networks – warlordism being militarised patrimonialism. This unlawfully recruited militia was trained, armed and enrolled into the *Forças di Governo* and given the popular name Aguentas, that is, Helpers or Supporters.

Enter Aguentas

As an irregular militia, it is difficult to find any 'official' data on the Aguentas, as they were not enrolled and registered following regular military procedure. We have a limited amount of statistical data on the Aguentas obtained after the war by a survey done by Rädda Barnen based on the captured Aguentas who attended a crash course in human rights arranged by the Guinean Human Rights League (Aimé 1999a, 1999b; Liga Guineense dos Direitos Humanos 1999).[40] We also have statistical data from a census of war veterans carried out by the PDRRI.[41] Yet what we know about the Aguentas is still sporadic at best. What we do know from the wartime data is that, by September

1998, the government side was reduced to 120 men, the foreign troops apart, but had succeeded in recruiting and sending an estimated 600 Aguentas to a training camp in Guinea Conakry, with further recruitment continuing right up to the final stages of the war.[42]

The statistical data from the post-war census show that the current number of Aguentas probably amounts to somewhere around a thousand individuals.[43] The exact number in the national survey totals 895 individuals; however, presuming that a number of Aguentas have been unable to register, or have chosen not to register despite the economic incentive to do so,[44] combined with an unknown number of unregistered Aguentas still based in Conakry,[45] who are currently believed to be involved in the fighting in the forest region bordering Liberia, we ought to augment the number considerably. However, being able to precisely define the number of Aguentas seems a somewhat trivial endeavour and the exact number of Aguentas as read from the statistical data, all their faults and uncertainties taken into consideration, is at best indicative. Nevertheless, what the available statistical data allow us to do is to straighten out a number of misconceptions, misunderstandings and misrepresentations concerning the Aguentas, by positioning them in relation to corresponding data on the general Guinean population.

Social Position and Stratification

Concerning these misunderstandings there are three major areas where the Aguentas have been misrepresented. First of all they were – locally and internationally – considered to be primarily children or adolescents. Secondly, they were seen to have been recruited primarily from the countryside, from the rural Papel and Budjugu areas. Thirdly, they were seen as illiterate, poorly educated agents and thus easily convinced or tricked into joining the Aguentas. However, if we look at the quantitative data we have on the Aguentas, we first of all see, contrary to popular belief, as well as to the misconceptions circulating along the murky information flow of war rumours, the NGO industry and political representations that by far the largest group of Aguentas were young men rather than children or adolescents.[46]

Age

Comparing the data from the social reintegration programme of the PDRRI and that of the Guinean Human Rights League, we see, in both cases, that the percentage of Aguentas under the age of eighteen is exceptionally small, being 2 and 1.6 per cent respectively.[47] Furthermore, according to the latter survey of the Aguentas who were taken prisoner by the Junta Militar, the youngest were seventeen years of age at the end of the war. Thus they must have been around sixteen years of age when they entered the Aguentas (coincidentally the minimum age for recruitment into the British army).[48] While there most probably have been cases of recruitment of soldiers under the age of eighteen, it is important to emphasise that the category of people who were recruited into the Aguentas were, both in terms of age and social position, youths rather than children, a fact that is supported by the data.

The fact that there is a classificatory difference based on generational rather than chronological age (see Fortes 1984) is exceptionally important to grasp, as it determines the way we position and analyse the actions and motives of the Aguentas. Viewing the Aguentas as children bears the analytical danger that, instead of seeing them as agents trying to navigate their lives through the uneasy waters of decline, conflict and war, we see them as mechanically mastered under the control of their elders, as objects in war rather than agents of war, a misconception that seems dominant within the international community working in Guinea-Bissau, as seen, for example, in the following quote by the former Swedish Ambassador to Guinea-Bissau:

> Recruitment [of the Aguentas] happens through disbursement of rice and a few bottles of alcohol to the head of the family upon agreeing to send a son on a month [of] military training. There has been controversy on the radio about these recruitments and the government radio broadcast an interview with a twenty-eight-year-old male who has been voluntarily recruited. He is most probably the exception which proves the rule that the majority are young boys. (Andrén 1998: 5–6, my translation)

As we shall see later, the above statement is a gross misunderstanding not only of the specific process of recruitment but also of the Aguentas and the process surrounding their recruitment in general. First of all, it entails an absurd generalisation that the fathers of the Aguentas will sell their 'children' to war for a couple of bottles of alcohol and a bit of rice, which, stemming from a lack of knowledge of both the inter-generational relations of power and authority, builds on a prejudiced stereotypification of Papel, Guinean or African fathers. Secondly, as said, the conception of the Aguentas as children leads to a flawed perception of the dynamics that caused at least my informants to mobilise. And, thirdly, as the statistical data as well as my own qualitative data show, the young man of twenty-eight mentioned in the quote being a man rather than a child was in fact not the exception but rather the rule. The data from the PDRRI survey show that 94.5 per cent of the registered Aguentas were between the ages of eighteen and forty-five, and were not, according to international standards, young *boys*, but rather youth or young *men*. The misconception that the Aguentas were young, underage soldiers is thus unsubstantiated and rests, I suspect, on two very different premises. In relation to the Guinean understanding of the Aguentas there is a social and reconciliatory aspect to their classification as children rather than youth, a fact that will be discussed at length in Chapter 9. Concerning the dominance of the international community's representation of the Aguentas as children, we should probably look towards the world of the NGO industry for the answer. However, although the position of youth or young men in war might not gain as much attention as that of children, their position as youth is nonetheless central to a proper understanding the Aguentas.

Residence

Furthermore, a general misconception seems to be that the Aguentas were from rural areas. Despite the fact that a slight majority of the Aguentas were born in the rural areas, all of my informants were recruited while living in Bissau and the PDRRI data show that, in 2001–2002, 67 per cent of the Aguentas lived in Bissau, with 34 per cent also having been born there. This could, of course, imply that the large majority of Aguentas moved to Bissau after the war ended in 1999, but my own data testify to the contrary.[49] Though not all born in Bissau, almost all of my interlocutors lived in Bissau at the time of their mobilisation, many of them attending secondary school or seeking employment, and, juxtaposing my data with the demographic data, the Aguentas seem more reasonably conceived of as urbanised rather than rural youth.[50]

As I looked further into the aspect of where the Aguentas were born it furthermore became clear that, although some of my interlocutors were born in the countryside, they were not first-generation urban dwellers. For spiritual safety reasons, many women will go to their ethnic 'homeland' when they are expecting. Upon closer scrutiny, the movement of people in Bissau points towards the need for a softening of the traditionally rigid dichotomy between urban and rural lives, as there is a constant movement of people between these areas. Many of my informants would have seasonal work in their *terra*, ethnic homeland, and spend an amount of time there during the harvest season,[51] in addition a number of rituals and social obligations, such as circumcisions, funerals and weddings, necessitate frequent returns to one's *terra*.[52]

Educational Level

Perhaps because of their perceived rural background the Aguentas were in popular perception equally supposed to be uneducated and intellectually sluggish – or *sin nivel* as they say in Creole.

Interestingly Rädda Barnen's survey seems to support this presumption as the sample of thirty-one Aguentas between eighteen and nineteen shows that the Aguentas were exceptionally poorly educated, with as much as 42 per cent of the sample being illiterate (Aimé 1999b: 43). However, the more exhaustive PDRRI data show us a low percentage of illiterates among the Aguentas, with 83 per cent knowing how to read and write,[53] and 81 per cent having received formal education.[54] The PDRRI data correspond better to my observations than the data from Rädda Barnen's survey of the Guinean Human Rights League programme, and the latter data might, in fact, have been influential in shaping the very myth of the rural and simple-minded Aguentas. This discrepancy between the two sets of data seems to be located in the fact that the sample from the Human Rights League programme is based on the Aguentas who did not manage to escape during the last offensive in May 1999, which many did. Rädda Barnen's data may thus be based on a biased sample and contain an over-representation of the rural – which in a Guinea-Bissauian context also means less educated – as many of the urban Aguentas were able to discard their uniforms, hide their weapons and run home or escape by using their social or family networks. Equally, networks might also be what we have to focus on if we wish to understand the ethnic composition of the Aguentas.

Ethnicity

Among the vast majority of anthropologists and other social scientists working on Guinea-Bissau, with the exception of Lyon (1980), most studies of political or conflictual processes in Guinea-Bissau seem to avoid or, at most, write off ethnicity as a factor. This blind spot could be related to the fact that many scholars first made acquaintance with Guinea at a time when the ethnic tones of the political processes were publicly denounced, or that '*tribalismo*', as ethno-politics is called in Creole, is locally taboo. Maintaining the perspective seems however to be characterised by wishful thinking rather than realism. The Aguentas present as clear a case as any of the ethnic dimension within national Guinean politics, with a large group of youth being drawn into the conflict by virtue of their ethnic relationship to both President Nino and the *governo* Chief of Staff Humberto Gomes.

On an academic level, one can thus only be puzzled by the avoidance of the subject when it seems to be a clearly identifiable underlying factor in a consecutive line of conflicts and, not least, clearly evident in the current political situation. In other words, despite the fact that the coup against the government of Luis Cabral had clear ethnic undertones (the Cape Verdean elite being seen as not adequately Guinean), which can be traced back to the separation between the

PAIGC and the FLING, to the assassination of Amilcar Cabral and to the Cape Verdean position within the colonial government and their role in the slave trade; despite the alleged coup or purge of 1985, which led to the execution and imprisonment of the political faction built around the Balanta war hero Paulo Correia, and hence the elimination of the political power base of the Balantas; despite the clearly ethnic aspect of the 1998 war, with the Aguentas being predominantly Papel and the Junta recruiting its soldiers primarily from the young rural Balanta population; and despite the clearly ethnic dimension of the distribution of votes in the election in the democratic election of 2000 and the subsequent 'Balantafication' of the state, government and military apparatus, after the victory of the Balanta president Kumba Yala it is still not *comme il faut* to speak openly of ethnic aspects of politics in relation to the Guinean political scene, nor does it seem to be *comme il faut* to do so in academic work on Bissau. The examples are numerous when in Guinea-Bissau, and they are equally easy to find in print. The otherwise outstanding political scientist Rudebeck states, for example, that: 'There was not a distinct ethnic dimension to the war, despite the fact that many ethnic groups are represented within the Guinean society, and despite the fact that the cultural self-images of the Guineans are characterised by this diversity' (Rudebeck 2000: 5). Yet if we look more closely at the ethnic composition of the government side of the war, with its majority of Papels, it seems unquestionable that there was an ethnic dimension to the mobilisation of the Aguentas. Equally, if we look at the casting of votes, from the election in 1999 to the latest in 2005, there is a correlation between people's votes and their ethnic identity. Yet, rather than simply judging the commonly held idea of an absence of ethno-politics within Bissau as wrong, we need to question instead what underlies this schism between the real and the ideal and what kind of rationale makes salient the ethno-political praxis as it is seen in Guinea-Bissau.

Taking Tribalismo Seriously

What seems to confuse the picture is that ethno-politics in Bissau is not overtly built on social polarisation. A major stumbling block in our understanding of ethno-politics appears to me to be the consequent fusing of the concept with inter-ethnic hatred. *Tribalismo* or ethno-politics is not necessarily about hatred. Although it is unquestionably about differentiating social categories it is, I believe, more often directed towards flows of resources and social obligation that provide a relatively secure foundation on which to build political networks in times of scarcity or instability. We might in other words have to start asking ourselves if we have been so focussed on Barth's theory of ethnic groups and boundaries (1969) that we instinctively look towards counter-identification when encountering ethnicity, at the expense of the dynamics of network (Hawthorne 2001)? Equally this representation of ethno-politics (as seen in the case of Rwanda), may very well be what lies behind the dogged denial of the existence of ethno-politics within parts of the Bissauian population, as the term connotes hostility between ethnic groups rather than, for example, competition between political complexes that build on ethnic networks due to aspects of safety and reliability.

Rather than being related to inter-ethnic hatred or political animosity, the tacit salience of *tribalismo* in Bissau is located on the interface between patrimonial political structures and an economy of affection in which one is obliged to help one's kin (Hydén 1983).[55] In the urban, multi-ethnic context of Bissau this means that networks are often built around ethnic affiliation,[56] to the point where there is a saying that in a political context people of the same ethnic group do not – and ought not, there being a normative aspect to it – *nega um otru*, i.e. deny each other assistance.[57]

The majority of Aguentas were Papels. Rädda Barnen's data from the Guinean Human Rights League programme documents that 42 per cent of the 120 interned militia were Papels, 20 per cent Fula and 10 per cent Budjugu. However, the large percentage of Fula and Budjugu Aguentas in the sample can, as with the educational statistics, once again be related to those who were imprisoned at the time the Junta Militar succeeded in capturing Bissau, who due to the distance from their *terra* and their primary networks had greater difficulties in escaping from the Junta patrols. My own data indicate a higher percentage of Papels (59 per cent) within the Aguentas;[58] yet, even if we disregard the specificities of the different samples, they still all testify to a significant over-representation of the Papels within the militia, as the Papel community only accounts for 7 per cent of the total population.[59]

To sum up, judged from the available data on the Aguentas we see that they were recruited during a stage in the war where the *Governo* side had taken to its heels, having suffered heavy casualties on the front line of the war; secondly, they were almost exclusively young men and predominantly from the ethnic group of the Papels; and thirdly, they had a better than average to average literacy rate – all characteristics that are of importance when trying to position their social navigation. But the Aguentas do not only stand out when socially positioned: they equally stand out if we look at their position within the military system they entered.

The Military Position of the Aguentas

Within the military hierarchy of the *Governo* forces, the Aguentas were, as an irregularly recruited militia, without military rank. In fact, the very name of 'Aguenta' (meaning 'helper' or 'supporter') was used to designate all government troops without rank, as the other soldiers fighting for the government side were either *antigo combatentes*,[60] that is, people who had fought in the Liberation War, or officers, sergeants or privates.

As military status is, at least ideally, ascribed according to military knowledge and experience, the Aguentas, being a haphazardly constituted, poorly educated force, were at the very bottom of the military hierarchy. This low-status military position was widely recognised by my informants, as this interview with Adilson reveals:

So what do you think I need to know to understand the Aguentas well. To understand them well, properly? It could be many things or just one.
You must know that the Aguentas were nothing. Aguentas are not like other troops. They are not troops that are written about in books, they are troops only to help in war ... Aguentas did not have a lot of experience. We had a month of preparation, one month, and then we came back. We had nearly a month. Expenditure was not there. That is to say, the Aguentas were a thing ... a thing made quickly, quickly, you understand? Only to know how to take up arms, how to fire arms. We did not have a lot of experience ... we were not complete troops. Do you know about troops? Troops have to be complete ... The Aguentas were not troops. [We] were not complete. The Aguentas were nothing.

Yet, despite sharing the same low position in the military hierarchy there were internal differentiations in military status, related to differences in military training and ability. Carlos, who was among the first group of Aguentas to be trained in Conakry, explains it in the following manner:

Were there different groups of Aguentas. Were there different groups within the Aguentas?
There were different groups, because you see that those that they call the true Aguentas,[61] are those that were trained in Conakry, but there are some that were trained here in Bissau. So like [the Junta Militar] they say: Aguentas they died a lot. But, no! Aguentas did not die a lot. We suffered thirteen to fourteen deaths in the Aguentas. People that died the most were the people that were trained here [in Guinea-Bissau], they died a lot, a lot, and they [the Junta Militar] ... they say that they were all Aguentas, but no. There were Aguentas and there were those other groups that were called Aguentas, but we were different.

Although we should put the death toll of the Aguentas who were trained in Guinea Conakry higher than thirteen to fourteen (the understatement was probably meant to increase the military standing of his own position), the quote shows the creation of internal subgroups within the Aguentas, differentiated by military knowledge, whereby the latecomers are placed at the bottom of the established hierarchy and the top of the mortality figures. Military knowledge was the ordering principle, but the differentiation seems to have been there from the start of their military careers, as the first Aguentas, recruited between August and December 1998 (Aimé 1999b: 43), were relatively better prepared after receiving between one and a half and two months' training at the military barracks in Kindia, Guinea Conakry. The later Aguentas, on the contrary, received only a shortened military training within Guinea-Bissau.[62]

The main reason for the difference in preparation seems to be related to the final withdrawal of the Conakrian and the Senegalese troops, which left the government side with a decimated military force. An apparent mobilisation frenzy was thus undertaken in the months of January and February 1999. In this manner, the government's answer to regional and international attempts at dismantling the sub-regional powder keg that the Guinean war had turned into was to recruit an additional number of Aguentas who were effectively so poorly prepared that their only function was to be fed to the cannons. The Aguentas were recruited as cannon fodder and they seem to have been aware of this.[63] The very name 'Aguenta' in itself refers to someone, or something, which only has the ability to support, preventing something from collapsing rather than being a constructive force or influence; eventually the supportive power of the Aguentas ran out and they were overrun by the *Junta* Militar in the *ultimo assalto*, the last attack.

Becoming Losers

So, despite the signing of the peace treaty in Praia on 26 August 1998 the war did not come to an end as tension continued to increase, resulting in a recommencement of the fighting on 9 October.[64] The initial violation of the ceasefire lasted only two days, but the war was to kick off again on 16 October in Bafata and reached Gabu and Bissau on the eighteenth, with the Junta taking control of Bafata on 21 October and Gabu on 22 October. During this segment of the war the government lost ground on all fronts and the Junta gained control over more or less all of Guinea-Bissau except for the city centre and the Bijagos Islands. The fighting in Bissau, in mid-October, was to be the first engagement of the Aguentas in the war. And thus the earlier rumours[65] that President Nino was recruiting young men primarily from the Papel and Budjugu ethnic groups were confirmed as the recommencement of the fighting on 18 October coincided with the arrival and subsequent assignment to the front line of many of my informants. In fact, many were driven directly to the front line, as Olivio explains when telling me how things went for him in the Aguentas:

> We liked the government so they took us to Conakry and we were there for two months. Two months and we came here on October 16 or 17, nearly at midnight, and at midnight they took us to the front line, to the war. We were at the front line at Bôr, Imperamento and Polon di Bra. After they brought us there, during the night, we were face to face with the Junta.

It would, however, seem that only one battalion of Aguentas were at the front when the fighting started on 18 October,[66] yet all those who had trained in Conakry were apparently in position on the front line as the war recommenced by the end of January 1999.

The fighting around Bissau at the end of October had come to a deadlock after a few days of intense activity and stayed so until it eventually calmed down with the signing of the Abuja agreement on 1 November 1998. However, progress in implementing the agreement had been slow, resulting in sporadic ceasefire violations by the middle of January and in a further four days of fighting from 31 January 1999 to 4 February, which once again included heavy and relatively indiscriminate shelling of the city. As in October, a new battalion of Aguentas was drawn from training camp in Guinea Conakry and taken directly to the front line. Lenny was sent to the front on the 31st, and was injured on the very same day.[67] In the following he sketches his history within the Aguentas, as he went from Bissau, to Kindia, and back to the war.

> *What did people tell you about the Aguentas before you left? What did they tell you?*
> My 'collegas', what did they tell me before I left? My own friends?
> *Yes, or other people, soldiers ...*
> Well, they said to me: 'Do not go.' ... But I left anyway. We left here. We went to Conakry. We went there for preparation ... like ... We went all the way to Camisar.
> *Where?*
> Camisar, in Conakry ... Camisar.
> *Okay.*
> We were there and then we went to Kindia ... Someone was saying that they should find us and bring us back [to the war], but they said: 'No, things have calmed down. Things have calmed down.' But they went and

found us there,[68] and they brought us. We came here and only ... the thing it started again,[69] tatatatata [he imitates the sound of a machine gun].
What war was this?
The war of the 31. War started again. They took us and they brought us to the front. We were here at this thing, here [Ponto Sibi] ... That is where we started firing. We crossed over to that side and the sun rose. But the mission was not fulfilled and they pulled us back again, and there, when we were going back, I was shot.

As both the above quotes testify, the Aguentas were taken directly to the front line and those arriving for the October war stayed there up till the end of the fighting in February 1999, when a Togolese delegation managed to secure the signing of the Abuja treaty, in which a sharing of power via a joint government was planned and a date was agreed upon for elections, only to be undone by a Junta breach of the ceasefire on 7 May 1999, sparked by a row over the disarming of the presidential guard, that is, the battalion of Aguentas at the barracks at the Presidença. As both sides fought to rearm their troops, the Junta managed to get hold of their weapons quickly enough to enter the city with only sporadic pockets of resistance to be overcome. The morning of 7 May 1999 was thus a dawning tragedy for the Aguentas as it marked their entry into the category of losers.

The War, the Aguentas and Failed Prospects

So, what can we conclude from looking at the formation of the Aguentas and their entry into the Guinean civil war? First of all, it becomes clear that the government side was effectively the underdog all through the war. Though it was able to secure equipment and personnel through its Senegalese, Conakrian and French backing it had neither popular support nor legitimacy. The reasons for this lack of support are most likely to be found in an amalgamation of co-determinant factors, among which are the general dissatisfaction with the long-term leader of the country, President Nino; a general dissatisfaction with the lack of development and abundance of unfulfilled promises; and, not least, anger at the influx of foreign soldiers to fight on the *Governo* side.[70] Equally, the fact that the government side showed a disrespect for the ordinary Guinean throughout the war, committing an array of human rights violations, many of which were committed by, or with the assistance of, the Aguentas, most certainly added to its unpopularity and, not least, to the unpopularity of the Aguentas.

The Aguentas were, in other words, not fighting on the side of a popular cause and seem to have been aware of the fact. Most of my informants enlisted at a point in time when the Junta Militar had demonstrated its military superiority by dramatically decimating the government forces and the latter were clearly lacking in public support. Enlisting knowingly as front-line soldiers, they had a fair idea of the risks involved and must have weighed the risk of engaging in warfare with the consequences of abstaining. Yet one is still left with the question of why anyone would volunteer to join the government side and the Aguenta militia at this given point in time?

When I came to Bissau I had expected their conflict engagement to be ideologically motivated and to be able to unearth it by focusing on political discourse and narratives. I expected, in other words, the Aguentas to be fighting for a cause, for a social ideal, an ideology. I therefore found myself probing for ideological orientations, but finding none, until it dawned on me that I was asking what they were fighting for when what I should be doing was asking what they were fighting against, imagining their war to be defensive or protective rather than rebellious or revolutionary. I assumed that finding out what the Aguentas were fighting against would be an expedient way of illuminating what they were fighting for.

I was mistaken.

Notes

1. My aim within this chapter is to frame the historical movement and constitution of Guinean society using the available historical interpretations. The historical account should be read as a contextualisation. As we shall see in Chapter 8, my general interest in historical interpretations is on the social use they are put to, rather than the factuality they are claimed to embody. In other words, I do not wish to debate the rights and wrongs of representations of Guinean history or Guinean historiography but rather to outline it so as later to be able to show, and frame, how my informants make use of it.
2. The first to explore the Guinean coast were Captains Gil Eannes and Nuño Tristão sailing under the Portuguese crown (Blake 1942).
3. The Diolas are not to be confused with the Manding Dyulas, that is, Manding traders.
4. The Mandjako and Mankanha are derived from the Papel, and the Felupe from the Diola (Lobban and Forrest 1998: Appendix C).
5. Also termed Mandingo or Manding.
6. Also termed Fulani or Peul.
7. The Fula, the Mandinga and the Senegambian groups all belong to the main Niger-Congo language stock, but whereas the Fula belong to the Berber language family, the Mandinga belong to the nuclear Mande family and the Senegambians to the West Atlantic language family (the semi-Bantu littoral) (Lobban and Forrest 1998:

Appendix C). There are also many social, religious and cultural differences between them as they have different histories within the general region. Among major differences are, for example: religious affiliation – the Fula and Mandinga are Muslims, whereas the mentioned Senegambians are primarily animist: Livelihood – the Mandinga are inland farmers as well as extremely active in the transnational, regional trade, the Fula are equally active in regional trade networks and inland farming along with a strong pastoral tradition; and the Senegambians are primarily – although it has been shown that they were, prior to the invasions, engaged in inland farming (Hawthorne 2001) – rice cultivators of the littoral Guinean delta.

8. Although my informants definitely see the Fula and the Mandinga as Guineans, they are nonetheless recognised as having come from the 'outside', as being invaders at an earlier point in time. The Senegambian are considered to be the 'indigenous' inhabitants of Guinea-Bissau and are referred to as *fidjus di tjong*, that is, 'sons of the land', by the Guineans themselves.
9. Also called Gabou or Kaabu.
10. The company had a monopoly on the slave trade from Sierra Leone to Senegal. It was later reorganised as Companhia do Cacheu Rios e Cabo Verde. The slave trade in Portuguese Guinea, the present-day Guinea-Bissau, was to be taken over in 1753 by the Brazil-based Companhia Geral do Grão Pará e Maranhão, which supplied the labour needs of the coastal states Grão Pará and Maranhão.
11. The first Fulas are supposed to have spread into the eastern part of the country in the twelfth century, but Fula migration was stepped up in the eighteenth century with the attacks on Gabu from the Fula-Jalonkas (Hawthorne 2001: 63–64).
12. In fact it is not till after the conference in Berlin in 1886 that we can actually talk about Guinea-Bissau in its present form. The conference saw the French incorporate one of the main agricultural areas of Portuguese Guinea and one of its primary centres of trade, namely the Casamance region and its major city Ziguinchor, into what is presently Senegal. As compensation France withdrew its claim on the southern area of Cachine. Casamance, however, had and still has significant links with Guinea-Bissau. The PAIGC (Partido Africano pela Independencia de Guiné e Cabo Verde) had important military bases in the area, and traditionally there has been a link between the two areas through the Diolas/Felupe, who inhabit the area on both sides of the border (Lobban and Forrest 1988: 39).
13. Four brutal 'pacification' campaigns were led by Major Teixeira Pinto and supported by a number of Fula chiefs and about 400 Fula and Mandiga troops, along with a number of foreign mercenaries, between 1913 and 1915, which resulted in the destruction of a number of Balanta, Budjugu, Felup, Mandjaco, Oinca and Papel villages. The campaign clearly showed the growing collaboration between the Fula and the Portuguese in the rural areas of Portuguese Guinea, but the level of brutality can be gauged by the public outcry it evoked in Lisbon (Lobban and Forrest 1988: 107).
14. The prefix 'luso' refers to Lusitania, i.e. Portugal, and Portuguese.
15. Partido Africano pela Independencia de Guiné e Cabo Verde.
16. The FLING (Frente de Luta pela Independencia National da Guiné-Bissau) was to become a Senegalese-based liberation movement, which at times was in direct conflict with the PAICG. The FLING was involved in the murder of Amilcar Cabral but after this lost political influence.
17. The *Commandos Africanos*, however, comprised a substantial percentage of the colonial forces. In general, the colonial Portuguese military and paramilitary forces were believed to have been 60 per cent African (Henriksen 1977: 32).

18. *Policia International e de Defesa do Estado* was the secret police of the fascist Portuguese regime.
19. For an ethnographic description of the change within the Guinean schooling system see Rudebeck (1992).
20. The changes coincide with the diminishing strategic influence of Africa after the end of the cold-war scenario, the global demonisation of Marxism and the diminishing possibilities of attracting foreign aid to Bissau.
21. ECOWAS, the Economic Community of West African States.
22. Factional conflict should, however, not be seen as a post-independence phenomenon. It was present before the liberation struggle kicked off, leading to the split within the MING (Movimento para Independencia National de Guiné Portugesa), and was also influential in the assassination of Amilcar Cabral.
23. The half-brother of the independence leader Amilcar Cabral.
24. The outrage created by the executions led to the formation, in exile, of the party Resistencia da Guine-Bissau/Movimento Bafata, currently the second-largest party within the political system.
25. Called the Ninjas by the younger part of the population.
26. Even if only alleged, and what we are seeing are in fact purges, they still testify to the existence of heightened political conflict.
27. Andrén (1998: 1–2).
28. On 12 January 1998, to be exact.
29. Casamance, the southern part of Senegal bordering the Gambia and Guinea-Bissau, has been the scene of a liberation war waged by the predominantly Diola (Felupe) based MFDC (Mouvement des Forces Democratique de Casamance) since 1982.
30. Guinea-Bissau: Human Rights in War and Peace (Amnesty International), p. 4.
31. Despite the public nature of the debate, it seems safe to say that both Mané and Vieira were aware of and gaining from the arms sales.
32. That is, the united military.
33. The presence of MFDC troops on the Junta Militar side was denied by its leadership; however, I have multiple eyewitness accounts, from both sides of the conflict, testifying to the opposite, and have also seen video footage from behind the front line showing irregular, francophone troops pointed out to me as MFDC by a person from the Junta Militar.
34. *Publico* 24 September 1998.
35. The areas of prime strategic importance were, according to my high-ranking informants, primarily Bissau and the Bijagos islands, securing the government side access to both a port and an airstrip.
36. Designated *Bissauzinho*, that is, small Bissau.
37. The battle on 16 June 1998 was supposed to have been decisive as the Senegalese contingent suffered heavy losses (Andrén 1998: 2).
38. Community of Lusophone Countries.
39. Report on the situation in Guinea-Bissau, prepared by the ECOWAS Executive Secretary, UN Security Council, 16 April 1999. ECOWAS is the Economic Community of West African States.
40. Rädda Barnen is the Swedish branch of Save the Children. The raw, demographic data, including age, names, ethnic affiliation and so on, from this course, based on captured POWs who were Aguentas, and who were subsequently interned in a guarded camp, have unfortunately gone missing, as one agency refers to the other in the search for the whereabouts of the documents. The registrational and analytical work that can be proved to have been done seems to build on a semi-completed survey of a subgroup within the larger group of captured Aguentas.

41. Programa de Desmobilização, Reinserção e Reintegração dos Ex-combatentes, a programme for the demobilisation and social reintegration of ex-combatants.
42. Only the first three battalions, approximately 900 Aguentas, were trained in Conakry, while the rest received their training at the primary barracks in Bissau called QG (*Quartel Geral*) or on the island of Bubaque (*Situationen i Guinea-Bissau – En Indledande Rapport*. Promemoria, Swedish Embassy in Guinea-Bissau, 2 September 1998, p. 5–6).
43. The data was collected from 2001 to 2002.
44. The war veterans being granted aid in accordance with their needs.
45. The exact number is not known but it seems, judging from information from other Aguentas, to have been approximately a battalion at the end of the war, that is, between three and four hundred men and youths, and somewhat less in 2002.
46. See, for example, Andrén (1998), Aimé et al. (1999a, 1999b: 43). See also Amnesty International (1999: 17), where it is stated that 'On the 13 May, 186 young Aguenta militia, including several between 15 and 17 years were released and returned to their families.' Of these 186 Aguentas, 120 are part of the survey from the Guinean Human Rights League, the word 'several' thus covering approximately 2 per cent or less of the total.
47. 18 out of 895 and 2 out of 120, respectively.
48. We see that the 'legitimate' use of youth in warfare begins from the age of 15, according to both the Geneva Convention and the UN Convention on the Rights of the Child (Furley 1995: 29).
49. Many Aguentas, despite being from Bissau, went to their *terra*, that is, their ethnic homeland, mostly Biombo, after the war due to the security provided in a place where ones ethnic group comprises the majority of the population. Despite being from the city nearly all still refer to a specific area considered as the major or primordial area of their ethnic groups as their *terra*, as a place of safety in times of trouble.
50. In times of hardship sending one's children to school is a luxury that many parents cannot afford and the age composition of secondary school students is thus spread much more widely than in the West. Currently, due to the period of warfare, the commencement of tuition fees (which disappeared mysteriously into the coffers of the Ministry of Education) and the constant strikes among the teaching staff over unpaid salaries, many young people have not had the chance to complete their education since 1998.
51. Women seem to be especially able to gain an income or a resource working their family's land, but it should be noted that the Papels are particularly likely to have an increased movement between the rural and the urban, as they claim the area around Bissau as part of their traditional homeland.
52. The function of the rural *terras* as ritual centres seems, however, to be changing as many young people now opt for the urban equivalents of, for example, the marriage and circumcision rituals, avoiding (in the latter) the hardship of spending time in the *matu* (forest) and the pain of the circumcision. Being circumcised in hospital is safer and cheaper and, furthermore, there seems to be no normative evaluation attached to this, as the stigma of being uncircumcised is attached to having a foreskin, rather than how one goes about getting rid of it. Being circumcised at the hospital is thus not referred to in a derogatory but rather in a factual manner of being 'from the hospital'.
53. There is a 0.15 per cent discrepancy between the two in favour of writing.
54. The national average illiteracy rate is 67.8 per cent (IMF 2002). The difference between the 81 and 83 per cent who are literate and who have received formal education is probably located in the ability to read and write the Latin or Arabic alphabet. Formal education uses the Latin alphabet, but a person is commonly recognised as able to read if literate in Arabic.

55. On the economy of affection, see Hydén (1983).
56. That is not to say that the economy of affection does not also include people of other ethnic groups, as there is a relatively high intermarriage between the different groups and as friends, neighbours and peers are all expected to help each other.
57. For example, *Balantas ka ta nega um utro*.
58. Nineteen out of thirty-two interviewed Aguentas.
59. From http://www.countryreports.org/content/guineb.htm.
60. For a further analysis of the *antigo combatentes* see Jespersen (2002).
61. *Aguentas puru.*
62. In Bubaque or at the barracks in QG. The Aguentas were placed in four different battalions, which again were stationed in four different barracks, that is: QG, Presidençia, Amura and Marinha. As my friend and informant Vitór explained, the Aguentas served four different military purposes as they functioned as artillery, infantry and naval troops, as well as paramilitary police.
63. Cannon fodder, or *carne di bazooka* as it is called in Creole, is just one of a myriad of derogatory names used to designate the low status of the militia. Monkey troops, *troppazinhos di Nino*, and even the name Aguenta all point our attention to their place at the bottom of the military pecking order, as there is not much status in being a 'helper'.
64. According to the Senegalese officers on the front line in Bissau the collapse of the ceasefire was caused by a Junta assault on their positions (Amnesty 1999: 18).
65. Cf. Andrén (1998).
66. A battalion generally consists of between 300 and 1000 men, with former Warsaw pact-backed armies, including the Guinean, tending towards the lower figures (Luttwak 1972: 40).
67. In Creole there is no differentiation between wars and battles, as the word war – *guerra* – is used for both.
68. *Ellis e bay busker-no la.*
69. *Ranka mas.*
70. It is in this perspective worth pondering why the MFDC rebel presence on the Junta side did not stir up any anger. That the same people that were to join the Junta in protest over the presence of foreign troops on the government side of the war did not oppose the presence of foreign troops on their own, indicates that the reason for their conflict engagement was located in other social and political factors as well.

Chapter 4

WARS WITHOUT ENEMIES

The small stalls by the roadside were packing up and blowing out their candles and as we approached home the street became enclosed in an almost tangible darkness. Dó was walking briskly. Having walked down the road a million times before he knew the way, knew where the holes, the caved-in sewers and storm drains were, and how to avoid them. In the dark, and without his adeptness, I was feeling my way forwards, treading tentatively, constantly expecting to feel the emptiness of a rut under my sole and trying to follow the flow of Dó's mumbled political opinions as an auditory path down the road. 'For all of them to die,' I could hear him say, 'all of them. This country will not know peace before they are all dead.' In his eyes the case was clear; the antigo combatentes, *the old liberation heroes, bore the brunt of the blame for the miserable state Bissau was in. Instead of worshipping the 'Heroes Cemetery', the burial plots reserved for the national heroes, Dó was longing for it to be filled up. 'Us,' the word now coming from right next to me, 'us here, we will not go forward before they have all died,' he repeated.*

No Martyrs, No Ideologies, No Enemies

There are no martyrs in Colombia, Malcolm Deas states, as the country is caught in myriad conflicts without clear causes (1997: 380). Equally, in Guinea-Bissau the social production of martyrs or heroes has stopped as conflicts within the country have somehow moved from the sacred to the profane. The lack of martyrs and heroes is, however, an important indication of what type of conflict is being fought, as martyrs are defined by their death for a cause, and the cause, by definition, is collective. One does not become a martyr if seen as fighting only for personal interest. Martyrs, in other words, are defined by offering their lives for the general good of the community that they are identified with and seen to represent. In this perspective, martyrs fight for a community's place and possibilities within the world. They become iconic of the community by dying for the good of the community. The lack of Guinean martyrs would thus suggest that the last couple of years has not seen war-related deaths in which the departed could be seen as fighting for the good of Guinea-Bissau.

Martyrs are, however, not defined by the context of the fighting but by the normative interrelationship between the combatants and can therefore be produced from any context of conflict or warfare that is characterised by normative rather than pragmatic positions.[1] In wars martyrs are, in other words, defined by dying for a collective cause at the hands of the enemy. The reason for the symbolic degeneration of the state-honoured heroes and the lack of martyrs since the war of independence is thus not a lack of radicalised conflict – the structural context for their production – but rather a perceived lack of normative difference between the fighting parties. The lack of heroes relates in other words to the fact that recent conflicts in Guinea-Bissau have been political in a pragmatic sense rather than in a normative, ideological one. In contrast to the war of independence with its ideological orientation and action combined to take the country towards realising its place alongside the world's other autonomous nations, the conflict and outbreaks of fighting in Guinea-Bissau since then have not been tied to a popular cause expressed in a narrative providing a clear sense of directionality towards a deified telos. Wars without martyrs are wars without collective teleologies; they are fought not against an enemy but for a possibility.

Grounding War in Enemies

As mentioned in the last chapter I expected to be able to uncover the Aguentas' motives for joining the militia by illuminating whom they saw themselves as fighting against: that is, by unearthing their idea of a perceived enemy and the threat that this enemy posed to their community. I expected that my informants' constructions of the enemy would elucidate a range of narratives that would position their activities by revealing their ideological orientations and motivations – why they were fighting, what they were fighting for and who they were fighting against. Yet, no matter how I went about it, I could not get detailed descriptions of the Other, and thus a window on my informants' ideological positions, points of view or understandings of conflict. Whether an example of how deeply rooted our general understanding of warfare is in an understanding of ideologically defined opponents, or an example of the sluggish nature of my intellectual motor I shall leave undecided, but I slowly became aware that I could not extricate a defined picture of the enemy from my informants because they had no radical vision of the Other.

From this perspective, the war in Guinea-Bissau does not seem to coincide with the political nature of warfare that we have come to expect in Europe and which can be traced back to Carl Maria von Clausewitz's *On War*. Clausewitz's dictum,[2] that war is a continuation of politics by other means (Clausewitz 1997: 22), has been the primary underlying perspective informing European theories and analyses of war and conflict for the last century and a half. Yet, whereas the dictum, at first glance, can be seen as an understanding of war as an instrument of naked interest, it in fact points our attention to the political character of warfare, as it should, according to Clausewitz, be seen and kept as an instrument of larger political goals, placed in the hands of politicians pursuing the interest of states (ibid.). Accordingly, we generally see war as intricately tied to the political realm of statehood or nationhood, ideally controlled by politicians and used as an instrument in the furthering of political ideals. In other words, in a European perspective, war is grounded in ideological differences between states. It evolves from the different perspectives on how a given society should be organised, resources distributed and territoriality demarcated.

Participating actively on the losing side of the Napoleonic wars Clausewitz witnessed first-hand one of the most decisive changes in European warfare. The Napoleonic era exhibited a profound change in the dominant mode of war, as it first of all saw the emergence of mass conscriptions of entire generations of young men via the logistics of the state apparatus and the backing of the state/war economy (Willmott 1997: xii–xiii).[3] However, the Napoleonic era also gave rise to a change in what people were meant to be fighting for, as they were recruited by the state and expected to fight for the welfare of an imagined community (Anderson 1993) to which the combatants were related via generalised kinship. That is, instead of fighting for the highest bidder, as a mercenary, for the personal aspirations of kings, the combatant came to be seen as fighting for the ideal of state and/or nation. With the Napoleonic wars we thus see a change in the dominant mode of warfare, from the former clashes of professional elite armies to large-scale wars of nationally recruited young men, backed by the entire state apparatus and economy, fighting for ideological orientations and nationalism. The connection between Western warfare and ideology is as such established via a simultaneous development, in which the profound changes in the mode of warfare are directly related to the very birth of modern politics. The Napoleonic mode of warfare emerged in the aftermath of the French revolution with it denouncement of the divine right of kings and the subsequent emphasis on the universal rights of the individual citizen and the socio-political organisation of societies around the bureaucracy of state and the community of nation.

The Napoleonic wars that were to inform Clausewitz's theories were the first instance of the modern political 'ideologification' of warfare, as the large-scale mobilisation of the French forces was made possible precisely by appealing to the ideological orientation of revolutionary nationalism (ibid.). They marked a turn away from military participation as primarily related to payment, social station or divine duty towards military participation as civic duty. In other words, with their point of departure in revolutionary nationalism, modern wars have been represented and understood as fought on state and/or ideological grounds ever since: that is, in the zone of tension between ideologies, competing ideas of the proper organisation of society and the territorial boundaries under which these socio-political systems should be able to exercise their authority. Our conception of war is integrally tied to the emergence of the modern state.

The consequence of the dominance of this perspective is that we, in both Western science and folk understanding, have a tendency to understand warfare as centred on ideology and territoriality. Consequently, any war that is not fought for ideological reasons comes, in a European perspective, to border on sacrilege. Being a mercenary was formerly almost the only way to be a soldier and the deterioration of the social value of the term amply describes the development in the Western mode and understanding of warfare, to the point where a mercenary is currently symbolically equated with prostitution, of making a living by using one's body in the most profane of possible manners. As the act of a prostitute is negatively valued, an act of emotion debased into an economic transaction, so too does the mercenary transgress normative boundaries as the motive for soldiering ought to be for a higher ideal: for the common good rather than personal material gain.

Ideology and Enemies

In this manner, modern warfare is seen as centred on conflicting systems of ideas – opposed societal visions expressed in teleological narrative constructions of the ideal order between society, resources, territory and movement through time – that is, around conflictual interpretations of the distribution and allocation of authority and resources.

At the most basic level, ideologies are thus about the distribution of resources and power, and yet, being teleological, they are directed towards the future as well as the past or the present.[4] My use of ideology thus does not refer to the process of mystification, false consciousness or other shrouding of the workings of power, as the concept has been used within the Marxist and neo-Marxist tradition,[5] but rather, following Geertz, to a symbolic framework for political organisation, which is not reducible to the narrow interest of elitist power but should instead be seen against the background of the cultural system it is generated in (see Geertz 1993). Yet it would seem that this idea of ideological warfare is difficult to maintain in a Bissauian scenario as indicated by the absence of heroes and martyrs and, not least, as we shall see, of enemies.

New and Old Wars Revisited

The conflicts and wars in Guinea-Bissau thus lead us back to the point of differentiation between 'new' and 'old' wars that is based on ideology, as sketched in my introductory chapter. Where old wars are about geopolitical or ideological matters or forward-looking ideas centred on the proper movement and formation of society through time, scholars such as Kaldor see 'new wars' as being about backward-looking political projects, termed identity politics (Kaldor 1999: 6–7). 'New wars' are non-teleologically grounded, that is, they do not look towards a normatively defined future but instead towards the past. As Kaldor states:

> Early nationalist struggle in nineteenth-century Europe or colonial Africa were about democracy and state-building ... politics has been dominated by abstract secular ideas like socialism or environmentalism which offer a vision for the future ... In contrast, identity politics tends to be fragmentative, backwards-looking and exclusive. Political groupings based on exclusive identity tend to be movements of nostalgia, based on the reconstruction of a heroic past. (Kaldor 1999: 77–78)

Yet on closer scrutiny, the difference between the two types of political projects seems perhaps not to be that great as they both end up in the category of ideology, by Kaldor's own definition. The difference seems to have less to do with teleology than with directionality. In other words, where the 'old' ideologies were linear, the 'new' ideologies are circular, but the narrative structure of identity politics is just as teleological as the 'old' teleologies. The quest is not to regress but to obtain the ideal state of the mythical past in the future, a classical narrative structure often seen in eschatological narratives, where the telos, that is, the normative future ideal, is anchored in the time 'before the fall' and will be regained after the apocalypse. The mythical past in this perspective is an ideal state of societal order – of the distribution of authority and resources – which can be realised again in the future. In identity politics the past is thus not 'finished' or confined to the past, but is rather dormant, ready to be realised in the future. In other words, if teleological orientation is what makes traditional party politics ideological and identity politics non-ideological, then somewhere along the line a major part of the differentiation between old and new wars collapses.⁶

Rebellions and Revolutions

I would, however, like to ponder the idea of teleology a bit further, since many of the present 'new wars', such as in West Africa, seem non-teleological inasmuch as they do not envision change in the social structures or political system of the country in question but rather within the existing socio-political structures. Instead of being revolutionary many of the so-called 'new wars' thus seem primarily reconfigurative or redistributive. We seem, in other words, to be looking at rebellions rather than revolutions (cf. Gluckman 1963), which effectively surpasses the distinction between 'old' and 'new'. In other words, wars in Africa seem increasingly to be rebellions and if we look at the range of civil wars in the Third World it would seem that revolutions (that is, ideologically motivated wars working to change the political structures and systems of the countries they are fought in) are limited to a few fundamentalist or secessionist wars.⁷ In contrast, West Africa, including Guinea-Bissau, seems to be characterised by incessant rebellions changing the internal power configurations but never the structures of inequality and marginalisation that produce the social situations that are contested in the first place.

In this perspective, the difference between fighting a rebellion and fighting a revolution testifies to a local or regional incapacity to change the poverty and calamity producing structures in the first place: that is, a lack of influence on ones position within the larger regional or global socio-political order. As governments in the Third World occupy the weaker positions in the global capitalist relation of extraction and accumulation of resources they are unable to better the general position of the country within the global competition for resources. What they can do instead is compete for the privileged positions within political networks of resource distribution and extraction (Duffield 1998; Kaldor 1999). Importantly, if we wish to gain a better understanding of these types of wars, we need to be aware of the fact that rebellions generally produce different dynamics of conflict from revolutions – that is, different motives for engaging in conflict and different relations between the fighting parties. The distinction is therefore an influential underlying parameter when looking at the construction of the enemy entailed in the two types of warfare, as one is characterised as a fight against a radical Other, differing in worldview and aspirations, whereas the other is characterised by the fight against a less polarised construction of the Other as an opponent.

As indicated by Do's statement at the start of this chapter, we can thus tentatively position the lack of martyrs and heroes, from the point of view of youth in Guinea-Bissau, as indicative of the demise of ideology. It highlights the lack of a forward-looking project as well as the withering influence of any such projects in the past. Combatants in Guinea-Bissau are currently not seen as fighting for the larger national community but for factions: not for a change in the socio-political structures or a better society, but for a better position and space of possibility within society. Our analytical take on the Guinean civil war must emerge from its make-up as a rebellion rather than a revolution. Currently, conflicts within Guinea-Bissau are fought for a change within the agents holding positions of power rather than a change of the actual socio-political structurations of power, a difference which is consequential to the type of relationship generated by and in warfare and thus in relation to reconciliatory processes and the possible re-emergence of warfare. Rebellions and revolutions entail different constructions of the conflictual Other, and these constructions have weighty social consequences. It is towards these constructions of conflictual Other or opponents that I shall now turn my attention.

A Brotherly War

As shown earlier, the Guinean conflict scenario consisted of the Junta Militar, primarily made up of *antigo combatentes* (liberation heroes), Adjuntas (primarily young, rural Balantas) and MFDC troops (Casamance rebel forces). The *Governo* side, on the other hand, consisted of a number of Guinean officers and non-commissioned officers, roughly two battalions of Senegalese troops, a battalion of troops from Guinea Conakry and the Aguentas. Obviously, the deaths of Junta and *Governo* soldiers alike testify to the existence of hostility towards the opposed forces. Yet from my informants' point of view we see that, despite the proportionally large percentage of war-related deaths amongst the Aguentas,[8] there does not seem to exist, or have existed, the hatred and contempt for the enemy that one would expect of such situations. And generally, in Guinea-Bissau, there were, apart from the foreign troops, who have been used symbolically to externalise the cause of the conflict, no easily defined discursively constructed enemies, heroes or motives for entering into warfare.

In relation to my informants, soldiers and civilians alike, the relationship between the fighting parties in Guinea-Bissau was not – and is not – characterised by radical stereotyping or dehumanisation, but rather by a particularly Guinean non-polarised construction of social categories and conflictual Others. Guineans like each other, *Guineense gosta d'um utro*, people continually say when one asks about the future of the country and yet they will most often subsequently slip easily into describing and debating the imminent danger of further trouble, positioning conflict and warfare as regular occurrences on a foundation of amity. In fact, the mantra of friendship continues paradoxically even in situations of actual warfare. My landlord Caetano answered my question about how long he thought the fighting would last, as we sat, seven people in his hallway seeking shelter from the shooting outside, with the sentence: 'It won't take long, Guineans like each other.' At the time, I thought the answer to be absurd, but somehow it seems strangely true, despite the recurrent bouts of fighting. Guineans really do like each other, and not even warfare seems to take the general amity out of the relationship.

Empathy, amity and relatedness are thus some of the main reasons that we can encounter for the existence of warfare without discursively defined enemies in Bissau. As a general tendency, this can be explained by a combination of the large degree of cross-cutting family and friendship ties among the fighting parties, and a consolidated ideal of national unity underpinned by the country's long independence struggle and its existence as a lusophone Other in the vast francophone West Africa. Yet, as said, it has equally to do with the rebellious character of the country's conflicts and a concomitant lack of ideological orientation within the political agendas of the two conflicting sides. Taken together, these facts come to mean that the opposing forces in the conflicts are familiar, and not seen as working towards a radically different socio-political system, but rather as being competitors within the existing one.

Whatever the reasons, or rather, whatever their configuration, the relationship between Guineans fighting on opposite sides in the civil war and later outbreaks of fighting shows itself, upon investigation, not to be characterised by the articulated hatred and aggressiveness one could expect to dominate the relationship between combatants. Actual battles and combat apart, there was, according to my informants, frequent and amicable contact between opposed Guineans troops during the civil war, pointing towards a level of non-conflictual interaction that makes the relationship between combatants in Guinea-Bissau stand out as an exceptional one, a fact which is recognised by civilians and combatants alike and which is expressed in the general conceptualisation of the civil war as a *guerra di hermonia*, a brotherly war.

Your Enemy as Opponent

The fact that the war (besides having a Senegalese, Conakrian and MFDC presence) was a civil war and thus primarily a conflict between Guineans is an aspect that is emphasised by soldiers and civilians alike via the concept of *guerra di hermonia*. Illuminating this conceptualisation of aggressive fraternity is important as it underlies my interlocutors' understanding of war and strife in Guinea-Bissau; it also very clearly influenced life on the front line, the specificity of combat and, not least, the subsequent processes of reconciliation and social reintegration.[9] Regarding the former, the fact that the war is seen as having been between kin seems to have been acknowledged throughout the chain of command of the government troops, and equally to have been noticed – albeit with annoyance – by the Senegalese commanders fighting on the government side. In the following quote, Olivio explains to me how the Senegalese officers who were put in charge of the Aguentas during the middle period of the war[10] would try to educate the Aguentas on the proper relationship between the warring factions:

> *What did your officers tell you about the Junta side?*
> The Senegalese, when they came, they said: 'You, must not trust the rebels!' This is what they told us. The Senegalese chiefs they said: 'You must not trust laughing with the rebels!' This was what they told us, the Senegalese chiefs [said]: 'You must not laugh with the rebel, because he is against you, he is not your friend so do not laugh with him. At the front line do not laugh with them, not even if you go to their side for a walk, do not laugh with them. This is no good in war.' But our Guinean commanders, when they gave us advice, they told us that we and the Junta – all these words – their way of marching or doing other things are exactly the same, so when he gave commands he would say: 'The war we are in is a war between brothers [*guerra entre hermons*]. This war has no reason to be. The war we are in is a foolish war because there is no reason for it to be.'

This quote directs us towards the fact that there was an ongoing non-conflictual interaction between opposed Guinean troops during breaks in the fighting. In fact, nearly all of the combatants I have spoken to in Guinea-Bissau have emphasised the positive relationship between the warring parties during ceasefires. But the above quote equally shows the different attitudes towards the opposed troops, exemplified by the different instructions given to Olivio by his Senegalese and Guinean commanders. What we are seeing in this perspective is an internal incongruity within the different groups fighting on the government side as to the perceived (social) nature of the war. Thus the Guinean 'brotherly' understanding of the war had apparently gained such dominance that Olivio's Senegalese commander found it necessary to lecture his men on the proper attitudes of aggression towards 'enemy soldiers'. Yet the Senegalese officer's apparent annoyance and surprise at the 'strange' relationship between opposed Guinean troops is directly related to the very issue of enemy and Other. In other words, the relationship between the groups in conflict and the appropriate behaviour between them is understood in two very different ways. For the Senegalese commander, the praxis of war between the different Guinean troops was seen as unwarlike behaviour that needed changing. From the point of view of his Guinean colleague, the amicable interaction across the front line, during pauses in the fighting, was related to the perceived nature of the conflict as a brotherly war: a war without a larger reason. Thus the efforts of the Senegalese officer were undermined by their local commander, who, instead of aiding the Senegalese officer in drawing 'proper' lines of aggression and engineering proper hostile behaviour between the parties, emphasised the common understanding of the conflict, as an unfortunate conflict between kith and kin. Olivio makes this evident a bit later in the interview.

> 'What we have here is a brotherly war, you should not have had this from the start, all of us should join each other in the barracks because we are brothers.' This is always the advice they [our commanders] gave us every day: 'We are brothers. This war has no reason to be. It is just because there is nothing to do about it, but we are brothers.'

The quotes above are Olivio's response to my questions on what his officers told him about the Junta. As such, they reflect the general understanding of the Guinean conflict as a *guerra di hermonia*: that is, a war which is not built around a polarised social scenario populated by allies and enemies and evident targets for destruction, but rather around a battle for social positions and trajectories.

Internal and External Others

In other words, in a gradation from enemy to opponent, the enemy end of the spectrum seems uninhabited when looking at the relationship between opposed Guinean troops. However, having said as much, I must make it clear that both the government and the Junta side of the conflict operated with a differentiation between foreign and national opposing forces. There is in Guinea-Bissau general agreement that the presence of foreign troops aggravated the conflict, and yet it should be emphasised, since many seem to disregard the evident, that the war started without the presence of the foreign forces and that it did not end at the time of their departure, but rather continued with intensity afterwards.[11]

Thus we cannot postulate that it was the presence of the foreign troops that caused the war or their departure that ended it but we can certainly speculate on the actual influence their involvement had on the period and intensity of warfare. Rather than instigating the development of full-scale warfare, the Guinea Conakrian, Senegalese and Casamance (MFDC) forces made it possible to symbolically localise the aggressive parties outside Guinean society, or the Guinean 'family', and thus to externalise the source of hostility so that it was outside the categories of both classificatory and actual kin. In effect, the presence of foreign troops seems to have made possible the very conceptualisation of the war as 'brotherly' by the contra-identificatory function the foreign troops served. As we shall see, this externalisation equally influenced the praxis of the war, as it was actually fought on different terms according to the nationality of the opponent/enemy. In Buba's words:

> Like there at the front we would talk with each other, even when we were not firing at each other we would greet each other [across the front] in the morning. We would say: 'How did you wake up?' If we had food [during ceasefires or breaks in the fighting] we would say: 'Come [and eat].' At this point we would have friendship, but the moment there was a Senegalese [it would break down] ... Because of what ... Because it is not the same troops and that is why this war lasted for so long.

Buba's quote indicates how the relationship between Junta and *Governo* troops changed depending on the presence of foreign forces and clearly shows that the foreign presence had a conflictual influence on the interaction between Guineans, thus overshadowing the underlying proximity between troops who were ideally less aggressively inclined towards each other. On a similar note Nome once told me, laughingly, that: 'To start with we were not mixed [on the front] ... we the *Forças Delta* and the Senegalese we were not together.[12] They were there and we were here, next to them, but then they [the Junta] killed many Senegalese, a lot, until [*tok*] they thought: 'This is no good' – and they started mixing us together on the front.'

Nome is thus testifying to the same phenomenon as Buba does in the former quote. Obviously there was also intense fighting between Junta and Aguenta troops but there was undoubtedly an increased hostility towards the foreign troops fighting in the war. The Junta would specifically target Senegalese troops when they were able to pick them out on the battlefield, and both quotes corroborate the fact that heightened aggression was spurred by the presence of – or was directed towards foreign combatants. This is also seen, for example, in the following fragment from a talk I had with Carlos, where we were talking about the composition of the Junta forces seen from the government side of the conflict:

> *Were there different troops within the Junta?*
> Yes, some were artillery, some were just soldiers ... some were old and some were younger like us.
> *Were there other differences?*
> There were also these rebels from Casamance.
> *How were they different?*
> They were Diolas, those people from Casamance ... If you caught one ... If we caught one of these we would kill him, you will kill him quickly.

> *What if you caught a Junta soldier?*
> No, we were told to bring him [with us].

This shows how the government side of the war also distinguished between nationals and non-nationals in their levels of violence. So, although it should once again be stated that there were indeed numerous examples of killings between Guinean troops, and equally many rumours of similar-style executions on and behind the front line, there seems nonetheless to have been a clear difference in the interpretation of – and action towards – different troops, depending on their identity as Guineans or foreigners, insiders or outsiders. In other words, where the relationship towards the Guinean conflictual Other is fundamentally seen as one of amity, though set in a situation of war, the relationship towards the foreign combatants is closer to enmity, due to a perceived illegitimacy of foreign intrusion. Carlos's views correspond with the general difference between the concepts of opponent and enemy, as shown by James Aho, where he differentiates between the two somewhat dramatically: 'While *opponents* in disputes can be rationally and temporally engaged, the enemy/enema is best flushed into oblivion' (Aho 1999: 117). Yet, despite the fact that the foreign troops were treated with a greater degree of brutality, they still do not correspond with the category of enemy, as they are and were not seen as a threat to Guinean society or to the lives of Guinean communities. They were a threat to soldiers during the period of warfare, but their role was restricted to the situation of warfare, and their existence was possible within what was defined as a *guerra di hermonia*, as Arno said during a conversation where I was seeking to get an idea of the current relationship between the large Senegalese community in Guinea-Bissau and the Guineans:

> *What do people think of the Senegalese now?*
> Nothing, nothing. All these things ... Normally we are like this (he puts two fingers together to symbolise relatedness), we are all brothers. It is the war that that caused [*é guerra ki pui*] that there came to be this anger between us.

É guerra ki pui means that the aggression, just as between the Guinean troops, is not seen as an immanent but as a situationally generated relationship (see Chapter 9).

Brotherhood and Kinship in Warfare

Upon a closer look, the concept of *guerra di hermonia* thus points our attention to the fact that not all combatants were equally related as 'brothers', that there was a differentiation between internal and external combatants, between insiders and outsiders participating in the war. Yet the general dominance of the concept of *guerra di hermonia* equally points our attention to the fact that, though the foreign troops might have been seen as kindling the fire they were not usually seen to be its cause. More exactly, the fact that the war was primarily seen as war between relatives, with the foreign forces seen as more distant than the Guineans, means that the cause of it, in my informants' view, must be placed somewhere within the 'brotherhood' of Guineans, as a family feud rather than a regional war. In fact, the kinship term of brotherhood is exceptionally useful in maintaining the 'unity despite division' implied in family conflict.

The designation of the war as 'brotherly' makes it possible, in other words, to encompass the paradox of simultaneous amity and aggression, of insisting on the fact that Guineans like each other at the same time as trying to kill each other through acts of warfare. Brotherhood, in this perspective, makes the fusion of acts of aggression and kinship possible, as fraternal social relationships are often characterised by the duality of solidarity and competition. Brotherhood, or siblingship in general comes to 'subsume rivalries and latent hostilities that are intrinsically built into the relationships' (Fortes 1969: 237) and in Guinea-Bissau, as elsewhere, brotherhood is a kinship relation in which it is possible to be in disagreement and competition (over favours, inheritance, women, status and so on) without breaking or endangering the underlying 'kinship solidarity' (ibid.: 241). In this manner *guerra di hermonia* makes possible the coexistence of such different intersubjective modalities as violence and friendship within the context of warfare.

Furthermore, the concept of brotherhood has the advantage of being able to encompass a large spectrum of the fighting forces. The perceived brotherly aspect of the war relates not only to consanguine or affinal kinship. Returning to Meyer Fortes, we are made aware that the model relationship of kinship is fraternity, as he makes the point using a quote from Pedersen stating that 'Wherever there is social unity, we have brotherhood' (ibid.). Equally, the role of kinship within the *guerra di hermonia* stretches from the imagined national community (Anderson 1993) to the consanguineous relationships between soldiers as brothers, uncles, nephews and cousins. Brotherhood in this perspective connotes a generalised social proximity, whether primary or secondary, as Denís and Buba's words show:

> This is a war between two brothers, you see? It is a war between two brothers so you must feel a lot. No matter what you do you must feel a lot ... this is my friend [*collega*],[13] my brother. It is all my family. (Denis)

> [T]here will be war between two friends that did not [initially] have these [ill] feelings. Some are here, some are there. But when the war reaches the middle they have been reflecting for a long time. All the time they say words like: 'No, we should not fight. We should not fight between us.' At other times your little brother is on the other side. Your older brother is on the other side. (Buba)

Where Denís emphasises the categorical kinship of the imagined community, that is, towards Guinean nationals and relatedness in general, Buba touches upon actual kinship of consanguine relations. Yet, being brotherly, the war should, by the logic of kinship, not have become a war at all but rather have been confined to the level of fraternal strife.

Compassion on the Front Line

> We could nearly see our brothers. My big brother – he is nearly forty – he was on the Junta side and I am here. He was a soldier in the Junta Militar, I went to the government side. He was here (points with his finger at the table). He was at Bôr. He was on the other side and I was here (points again). All the time I told people to give him my regards. It is a brotherly war. That was the feeling towards it. But after ... After they violated the ceasefire ... on the 31st ... We had a hard battle, hard battle, I told people to go and say hello to him and to tell him to stop shooting, because I was here. To stop firing from brother to brother, for us to talk, and for people to stop the war and talk. After the battle of the 31st passed, time passed and they [ECOMOG[14]] came and told us to disarm. (Olivio)

As can be seen in Olivio's description, the brotherly aspects of the war had very real consequences, creating, among other things, a strange front-line scenario. Contrary to many conflicts or wars, the Other in the Guinean context is and was not easily dehumanised and excluded from the social sphere, as is typical in the social construction of hatred, and was thus not easily constructed as a symbolically polarised enemy.

Rather, what we see in Guinea-Bissau is a conflictual relationship that is saturated by kinship idioms.[15] Kinship complicates warfare as it makes one hesitate and makes one retain compassion where there ideally should be none. Yet, as other civil wars will testify to, wars between people with intimate knowledge of each other's lives do not necessarily guarantee a diminished amount of bloodshed or a more humane construction of the Other as enemy. In fact looking at Burma, Rwanda and Bosnia, we might be tempted to conclude the opposite. Yet the important difference between the Guinean civil war and these other wars is that they were fought by parties with different ideas of the future, for radical changes in the political structures, and thus far from the rebellious point of departure of the Guinean civil war.

In comparison, the Guinean civil war is a war in which both sides fought for positions of power and accumulation of wealth within the same political system, meaning that the warring parties were able to imagine the motives and rationales of the O/other. The Other as kin is related by means and motive and when combined with a lack of ideology, of a collectively defined societal goal in the future, and with intricate knowledge of the opposing forces, the emergence of an understanding of the war as one between brothers is made possible. This subsequently influences the acts of aggression expected and facilitated towards the conflictual Other, as can be seen in Carlos's description of a battle situation: 'Sometimes if you went like this [he points to a map he has drawn of the front line], you would see your good friend, and you would see that he slept, and you would not have courage to kill him. If you kill him you feel a lot ... You cannot.' 'You feel a lot' expresses compassion where, from a military point of view, there should ideally be anger and hatred; this has consequences for both the modes of actual war and those of reconciliation. It is one thing to overcome the taboo on killing: it is quite another to overcome the taboo on killing those you are supposed to protect, fratricide and patricide being powerful cross-cultural symbolic transgressions.

However, the brotherly aspect of the Guinean war comes even more strongly to the fore during pauses in the actual fighting. As seen earlier, there seems to have been an unusually high level of interaction across the front, as Denís explains:

> *When you were at the front, these people ... These people ... How was the relationship between people from the Junta and people from the Governo? I mean, clearly, when you fought, you fought, but when you did not fight?*
> When the war was not on, you would sit on your side and chat and they would sit on theirs. Like this you could call them [over] and they would come and they would call us and we would meet halfway... Sons of Guinea-Bissau would do that. Us Guineans we would come, they would come and we would come. We would meet. We would greet each other.

Or in the words of Carlos and Vitór, who served together in the Presidential Guard at the barracks of the Presidença:

> People from the Junta were very tired because ... They were very tired because they did not have a lot to eat, they did not have enough to be full. Other days we asked our big people if we could – if there was food enough – if we could call them. And they would cross the front, and we would sit and eat, and then they would go back. Other days if they had enough to eat they would call us, and we would come and eat.
> [Vitór cuts in] ... it is a war between brothers.[16] When two brothers fight they can [still] sit down and eat.

The influx of foreign troops did not, in other words, change my informants understanding of the war as one that evolved and was fought between kin rather than between ideologically opposed enemies or group that were in other ways mutually exclusive. The war was, despite the presence of foreign forces, not one fought between enemies threatening community life (Aho 1994: 10–11), but rather between opponents from the same community with the assistance of outsiders. In this manner, the 'brotherly' aspect of the war is an important point to understand when trying to make sense of my informants' actions, as it was influential in shaping the actual fighting and the general interaction on the front line, resulting in a very strange combat scenario, as seen in the mode of interaction between Guinean troops, as described by Buba:

> A lot of other people, a lot of people, when they heard of the violation of the ceasefire, they refused to fire. They refused. They would run and return [home]. They ran to their villages [*tabancas*] and [they] stayed there.[17] Others refused. They would say: 'I am not going to fire at my brother any more.' At the front line some would refuse. But others fired because they defended their own heads. Even if it is your brother – you see him because he is on one side and you are on the other side – you will defend your side so it does not fall, and he is defending his side. So it is necessary that you kill each other. There were these kinds of pressures to fire on each other between two brothers.

'Defending your own head' is what makes one fight actual or classificatory kin, it is the ultimate pragmatics of warfare, indicating that at some point all acts of war become defensive even when ordered to attack. However, in our larger perspective it equally shows the lack of ideological motivation, which is expected to precede and fuel the act, and very often enters in retrospect when making sense of acts of armed conflict. That is, not even in *post facto* narrativisation is it possible for the Aguentas – or generally for any of the Guineans I have spoken to – to construct ideologically opposed agents of war or to make sense of the fighting using ideological narratives, when referring to the fight between Guineans, as Carlos shows below:

> *What did people tell you about the Aguentas before you went?*
> Nothing ... I just went.
> *What did your friends, your family say?*
> They said 'Do not go. Do not go. The government will lose the war.'
> *What did you think about that?*
> Nothing. I just went ... I knew that perhaps they would lose, but everyone fights for his side, for his head.

To sum up, the war in Guinea-Bissau was unusual as it was built around an idea of family relationships, amity and a related Other, going beyond the polarisation of the social world into friends and foes, allies and enemies, which become hardened polarities in situations of warfare. From an academic perspective, the general understanding of the war can best be made sense of – and the relationship and interaction between the internally opposed military forces best be understood – as being between opponents rather than enemies. The presence of foreign troops, which made it possible to symbolically externalise acts of aggression, combined with a minimal existence of ideology in the war, and a high level of knowledge of each other's social lives and possibilities, made it possible for the Guinean forces to see each other as navigating the same terrain along similar trajectories, or, in a Bourdieuesque idiom, as opponents in the same 'field' competing for the same capital. The opposing Guinean forces had, in other words, sufficient knowledge of each other to see that both sides were fighting for the same possibilities and from the same point of departure.

However, this analysis should not leave us with an idea of peace and harmony between what were, and to a certain extent still are, opposed troops. We should beware of painting too pretty a picture of the interaction and neglecting the existing animosity between former and present conflictual parties in Guinea-Bissau, be they troops or civilians. Atrocities and abuse committed during wartime are not easily forgotten or forgiven. But what stands out in the above is the coexistence of hostility with the idiom of kinship, which in itself borders the oxymoronic. Yet this rather paradoxical understanding and behaviour can be explained via the concept of situationality.

Situating Acts of Aggression

Explained in another way, there is nothing brotherly about actual warfare. The Aguentas killed and were killed, and the wartime activities created just as much fear in my informants as they do in any soldier anywhere in the world. The reason that my informants could, and can, maintain an understanding of the forces they were fighting against as symbolic brothers has instead to do with a remarkable awareness of the relationship between action and situation that seems to exist in Bissau. The brotherly feelings my informants tell me about are, in this point of view, not reducible to mystification or the pleasant, retrospective acquisition of a convenient lie. Rather, the discrepancy between the two modes – between being brothers and killing each other – must be located in the realm of situationality, or a situationalist understanding of violent action. This refers to the understanding of action as situated in specific contexts and interpretational frames.

As such, the period of time my informants spent on the front is not seen as a homogenised unity but rather divided into isolated, numbered events. Rather than referring to the war as a year of overt conflict between visible parties, my informants see the year as containing four or five wars, depending on whether or not one counts the outbursts of fighting on 9 October and 18 October as one or two. Wars, *guerras*, refer in Guinea-Bissau to any period of actual combat, as a radicalisation of conflict. People thus refer to 'the first war' or 'the second war', which in turn entails the existence of intermediate periods of relative peace, again acknowledged as differently framed from those of war. These framings in turn imply different interpretations of agent and action, leaving us with a situational understanding of the opposed Guinean troops ranging from brotherly to dangerous, and not least with an understanding of the act of violence as related to its context rather than to the person committing it.

Furthermore, the fact that my informants saw each other as motivated by and working towards the same goals of social positions and relations – rather than towards two different ideologies and futures – equally made it possible for them to situate acts of aggression as contingent rather than as essential traits of the Other. Whereas aggression, in situations of crisis, usually enters into symbolic constructions as the Other, as the enemy, by becoming testimony to his dangerous nature, in Bissau, it seems to be related to the situation that demanded it, rather than the Other that enacted it. It was seen as specific to periods of actual combat during the war, rather than as characteristic of the relationship between the two parties in general.

For anyone who has ever studied warfare the fact that the period of war contains differently framed sub-periods might seem somewhat evident, but the important fact is that action in these differently framed periods itself becomes differently situated and thus interpreted. This can account for the fact that the soldiers seem to have shifted relatively easily between fighting each other and sharing a meal. As in Carlos's experiences:

> If the war lasted for six or seven days and they called a ceasefire, or if it lasted one week or two weeks and if the ceasefire lasted two or three days, they would call us and we would come and eat, or we would call them and they would come eat. Sometimes we would eat together for more than a month, but you see, if war started they would not dare come and us as well, we did not dare.

Battle and ceasefires are thus differentiated events, instead of being part of a longer period of 'unrest' or 'conflict'. This entails acts of war or peace being situated within different contexts and understood and evaluated contingently. This comes to the fore in Toto's explanation given below. Toto is a Papel living in Bairro Militar in Bissau and had both friends and family on the Junta side, and when I asked him how he could get himself to fire his gun when literally fighting friends and family, he replied:

> Well, you know, when you are a soldier you do not have that way of thinking, that this is my family. If they say go and kill, you must go and kill. Even if your father has come there, if they say fire, you must fire. That is the reason that if you take up arms you do not put it down again ... When the ceasefire ... When these people violated the ceasefire ... At that moment you do not reflect upon the other ... your family, your uncle and that. At that moment you just think about defending your body.

'Defending your body' and the statement made earlier about 'defending your own head' both point our attention to the fact that in actual warfare the opposed forces, Guinean or otherwise, are seen as dangerous. But it would seem that my informants construct this dangerous Other without a concomitant symbolic polarisation, or without greatly straying from the sphere of brotherhood. Even if you add the further elements of fear of persecution or death if you were to lose the war,[18] it still does not seem to exclude or remove the category of brotherhood from the relationship. Rather, aggression is seen as punctuating brotherhood, but without soiling the relationship. For my informants the step from dangerous to brotherly was thereby easily traversed as the situation changed. In the words of Vitór: 'The first time you would go close to the front after a battle you would be a bit nervous, but then the others would go a bit closer as well and we would talk and some would come here and others would go there.' It is clear that actual warfare changes the interpretation of the opposed troops but these changes are clearly related to periods of 'defending your own body or head'. So, while the horror of warfare centred my informants' attention on defending themselves against danger, the violent acts committed are situated within the specific period of warfare and secondary to a primary relationship of brotherhood.

Imagining Oneself as Other

Situationalism thus refers to the 'ability' of my informants to make sense of the actions of others by relating them to their specific context rather than locating them in essentialised characteristics, such as personality or instinct. Yet, in order to situate the violent actions of others within context, rather than as internal flaws, an empathy is needed that differs from the negative empathic projection in the construction of enemies. A negative empathic projection would include transference not only of my own 'excremental qualities' (Aho 1994: 113) but equally, or even more so, of my understanding of myself as enemy onto the Other. What makes some people kill and others suitable to be killed is thus not only that they are seen as 'rats', 'vermin' or, in Aho's Freudian-inspired preference, 'excrement', but also that we project upon them the (fear-derived) aggressiveness that we hold towards them.

Thus enemy, opponent and other are created via projections of the agent's own understanding, perspectives and motives onto the Other (ibid.: 114), but the fact that we are able to imagine the Other through ourselves does not mean that we, in dialogue with our own projection, imagine them as ourselves. Rather, I believe, the reason my informants are able to situate the violence of the Junta is because they are seen as being part of the same social context and having the same life chances open up for them at the onset of war. Relatedness, in the brotherly war, is thus a question both of actual or generalised kinship ties and of similarity of motive and possibility. Instead of constructing the Other as enemy, via a negative transference of putrid inner qualities and aggression towards one's social group, my informants are able to imagine the processes and social constraints that made war an opportunity for the other, constructing him as an opponent in a shared terrain. In other words, as opposed troops faced each other, they were aware of coming from a similar place, of having similar possibilities open up to them via the situation of warfare, and of navigating the same terrain. The whole brotherly war was fought on the premise of a change of power configurations rather than a change in political system. It was not a revolution, but a rebellion, fought for a change in the hierarchy of people holding positions of power, rather than for a change in policy or ideology.[19]

The lack of enemy in my informants' perspective of the war thus leads us towards some key aspects in understanding their war engagement. First, we see that the war was not ideologically motivated. There was no perceived movement towards a normatively defined better future and no teleological stake involved. Secondly, the lack of enemy substituted by the presence of opponents leads us to see that the terrain of war is one that is being navigated with a focus on possibilities rather than hostilities. However, in order to make sense of why joining a militia in the midst of a war which is most likely to get you killed can be seen as social navigation, we must gain a better understanding of the terrain young people seek to navigate and their social position in it. As we have seen, my informants share the characteristics of being urbanised men, but the social position that is most decisive for their social navigation is that of youth, which is what I shall now turn my attention towards.

Notes

1. We can, in other words, produce martyrs from any radicalisation of conflict, from riots through to world wars.
2. This appears in Chapter 1, of Book I, the only part of Clausewitz's work that is believed to have been completed at the time of his death (Beyerchen 1992: 60).
3. Introduction to Clausewitz's *On War* (1997). Much the same arguments are later made by Kaldor (1999).
4. This holds in both interest and strain-theoretical perspectives. Ideology as a means to pursue interest is complementary to ideology as a means to avoid the strain of societal discontinuities and discrepancies (Geertz 1993: 202). The two theoretical approaches are different sides of the same coin and pursuing one at the expense of the other relates more to a scholastic urge towards the neatness of one-factor analysis than to scientific reason.
5. I find the idea of mystification problematic on two accounts. First of all, it creates a picture of a layered society in which the strata of the powerful and the powerless only overlap within the workings of power and exploitation. Not that I wish to deny the existence of differences in degrees of power between agents, but I believe that the relationship is not confined to isolated modes of interaction, nor is the divide categorical. It is, in other words, one of graduation rather than division. Secondly, the idea of society being divided in two relatively separate strata has the unpleasant implication that the powerless haven't the capacity to recognise their own exploitation. I believe it instead more accurate to say that they are unable to act in a manner that would increase their social position and opportunities and thus benefit from the workings of power.
6. The differentiation is even further blurred if we look at the construction of the enemy made possible within the two scenarios. Linear and circular narrative ideological constructions yield us very similar constructions of the dangerous Other as one who prevents us from realising our future potential (Vigh 1998). The enemy in wars characterised by identity politics, as well as in the linear orientation of traditional ideology, is one who works towards a different system of distribution of symbolic and economic capital. Identity politics and the wars fought in their shadow are, in this perspective, as ideological as the more clearly defined conflicts between, for example, 'leftist' and 'rightist' political movements, and are equally directed towards the future, despite their anchorage in the past.
7. A note on fundamentalism. Much journalistic and academic attention is given to what is seen as the immanently fundamentalist aspect of Islam supposedly located in Sharia. Yet, if we look at the countries that have turned towards implementing *Sharia* law just prior to their 'fundamentalisation', we nearly always see states where the secular power of the government was either weakened by war or being misused to the extreme by brutal regimes (Iran, Nigeria, Afghanistan). Fundamentalism, coincidentally first used to designate Protestant sects, is thus a phenomenon that historically has come to the fore in relation to societies characterised by heightened secular disorder and lawlessness, and thus, historically, fundamentalism most often designates an impositions of (religious) order onto social and societal settings where none exists.
8. If our estimation, as seen in the previous chapter, is correct, that there were approximately 1000 surviving Aguentas and between 1500 and 2100 to start with, then the death toll of the Aguentas amounts, at a minimum, to 33 per cent.
9. See Chapter 9 for a detailed discussion of the process of social reintegration and appeasement.

10. Initially the Aguentas and the Senegalese troops fought in different units on the front line with Guinean and Senegalese commanders, respectively; as we shall see, this was to change during the war as the Senegalese units were singled out by the Junta troops and subsequently bore the brunt of Junta aggression.
11. Despite the departure of the Senegalese and Conakrian troops on the government side, there are no indications that the Junta parted with the Casamance troops backing their war efforts.
12. *Forças Delta* or *Forças Delta II [dois]* is another name for the Aguentas, taken from the American action series Delta Force.
13. A *collega* is a member of one's *collegason*, that is, of one's peer group.
14. The Economic Community of West African States (ECOWAS), the Economic Community of West African States Monitoring Group (ECOMOG). Formed as a response to the civil war in Liberia, the ECOMOG have performed 'peacekeeping' operations in a number of West African countries. The role of the ECOMOG has, however, been the subject of much debate as they have been accused of having hidden agendas and have become notorious for their frequent lack of discipline. Unflatteringly, a special military unit on the government side of the war in Guinea-Bissau were nicknamed ECOMOG, after the ECOMOG force in Liberia, 'because they were bad', that is, particularly ruthless, as my informant Vitór phrased it.
15. The younger of my informants would not only refer to the war through the concept of brotherhood but would also refer to elders on the Junta side as their uncles.
16. *Uma guerra entre hermons.*
17. The word '*tabanca*' refers to a rural village, but is equally frequently used as an (ironic) pseudonym for *bairro*, or suburb.
18. The government troops were told that, if they lost the war, they would be persecuted by the *Junta*. Toto himself explains it as follows: 'They said that they [the Junta] were going to kill us all. If they caught us they would kill us all. This was also what the *Junta* thought, that if we succeeded we would kill them all. They said, many of them said – people of rank – that if we take them, we will kill them ... We took them to lock them up. But you, if you are caught they will kill all of you. They did this so we would feel threatened in the field.' Besides most probably being a motivating factor in the atrocities committed by the Aguentas, this was also the main reason for the 300-odd Aguentas fleeing to the barracks at Kindia, Guinea Conakry, after the final assault. These Aguentas are still in Conakry, allegedly financed by Nino, and are, according to numerous of my informants and other sources (see Chapter 10), serving as mercenaries in the region's wars.
19. Equally, the reason behind the large influx of veterans of the war of liberation into the Junta side can be explained via rebellion rather than revolution. Prior to the war, the *antigo combatentes* were losing their positions within patrimonial networks as well as their overall influence and standing within Guinean society. From the perspective of the *antigo combatentes*, the military uprising of the Junta offered a way to regain what had been lost.

PART III

SOCIAL NAVIGATION

Chapter 5

THE SOCIAL MORATORIUM OF YOUTH

'Blufo, blufo, bluuufo.' *The word was being hurled across the street at a local lunatic: a man in his fifties, gone mad during the war and now roaming the streets of inner Bissau competing with the local dogs for leftovers in the city's myriad rubbish heaps. Whereas the mentally ill are generally shunned in Europe, they seem to attract an abundance of abuse and bantering in Bissau, and verbally* blufo *was just about the worst anyone could yell at you.* 'Bluuuuufo,' *Vitór bawled again.*

I had earlier learned that a blufo *was someone whose penis still had a 'hat', that is, an uncircumcised person of age, someone who, despite being old enough, had not yet gone to his 'feinadu'.*[1] *Further exploration revealed that it referred to a man who would never become wise, could never become someone important in Guinean society, could never have a wife. A* blufo *is, as such, a betwixt and between category defined by a discrepancy between chronological and social age. Being a* blufo *means being symbolically stuck in the position of youth never to gain the authority of adulthood. It is any Guinean youth's nightmare, and yet close to being the predicament of a whole generation.*

As shown, my informants did not enter into war in order to bring forth a revolution or to consolidate a political order. Rather, I would argue, we should see the Aguentas' engagement in warfare as an attempt to navigate the social terrain opened up to them by the onset of war. However, in order to illuminate how warfare could grant my informants a possibility for social navigation, I need first to account for the social positions and conditions from where they seek to move and, as we shall see, escape.

In this chapter, I seek to go behind the actual context of warfare and explore my informants' socio-political position as youth within Guinean society as well as to illuminate the navigational possibilities this position encompasses. Being immersed in a web of socio-political relations my informants evidently occupy a multitude of different social positions. Yet the one position that they all share and which seems to be most directly related to their life chances and socio-political possibilities is that of youth. In this chapter I shall therefore examine how people seek, and are confined within, the social space of youth, and attempt to understand my interlocutors' social possibilities and options from within this position. I shall illuminate what political space my informants claim, are confined to and participate in (Durham 2000: 113).

Youth in War

That youth are particularly closely connected to warfare should come as no surprise. Due to their physical abilities and marginal socio-political position young men have always constituted the bulk of armies, and the category of agents most visible in warfare, be it through images of their maimed and twisted bodies on the battlefield or that of hazy-eyed youth killing indiscriminately, are consequently young men. In fact the centrality of youth to warfare is so great that the lives they take or the lives they lose on the battlefield are seen as the legitimate waste product of the process of war. Thus, integrated into the very systematisation and praxis of warfare is the apparent proximity of youth to violence as military structures place seniority behind the front line and juvenility in the very centre of it. Proximity to violence is in other words ordered along a continuum of age, or seniority, with youth doing the actual killing and maiming and their seniors controlling the flow of events and pondering the subtleties of military tactics and strategy.

Currently, 60 years after the last global extermination of young men in the second World War, the role of youth in war is once more being accentuated: not, however, by the large-scale destruction in wars between industrialised nations, but by children and adolescents working violence in the in-between category of civil war. What stands out from this apparent shift in the mode of warfare is that somehow the rules have changed, dismantling the categorical boundaries and making potential victims of us all (Lutz 1999: 614–15). As we are appalled by images of youth not just killing other youth any more, but killing indiscriminately, blowing themselves up in busy market squares and staging military assaults on civilians, it seems that warfare has quite literally lost its rules. Yet, contrary to many popular representations, this is not necessarily due to an escalation in the levels of brutality or the sadistic and violent potential of youth. Whereas it seems plausible that the dominant mode of warfare has changed the general understanding of modern warfare as increasingly bloody and unregulated seems to be related to the relationship between generational categories and violence and to representational proliferation of atrocious acts as 'infotainment' (see Kleinman and Kleinman 1997), rather than to a decisive change in the praxis or agents of war.

The perceived relation between the proliferation of civil wars and the increased vulnerability of civilians as targets (see Kaldor 2001: 7; Kalyvas 2001: 100) is explicable from the difference between the identification of friend and foe, soldiers and civilians in relation to interstate as opposed to intrastate warfare. Where interstate warfare is often fought on the battlefield – a space of war with clear distinctions between the warring parties, soldiers and civilians[2] – intrastate wars are generally characterised by unclear differentiations between the fighting parties. This is, of course, related to the fact that civil wars are fought between internal enemies who are not necessarily distinguishable on the basis of language, appearance or uniform and often in non-demarcated areas of warfare using paramilitary strategies, entailing a deliberate switching between the category of civilian and soldier and blurring the differentiation between the two. Yet, contrary to popular belief there is nothing novel in this (Kalyvas 2001), and historically isolating a civil war which has not been fought with diffuse boundaries between these categories seems difficult, the Bissauian civil war in fact being one of the few to come close.

Secondly, I cannot help but think that there is a moral aspect to the debate. Why are we more outraged at the death of children and the elderly than the death of young men? Would the images be equally disturbing if what we saw was the same transgression of the divide between soldier and civilian but the ones dying being young men? The answer, I believe, is no. Young men murdering each other, soldiers or not, coincides with our understanding of which generation embodies violence, and the outrage of 'illegitimate' killings makes us aware of the acceptance of 'legitimate' war-related deaths, and thus points our attention towards the perceived close relationship between the social category of youth and the phenomenon of violence. There is something immensely perverse about the fact that the death of young men on the battlefield disturbs us less than the loss of other life – as if there was a qualitative difference between deaths – and we need to ask ourselves if the ordered, targeted and systematised killing of young men truly makes their violent deaths any less outrageous. The problem is not who gets killed in warfare but the fact that people get killed in itself.

Mechanically Mastered or Loose Molecules

When we narrow our focus and look more closely at our representations and understandings of children and youth in civil wars, we become aware of the existence of two primary, yet often opposed, understandings of youth. Most interpretations and representations (folk as well as professional) emphasise the role of youth and children in warfare either as being that of potential victims of manipulation by powerful seniors, or that of potential perpetrators as non-socialised 'loose molecules', that is, as destructive forces that are uncontrolled by social and societal constraints (Kaplan in Richards 1996: xv). In relation to violence and war, youth are seen either as risk or as at risk (Honwana 2000; Bucholtz 2002: 532–34).

In other words the acts and role of youth in warfare, and especially civil war, are currently seen as either determined by the generational order or detached from it as opposite poles on the autonomy continuum: that is, as agentive to the extreme or determined to the extreme. They are opposing views on youth, as being mechanically mastered by their elders or social institutions or as being unrestricted agents living out the social pathology of incomplete socialisation and doing as they please by way of a gun: a schism noticed by Durham's when she states: 'Warfare is one of the sites where the agentive nature of young people is most ambiguous ... are [war engaged] youth victims or perpetrators of violence?' (Durham 2000: 117). The primary point of divergence in analysis is, as seen in the above, the perception of the level of freedom of youth to choose what to do and how to act in situations of war.

Youth as Position and Process: Being and Becoming

This difference in perspective roughly coincides with two primary conceptualisations of youth within the social sciences. Youth can either be studied as an entity in itself, that is, a socially and culturally demarcated unit producing a 'sub culture' (see Wulff 1995), or it can be viewed with an emphasis on its position and dynamics within a larger social or societal corpus, as a social category defined by its inter-generational position. From the first perspective, youth constitutes a site of construction of ideas and praxis specific to the group in question, while the second defines youth as a period of liminality within a larger societal order – as a transient inter-generational stage between childhood and adulthood (Turner 1967): that is, the study of youth as a social and cultural entity or, in contrast, as a the occupiers of a (transitory) social position (Durham 2000; Olwig 2000; Olwig and Gulløv 2004; Cole 2004).

However, to gain a proper understanding of the role of youth in war, we need to see youth both as a stage within the generational dynamics and a social space in which its agents share similar horizons and points of orientation (see Schutz and Luckmann 1995: 115). We need to see youth as both social position and process (Vigh 2003). In a Mannheimian perspective youth, as generation, should be seen as being closer to class than to a 'consciously willed or developed group' (Mannheim 1952: 289; see also Cole 2004), defining it within a field of forces as an experiential demarcation.[3] Generations as experiential strata are not concrete groups, being bound together by formative experience and interpretative horizons instead of actual personal contact and knowledge of one another (Mannheim 1952: 288, 299, 306; cf. Anderson 1993).[4] Youth must, in this manner, be seen both as a point of acquisition, continuation and reinterpretation of social norms and values and as part a social whole (ibid.: 290–91). To make sense of the actions of groups of youth, we thus need to focus both on their orientations, possibilities and actualities, which Mannheim informs us are always 'differentiated and polarised' (ibid.: 316), and on their social locations, movements and positions, which underlie their possibilities of action and are integral to the generational and social order. From an interpretative position, youth are part of a larger social order and yet never internally undifferentiated, as well as being united and differentiated by their historical becoming, as a specific generation growing up in specific circumstances, that is, as a strata of experience, of shared historical constitution. In other words, Mannheim's idea of 'generation'[5] makes it possible both to contextualise youth within a field of forces and to analyse it as an experiential demarcation (Mannheim 1952: 289).

The Mannheimian dual nature of generation mediates the two primary conceptualisations of youth within the social sciences. It makes it possible for us to analytically approach the concept of youth as being both social process and position, located within a generational flow as well as being bound together by formative experience and interpretative horizons (ibid.: 288, 290-91, 299, 306). A Mannheimian perspective provides, in other words, a step towards synthesising the bifurcated view on youth within the social sciences as it shows us that 'youth' is always both being and becoming.

Affluence and Life Chances

If, however, we ask ourselves why this general bifurcation of the concept of youth as either position or process rather than both position and process exists and persists within the social sciences, the global politico-economic position of the community in focus seems to provide part of the explanation. We thus gain an interesting perspective on the two opposed approaches to youth if we locate them geographically, that is, in relation to the region of the world that our analysis is directed towards. If we look more closely at the social-scientific work done on youth in general, we see that the portrayals of youth as cultural entities, as the 'owners' and producers of a specific (sub)culture, seems primarily to be focused on the West – with the Birmingham school as its major academic advocates.[6] In other words, when we, as social scientists, look at youth in the West, we tend to focus on and construct youth as an independent cultural unit. In our perspective on youth in, for example, Africa, we tend, on the contrary, most often to construct youth as a period of transition.[7] So, as we move our scientific focus from youth in areas of affluence (such as in much of Europe) to youth in areas of scarcity (for example, in much of Africa) the movement appears to have the analytical implication that the agentive potential afforded youth shrinks together with the status of the social position.

Within the dual nature of the emergence of social-scientific analysis, that is, in the meeting between the conceptual categories of the researcher and those of the researched, the difference can be related to our understanding of youth, to our representations of the societies in question and to the fact that generational categories vary across societies as do the ways in which they are valued.[8] Yet, taking the rapid change within the status and representation of youth in Europe into consideration, it seems reasonable to conclude that such differences are most often related to the specific social role of youth within the generational order and the allocation of access to resources, power and authority within the given social terrain. In other words, the easier it is to gain access to resources and to obtain social mobility in a given society, the more status does the social position get and the more do we as social scientists tend to analytically construct youth as a social entity rather than a transitory position. It is access to resources and authority that apparently determines how independent and autonomous the social category is represented as being.

The concept of youth is, as such, differently analysed and theorised in relation to the affluence of the societies and the level of life chances of the agents it refers to. Our way of understanding 'youth' is thus dependent on the specific social stratification of generational categories in relation to the space of possible action which is socially afforded it: a possibility of action of which Bauman says: 'the ultimate meaning of a relative superior status is always a wider range of possible choices, and the lower down a status is in social hierarchy, the less freedom their incumbents possess and the less they can be seen as genuinely 'voluntary subjects'. To be higher means more freedom; to be lower means more dependence. (Bauman 1992: 27).

If we follow Bauman's logic, youth in Bissau thus suffers the space of minimal possibility and value.[9] The level of freedom or status of youth can in this perspective be said to correspond with the level of gerontocratic control over social mobility and inter-generational dynamics, that is, with the level of political power, de jure or de facto, granted along the variable of age. Or, put differently, the fewer social possibilities available to youth, the more they become dependent on the flow of power and resources along the inter-generational order and the more we tend to analyse them as belonging to a stage of transformation rather than as social and cultural entities.

It would thus seem that the conceptualisation and status of youth are both analytically and socially dependent on the relationship between the position and importance of age as a political variable and the relative ability of youth to build a life for themselves independently of the resources and authority of their elders. So, although the category of youth, in an inter-generational perspective, is located between childhood and adulthood, what constitutes or actualises the movement from one category to another is, despite the apparent universality of this social space, socially and culturally specific, as it relates to the access to authority and resources as well as the valuation and understanding of age and generation.[10] The two different analytical perspectives outlined here might be related to different cultural understandings of the concepts of age and generation, with the specific status of youth being related to the degree to which resources (symbolic, cultural or material) are controlled and allocated along factors of seniority. In other words, the more age becomes a political factor the less 'freedom', in the sense of social, political and economic possibilities, is granted the incumbents of the category of youth and the less status is it granted as a social position; this implies a massive difference in the conceptual packaging of generational difference.

From a Cultural to a Social Moratorium of Youth

'Contrary to the Western view that youth is the most desirable station in life, adolescent Africans hunger after the age which will endow them with an authority currently denied' (Chabal and Daloz 1999: 34). Chabal and Daloz's comparison between the status of youth in the West and in Africa merges the above discussion with the title of the present chapter. In a Baumanian perspective, we can say that the wider range of possibilities for youth in the West has entailed that the social category has been granted ample status and has become a social position to aspire to. Going back to the title of the chapter, the original concept of youth as a 'cultural moratorium' was coined by Helena Wulff, in two enlightening articles, in order to describe the efforts that people in the richer parts of the world put into staying in the social category through 'extending their youth by way of experimenting with different roles and thereby delaying adult responsibilities' (Wulff 1994: 133; 1995: 7). In the North, with its generally wide range of opportunities and life chances for young people, youth has become endowed with an abundance of status, being seen as the space of social and cultural production par excellence. However, it would seem that in societies characterised by a higher level of gerontocratic control, crisis or decline, where the acquisition of resources is far more difficult, the characteristics of the category are defined instead by relative dependence. Consequently the understanding of youth which is currently dominant in Bissau is closer to the perspective described by Daloz and Chabal, as youth is seen as a period of stagnation, limitation and marginality, of restriction rather than opportunity, making youth a social moratorium rather than a cultural one. In fact the category of youth in Bissau brings us as far from the idea of a willingly sought after cultural moratorium as we can get, as it designates a social position that people are involuntarily caught in and are trying their very best to get out of – a confinement which is directly related to a prolonged decline and drastic reduction of social possibilities.

The difference between the cultural and the social moratorium rests, in other words, on the space of possibility afforded youth. It rests on life chances and opportunities of social becoming. We all live our lives along multiple paths of transition (see Jones and Wallace 1992), rather than along a single path or predefined set of stages, and yet the amount of transitional possibilities available to youth varies greatly from context to context. The fact that youth in Bissau has become a social moratorium is thus related to economic hardship and a generationally asymmetric control over access to resources, which has greatly reduced their space of possibilities. It is caused by two decades of scarcity combined with a system of resource distribution that, to a large degree, is structured along a generational variable.

Immobility, Anomie and the Emptiness of Diversion

When I ask in Bissau what is good about being young, the answer is nearly almost *divirti*, meaning diversion, leisure activities, or just amusement. *Divirti*, amusement, be it in the shape of partying, romancing or playing sports is what youth do – or rather, all that it is possible for youth to do. The positive aspects of *divirti* should not be underestimated, and yet lack of possibility seems to a large degree to account for the conformity of the answer and, whereas *divirti* figures prominently on the plus side, the negative aspects of youth by far overshadow it.

As I commenced my fieldwork, none of my informants held a paid job, none had economic possibilities beyond everyday survival and none had their own household, sharing instead a room with friends or living at the mercy and expense of the father, mother, uncle or aunt, or others from the older generation.[11] Being unable to forge lives for themselves, to realise culturally defined and socially prescribed trajectories of maturation, the fluffiness of *divirti* seems a poor compensation for the truncation of social being and the general strain of being young in a society characterised by the lack of opportunities that follow in the wake of thirty years of socio-political decline. Thus the social becoming which was possible for the liberation generation has stagnated both ideally and in praxis, with resources being, for the most part, concentrated in the hands of those who became figures of authority due to participation in the liberation struggle,[12] and any others who could access and accumulate resources before the general onset of economic decline struck Africa south of the Sahara in the early 1970s (Bayart 1993: 69).

As resources are needed in order to obtain social mobility and gain a higher status than that invested in the category of youth, the combination of uneven distribution and access to resources and the ongoing period of decline has led to the social dynamics of the generational order being replaced by social inertia (see Gable 1995), with the result that those already in control of resources become older and older and the group waiting to gain in status and societal position becomes larger and larger. In other words, as social networks contract as a result of decline, an ever-increasing group of youth finds it increasingly difficult to acquire the resources to fulfil the ritual and social obligations needed to set up a household, consequently making generational and social mobility impossible to obtain. The result is a smouldering inter-generational tension,[13] which can, in fact, be seen all over sub-Saharan Africa. As pointed out by the Comaroffs, 'the hardening materialities of life' have placed youth in an especially marginal position, and as a result 'rather than the more familiar axes of social division – class, race, gender, ethnicity – the dominant line of cleavage here has become one of generation' (Comaroff and Comaroff 1999: 284).

Bearing resemblances to the anger noticed in the above quote, my informants locate their inability to ensure a future for themselves in the greed of their elders (ibid.: 289). Moreover resentment remains simmering as the networks that youth are currently desperately trying to navigate contract even further. My friend Seku provides a good example of the tension within such relationships.

Seku

I was hanging out with Seku. We had just eaten and were chatting, leaning back in a couple of chairs with a lazy, digestive ambience settling over the place. Seku shares with a couple of his friends a *congo* – a room outside parents' or elder's households shared as sleeping quarters by groups of youths, which is a common alternative to living under the roof and rules of your father or uncle.

Seku's *congo* is an annexe and much like any other such rooms in Bissau. It is a small, damp, mud brick room with a stamped earthen floor, furnished spartanly with a couple of beds, a few chairs (or stools), a hole for a window, and patches of lush green mould for wallpaper. Normally Seku and his room-mates, Aliu and Nomé, will spend only their sleeping hours in their *congo* and the rest of the day outside either in their *collegason*, in the stadium playing football or basketball, or running errands. But in the rainy season the place becomes a refuge for their entire *collegason*, as they cram together seeking shelter from the rain, turning the small room into a sauna with a malodorous twist.

Seku loves his *congo*, as it grants him the freedom to do as he wishes, to bring girls home, drink, party and generally behave without the condemning interference of his father or other family members. Yet, despite not living in his father's house any more and thus having attained a degree of freedom, Seku is still nearly totally dependent on the goodwill of his family for food and handouts. In other words, though ideally being expected to be able to take care of himself, and eventually expected to provide for his elders and a family of his own, Seku, at 26 years of age, shares, with the rest of my interlocutors, a common position of dependence.[14] Yet, despite being a bit older than many of my other interlocutors, Seku's situation is neither odd nor exceptional. The current situation for youth in Bissau is recognised as difficult by all, and his difficulty in finding a daily meal without the help of his father, mother, uncle or aunt is more usual than unusual.

How and on whom one depends is related to economic possibility as well as obligation. In general, the entire family is supposed to look after and assist a family member in need, with his closest relatives of course being more obliged than others. The parental household is the main provider but if the parents are divorced, as is not infrequent, the father is expected to contribute, although among the matrilineal Papels it is – traditionally – the oldest brother of one's mother who is ritually obliged. If both parents are deceased or unable to provide, one's oldest aunts and uncles take on the obligation. In general, however, within the urbanised community there is a move towards patrilineal rights and obligations, related to a general move from 'black law' to 'white law'.[15] Yet for the matrilineal groups this 'patrilinialisation' seems rather to entail a process of bilineality, in which the agent is able to activate both lineages, evoking different obligations and rights. In Bissau a man has authority over his son if the son is dependent on him,[16] and the period of youth is usually defined by the amount of time it takes the son to free himself of this dependence. For Papel youth, this is said to start when a boy is circumcised or when he begins to *kunsi mindjer*, 'to know women', and he passes into adulthood when he marries, which is possible when one is able to take care of a household (see Fortes 1969: 205).

It is this state of independence which Seku and my other informants are struggling to reach making generational relations problematic, as youth who are not able to establish their own household remain a burden on their father or uncle at the same time as they are aggrieved by their lack of ability to achieve autonomy. 'Fathers want to be in control of their sons' Seku would complain,[17] but, aware that challenging his father's control would probably entail going to bed hungry, he made himself eligible for meals by being subservient, by doing as he was told, doing favours and running errands, whilst all along complaining bitterly at the humiliation of having to act like a boy when in fact he sees himself as a man. When I asked him what he wanted to do if he could, Seku answered:

> I want to be the man of my [own] head.[18] I want to be a man of respect, a complete man, complete [*completo*]. You understand? I want to have my own house, children, a wife. I want a job. If you have this then no one can tell you that you are young. You will have your own family, your own job. If you are a complete man then you are the [sole] force of your head.[19]

Neither Seku's situation nor his aspirations are unusual, as young people in Bissau in general live their lives at the margins of resource flows. In fact, in the present context, the sentence 'then no one can tell you that you are young' points our attention exactly to the generally perceived stigma of youth as the category becomes derogatory in use when related to relations of power. The concept frames an interaction within a relationship defined by power, showing the use of the label 'youth' as belittling in effect.[20]

Not being 'a man of your own head' furthermore points our attention towards the position of youth as one without the authority and possibility of doing what one wishes, but instead having to follow the wishes of a significant other. 'Being in control of one's head', as the opposite is phrased, involves having the freedom to choose, to make up one's own mind and follow one's own desire, all of which are ideally encompassed in the category of adulthood. In a Guinean perspective, Seku is thus not a complete man as he does not control his own life and cannot get a wife or support a household, but is dependent on the goodwill of his parent. Yet, as said, it is a common complaint, an aggravation felt by all of my younger informants, especially given their distance from realising what they see as their social being. They are, moreover, equally unable to heal their 'trajectoral' impairment.

The relationship between the generational position of youth, social mobility and access to resources has, in other words, entered into a vicious circle in Bissau. Persistent decline in resources has entailed a retrenchment within family, socio-political networks and state, resulting in diminished access to resources and life chances among young, urban men,[21] making it impossible for the majority of them to support a family, marry and thereby become a man of respect, an adult. The consequence is, as we shall see, a situation of generational anomie in which it is currently unachievable for youth to attain the role and position,[22] which is socially prescribed and expected of them (cf. Merton 1968).[23] The current position of youth thus sets the frame for a wide range of inter-generational conflicts and tension, as the decline of the Guinean economy has made it difficult to gain access to the resources needed to become a 'complete man', with marriage being the primary, but unattainable, ritual that heralds the move into the status that being a provider provides.

Poverty and the Possibility of Marriage

Despite having suffered the ordeal of warfare, of being badly wounded and of losing rather than winning a war, Bernardinho is one of the luckier of my informants. Having found a job after the war, he is currently better off than most other Bissauian youth, and much better off than most Aguentas. Nonetheless, he still provides a good example of the precarious situation of youth in Bissau, as he is equally unable to move within the generational order.

Currently Bernardinho works as a kitchen helper in a local bar and is paid in meals rather than money. Not being paid cash for the work you perform is common in Bissau. In fact, many youth do not receive any returns for the odd bits and pieces of work they do, as they are repaid in favours, both past and future.[24] Furthermore, employers are notoriously unwilling to pay what they owe, and being paid in food seems to please Bernardinho, as it is at least tangible payment. So, despite it being in *naturalia*, Bernardinho's job is an asset for him and, even though he is just as poor in economic terms, he is a muscular, well-fed man who is unmistakably stronger and better fed than most of my other informants.

Bernardinho has had the same girlfriend for the two years I have known him, and our conversation would often drift into the sphere of partners, families and marriage. This particular day, we were standing by the counter of the bar, chatting. Normally, it was used to serve food and drinks, but currently Bernadinho was using it as a chopping board, slicing liver for the evening's main (and only) course. Standing there for the duration required to chop the best part of three kilos of liver, our conversation drifted from thoughts about the future on to the subject of women:

There are lots of women in Africa, lots. But money ... you must have money. If you have a woman but you do not have money she will go and find it where she can. If you cannot give her [money] for the market,[25] she will find someone who can.
So she will leave you if you do not have money?
If she needs a thing where will he [her boyfriend] see [i.e., get] it? If you do not give her, where will she see it? It is the same with marriage ... That is why marriage has nearly stopped in Africa. You can know a woman ten years, but you will never have enough money to marry her. To be a respectable man you need to marry. If you are not married you will not have respect in society. It is the same thing with work. If you have work you can organise your life, you can get married, and afterwards you can start a family ... But only someone who knows you... Only someone who knows you will give you a job ... These days, young people are frustrated. It is this that makes young people want to leave, so you can have a level of life. You go there [abroad] and then you can send money to your family ... But it is sad, because you are far from each other. It is difficult. Africans have difficult lives.

In spite of being lucky, having found a source of regular and generous meals, Bernardinho clearly feels the common sting of the present decline in Guinea-Bissau, as he is socially stuck, locked in the category of youth without possibilities of attaining social mobility. Furthermore, he is acutely aware that his dream of wedlock and social mobility can very easily be played out as a nightmare, since, instead of being able to marry his girlfriend with all the positive consequences it would have, he is faced with the constant possibility of his girlfriend leaving him for someone who can support her. There is, in other words, a massive discrepancy between the desirable and the possible within his prospective orientations.

Not being able to marry leaves Bernardinho without the means of becoming 'a respectable man' and thus locks him in a social moratorium of youth with few options for escape other than leaving the country. Yet migration is, in itself, highly dependent on receiving support from ones networks, not only in order to accumulate sufficient money for the actual journey, but also to get a passport, pay for a visa and establish connections abroad. As the quote shows, migration is, despite the difficulties it entails, seen by the majority of my informants as the only means of having a tolerable life, indicating that a locally generated way out of the social moratorium is currently not deemed possible. Or, as Amadu said, showing me the newly received EU visa in his passport: 'Look, is it not beautiful? I am so afraid that I will lose it ... You know, [if I lose it and] if someone finds it, it is like a dead who sees life.'

Buba

Buba was, to a large degree, in the same situation as Bernardinho, though he had no job and no prospect of receiving regular meals, as he relied for support on the goodwill and already strained finances of his uncle. Buba's reasons for joining the Aguentas were directly related to his family network. His uncle had been an officer, 'loyal' to the former president, and had encouraged Buba to enlist; this, combined with the fact that most of his friends were also going, had been sufficient motivation for Buba to join. However, as the *Governo* had lost the war, Buba's uncle had lost his privileges, had his house and property taken away from him and was left with a bare minimum, of which there was no longer enough to see to Buba's needs.

The first time I met Buba he was in a bit of a state. Having faced a traumatic period at the end of the war, he was a nervous and extremely vigilant person, who in many ways gave the impression of being trapped or cornered.[26] He was terrified of possible persecution and constantly afraid of being caught by the Junta Militar. Even though he agreed to participate in interviews, our first few attempts were unsuccessful because he began to whisper as soon as I started the tape recorder or even took out my pen and notebook. It should be said, however, that Buba really was in a specially difficult position, for he was as afraid of his own community as of the Junta in general, since he had been one of the few Muslims from Bissau to have joined the Aguentas and in this way was somehow seen to have been fighting against his own, Asumané Mané and a high proportion of the Junta officers being Muslims.

However, despite Buba being Fula on his father's side, he is Papel on his mother's side and maintains a close relationship with his mother's eldest brother, the *Governo* officer, who, the Papel being matrilineal and avunculo-local, is traditionally the most important male figure in a Papel perspective. Moreover, his girlfriend, with whom he has a child, and most of his friends are Papels. Whenever I met Buba, he was thus in the company of Papels, when it came to both friendship and romance. 'You are fucking my kin', Vitór, his best friend, and both Papel and Aguenta, would tease him. Yet, honouring the wishes of his mother's brother to join the Aguentas and not being a practising Muslim, Buba sometimes seemed as much of a Papel as many of my other informants.[27]

When I came back to Bissau after a year, I went to see Buba again. When I had left, he was living by himself in a small, windowless annexe built of *dubi*, mud bricks, with a corrugated-iron roof. The room had been provided for him by his uncle and can at best be said to be better than nothing. However, he was planning to move into something better when circumstances would allow, evidently thinking that better times were looming somewhere around the corner; his main concern was for his girlfriend and baby. 'When I get work, I will get my child and girlfriend,' he had said in our last interview. I left Bissau with the hope of Buba improving his life and life chances, finding a better place to live and being able to establish a household so he could be with his family.

Returning in March 2002 I was therefore eager to see how he had got on. But not much had changed for the better. Buba was still living alone in his annexe, and the possibility of life improvements coming his way had not materialised but rather deteriorated. He had become noticeably skinnier, wilted in fervour and physique, and I found it hard not to show my alarm at the sight of his weakening. 'Now things have got even worse,' he said. 'Before we had enough for one shot a day [one meal a day],[28] but now, not even that,' continuing:

> Young people are tired here. If you do not have work, and your father does not have, then it is a great tiredness [*kansera*] for you. If you do not work, if you do not have money, you cannot get married. My son is there (he points towards Pilun). I cannot take him ... Because I do not have a job, so I have to leave them there. I cannot go and look for them ... You know ... women cannot suffer like men. They cannot sit [for] one day, two days without eating. They cannot! So I have to leave them there [with his girlfriend's family].

Buba's circumstances are a good example of the unpleasantness of the social moratorium as lived. 'Women cannot suffer like men' is Buba's way of explaining why he cannot live with his girlfriend. As he is incapable of finding the resources needed to grant himself a meal per day, he is aware that he cannot tend to the primary needs of his girlfriend and baby, and is therefore unable to fulfil his social ambition and obligation. Not having money to pay for the wedding ritual and host a marriage celebration and to thus publicly mark the transition from youth to adulthood is one thing. However, even without this, Buba is not capable of taking care of his child and girlfriend. The social moratorium as lived is in other words more than just generational anomie. It is a state of massive marginalisation, abject poverty, impairment of one's social trajectory and *um tiro kada dia*, one shot of food a day – if lucky.

Social Death

Yet, like my other informants, Buba is not dying of starvation. His imminent death is not physical but social. Buba is able to feed off his family and friendship networks in order to cover most of his daily needs, yet, due to the prolonged period of decline, he is unable to attend to his social needs and fulfil a process of social becoming. A key social feature of youth in Bissau is, as such, social death, that is, the 'absence of the possibility of a worthy life' (Hage 2003: 132). Due to the disastrous social and economic situation the possibility of progressing meaningfully in life is, for Bissauian youth, close to being non-existent. *Bissau murri'dja*, Bissau has already died, people say, indicating that generalised social death is seen to have frozen the city in a futureless state of decline and hardship, of crisis, conflict and warfare (see also Gable 1995: 243; Allen 1999; Ferguson 1999). Yet in Guinea-Bissau this process of decline and crisis seems especially severe in relation to young, urban males. As they do not inherit land to cultivate and settle on or benefit from the services of a diminished state, their lives are characterised by abject marginality. In fact, were it not for the support received from family networks, almost none of my informants would have the means of securing themselves a meal a day. So, despite family relationships being perceived as tedious, they are nonetheless a resource which they would not wish to be without. Moreover, these networks are often what connect them to larger sociopolitical networks.

The Navigational Space of Youth

What we have seen thus far is that the social position of youth in Bissau is characterised by social confinement, deficient inter-generational mobility, a lack of life chances and an impossibility of social becoming. However, my informants obviously do not embrace their marginality, and what I shall now look towards are the social relationships and networks that they navigate in order to increase their life chances, in order to understand what socio-political lines of movement and strategies are available to them, and how they seek to make the best of these in order to tend to their physical and, not least, social needs.

Concerning the more immediate survival imperatives, Lourenço-Lindell (1996) has shown, in her article 'How Do the Urban Poor Stay Alive?', that people in Bissau rely heavily on the obligation of networks to share their supplies of food, however limited, in securing their survival. They rely, in other words on what Hydén has called the economy of affection – 'a network of support, communication and interaction among structurally defined groups connected by blood, kin, community or other affinities, for example religion' (1983: 8).[29] But the economy of affection and obligation also has its limits.[30] As we have seen in Guinea-Bissau, it has also been struck by the process of decline, and, since youth should ideally be able to fend for themselves, they are the least likely to benefit from the economy of affection when resources are restricted, and thus become especially prone to feeling the sting of decline as they are the first to be cut off from the distribution of resources within primary networks. In a similar vein Mary Douglas writes that:[31] 'the emergency system starts with a gradual tightening and narrowing of the normal distributive principle. It is foreseen that there will not be enough food for everybody. The emergency system starts to give short rations to the disadvantaged, the marginal, the politically ineffectual' (1987: 123). The brunt of this constricting of the 'distributive principle' within the last few years in Bissau has to a large degree been borne by youth.

Living in this social moratorium, the largest part of my informants constitute what has been termed the 'lost generation', as 'young people [who] have finished their schooling, are without employment in the formal sector, and are not in a position to set up an independent household' (O'Brien 1996: 57; Seekings 1996). Yet whereas 'the lost generation' implies an irretrievable abjection, a moratorium refers to a possible gaining of momentum, which is the underlying reason behind the continued efforts of social navigation that characterise youth in Bissau. However, despite the fact that both O'Brien and I are working in West Africa, youth as a predicament seems to apply not just to the Aguentas or to West Africans but generally to youth in areas characterised by economic hardship and decline, where young people are forced to remain dependent far longer than they prefer.

The Collapse of State and the State of Collapse

Youth in Bissau are, as such, in a continuous state of crisis. As the social moratorium has come to encompass generations, due to the prolonged decline and instability of the country and the ensuing scarcity of resources in families and networks, the crisis has gained an edge of chronicity (see Estroff 1993). The concomitant inertia of the intergenerational process during the prolonged period of decline has had dire effects on the lives of my interlocutors. They find themselves unable to actualise the sought-after life trajectory, the move towards being socially localised, towards being a social entity,[32] and the movement from being dependent on others to being independent, or having dependants, by becoming the master of ones own household. What is longed for by my informants is, however, not just attaining social status, by being a provider and having dependants, but just the possibility of being able to navigate the social terrain in such a manner that they will be able to gain a domain,[33] a social space of one's own or, literally, a place, a *kau* as it is called in Creole.

Where the state might formerly have provided an alternative exit from the social moratorium by furnishing youth with the means for achieving social mobility through, for example, education, these possibilities for social movement have effectively been either abandoned or colonised by patrimonial networks. In other words, as youth become marginalised within the economy of affection, the only social structure left to navigate, if they wish to escape the social moratorium that their lives are caught in, is patrimonial. Yet, due to conflict and instability, patrimonial networks are themselves receding and concentrating their resources around key points, putting my informants in a situation where finding an 'effective' patron of even minor status and importance, such as a petty gatekeeper to a patrimonial network, has become difficult.

Migration, Patrimonialism and the Economy of Affection

Refocusing on the political space – or non-space – of youth, we can thus summarise that there are ideally three more or less available options for my informants if they wish to tend to their material and social needs. Of these, migration stands out as the most desirable but the most difficult to attain, as it demands considerable resources, not only to pay for the journey, but also for the entire system that provides you with the passport and visa; it is, in Bissau, a very expensive exercise in bribery. However, migration makes it possible to rapidly become someone, *un algin*, without having to depend on the goodwill of one's elders or having to work one's way through a network. In other words, by becoming migrants, youth can quickly gain an adequate income to support one's household and extended family in Guinea-Bissau. Thus, ironically, the prize for gaining rapid status at home would seem to be to endure minimal contact with the household one supports as well as being placed in the lowest status in the host country in the West.

Family Networks and the Economy of Affection

An agent can also tend to his needs through the economy of affection and obligation, relying on the fact that the primary family will feed him when in need and that he – if lucky – will gain an inheritance of worth. Yet, as we have seen, due to the prolonged decline, youth are increasingly being marginalised within this economy of affection, as they are last in the line of obligation, that is, the ones that nuclear families are least obliged to feed or help financially. However, many of my informants do nonetheless survive via the economy of affection, but it becomes important to note that family relations are used to cover one's immediate needs rather than offering a way out of the social moratorium. In fact, only very few are able to acquire sufficient resources from family networks to secure themselves a future. *Si bu familia ka tene ...*, 'if your family does not have ...', people say, not needing to finish the sentence as the resulting hardship is evident. In this manner, being of a normal family means that it will be a financial strain for them to support ones everyday existence.

Patrimonial Networks and Possible Futures

'If your family does not have' thus means that escaping the social moratorium is going to be tough, seeing that the few resources there are are in the hands of a few patrons, *homi garandis*, who control the access to and flow of resources and their flow through Guinean society.[34] As youth are normally not able to access the amount of resources needed to maintain a household through family networks, one of the only possibilities left is to find the backing of a wealthy patron, thus entering a patrimonial network. Patrimonialism has been defined by Bangura as: 'a system of resource distribution that ties recipients or clients to the strategic goals of benefactors or patrons. In the distribution of 'patrimony', or public resources, both patrons and clients attach more importance to personal loyalties than to the bureaucratic rules that should otherwise govern the allocation of such resources' (Bangura 1997: 130).

We thus see a possible navigational continuum from relations of affection and close network obligation to patron–client relationships to actual patrimonial networks as socio-political structures, which distribute public resources on the basis of personal relations. Youths seeking to enter patrimonial networks do so by trying to gain a reciprocal relationship to a patron, at any point in the patrimonial network, who controls a flow of resources exceeding that needed to fulfil his family obligations. While youth in Bissau will often fall back on family relations to help them in times of need, seeking to enter patrimonial networks is clearly directed towards both the here and now and the future. Most youth are aware that they will have to bow and scrape their way through such networks before gaining a possibility to actually prosper from it; yet they seek to enter such networks more than willingly. In fact, most of my informants were living off the economy of affection and obligation while simultaneously looking for a way of forging patrimonial ties and thereby gaining a possibility to tend to both to their material and their social needs, their immediate and future situation. Furthermore, the dominance of these forms of possible access to resources is made evident upon the very first contact one has with Guineans. The attempt to construct a relationship centred around patronage or affection is made evident to the wealthy on a daily basis as one is, as a wealthy, white, First World person, constantly approached by the phrase 'I want to be your friend' or by being called 'patron', that is, through the construction of a relationship based either on the economy of affection or patronage.[35]

Crisis in Patrimonialism or Crisis in the State?

Patrimonialism is not unique to either West Africa specifically or Africa in general (see Bayart 1993). Rather, the apparent surge of patrimonial politics in sub-Saharan Africa since the 1970s seems related to the impact of the economic crisis on the newly established post-independence states. It is, in other words, not a historically 'deep' mode of politics related to the continent and its sub-Saharan inhabitants (Chabal and Daloz 1999), but a mode of politics that is intimately related to scarcity. Patrimonialism is the politics of poverty and marginalisation. It is what we actualise when resources are too scarce to go around and when communal political systems lose their ability to provide for subjects.[36]

Yet, as a result of persistence of decline we see that the concentrically organised circles of agents that these networks of redistribution can afford to patronise have started to shrink (ibid.: 36). In other words, in situations of chronic crisis the retrenchment of state is followed by retrenchment of patrimonial networks – or, as Richards would call it, a crisis of patrimonialism – which to a large degree creates and maintains the social moratorium of my informants, as it cuts them off the networks in question. Yet we might nonetheless have to ask ourselves if it is really patrimonialism that is in crisis, due to the decline in prices of raw materials and the drying up of the sources of aid in the 1990s due to the end of cold war (Richards 1996: 36). Perhaps it is even the contrary: patrimonial networks gain strength by controlling access to resources and affluence makes access difficult to control. The result is that youth in situations of plenty are able to tend to their material and social needs without having to run errands and do favours for patrons.[37] In fact, patrimonial networks require a minimum of economic shortage to secure their influence, and rather than being affected negatively by economic crisis, they seems to be built on it, gaining their very power and dominance from scarcity and decline. The shortage of resources can very well be seen as strengthening the position of patrons and the power base of patrimonial networks.

The State of Patrimonialism

As resources decrease, my informants are thus increasingly dependent on finding an entry into patrimonial networks in order to secure themselves a way out of the social moratorium. And, as these networks become increasingly difficult to access, youth are willing to do almost anything to oblige them, having so few options available that being exploited by a patron, through an unequal exchange of resources, favours and obligations, is currently the best they can hope for (see Hinkelammert 1993). Currently, in Bissau, even negative reciprocity induces a social relationship with, at least, the possibility of reciprocation (see Sahlins 1974), granting youth an opportunity for bettering their lives in the future. Beyond being exploitative the relationship encloses, in other words, a possibility.[38]

So, while family networks may sustain one's existence, they do not and cannot normally support an agent in his efforts to become *homi completto*, a complete man, that is, in facilitating his process of social becoming. For this the youth must turn towards patrimonial networks. The way youth go about navigating patrimonial networks is thus a social praxis of utmost importance for us to understand if we wish to gain an insight into the actions and motives of the Aguentas. Yet to gain a better understanding of the workings of patrimonial networks in general, as well as specifically in Bissau, we need to first move our perspective away from seeing patrimonialism within a Weberian scheme of progress towards a bureaucratic structuration of power. The only way to avoid essentialising or culturalising patrimonialism is to see it as a political process that is related to poverty and marginalisation. Whether within lay discourse on African politics or within development discourse and its focus on 'good governance', 'civil society' and 'citizenship', patrimonial systems are constantly mirrored against our conception of a state as a bureaucratic order, making it difficult for us to see them as other than atavistic and negative structurations of power,[39] consequently preventing us from getting a proper picture of their working, of their contemporary dynamics within a local, regional or global political arena and their influence on the social possibilities of agents trying to navigate them. Gaining a proper picture of patrimonial networks thus demands of us that we do not just juxtapose and evaluate them in relation to a bureaucratic conception of the state (Herzfeld 1992: 2–4), but that we trace and follow them through societies from, for example, the 'top' position of accumulation of state finances through to the outer links of the economy of affection.

If we go back to Bangura's statement that 'both patrons and clients attach more importance to personal loyalties than to the bureaucratic rules that should otherwise govern the allocation of such resources' (Bangura 1997: 135), we find ourselves directed towards two generalities in academic work with non-rational-legal state systems: first of all, that they are constantly positioned and analysed against the background of Western conceptions of the state and, secondly, that their dominance tends to be seen as a puzzling pathology. Yet, while patrimonial networks are seen as parasitical on state structure, that is, as a bitter by-product of implementing 'state' in a specific cultural context, the question we ought to be asking ourselves is rather whether the concept of state is at all valuable in making sense of the type of political networks in question. Can we disentangle our concept of state from our understanding of its relationship to bureaucratic structures?

Gaining a better understanding of the current function and remains of state structure in Guinea-Bissau might be facilitated if we see them as patrimonial points of absorption and distribution, as centres or crystallisations in a web of rhizomatic networks tying the individual to the political and societal. Primarily, such a perspective would aid us in avoiding unfortunate social-scientific ruminations on war and conflict that see fragmented structures of 'state' as institutional agents, directing our attention towards the constellations of agents working the state instead (Douglas 1987). It would furthermore allow us to illuminate how patrimonialised state structures and networks constitute fields of possibilities for political agents in their efforts to better their situation. The postcolonial state is, as Bayart informs us, 'not one-dimensional, formed around a single generic trunk, like a majestic oak tree whose roots are spread deeply into the soil of history. It is a variable multiplicity of networks whose underground branches join together the scattered points of society' (Bayart 1993: 220). From the perspective of young men in Bissau, it is exactly these underground branches that constitute the political space, which it is possible to navigate in trying to improve ones life situation and enhance ones life chances.[40]

When trying to gain a better understanding of the youth that became Aguentas, it becomes especially clear that the focus should be drawn away from political science and statist macrostructure if we are to understand their participation in conflict and war. Navigating networks, from the economy of affection and obligation through to patrimonialism, is, for young men in Bissau, not just the primary way of gaining access to resources, ranging from a ticket to Europe to a daily meal, but the only way. Yet focusing on how my informants plan their life trajectories and tend both immediate and future needs reveals that it is not the specific patrimonial network that takes centre stage but rather modes and styles of navigation. Attention to the latter illuminates the extent to which my informants navigate the possibilities opened up by factionalist politics while not being bound by factional loyalties.[41] Factionalist politics and warfare provide, in a Dahrendorfian idiom, the social options that open social ties and networks for the navigational efforts of youth,[42] and the focus of my informants is not on charismatic leaders, ideology or religious enlightenment but on possibilities opened in the social terrain by the dynamics of different networks and network competition. It is 'political' movement, which counters our 'normal', hierarchical understanding of the state and our normal idea of the movement within political structures as ideologically motivated and differentiated. In other words (combining Weber and Hobbes at will), in Guinea-Bissau the 'state' as a bureaucratic structure allowing for centralised civic rule and serving to protect its citizens and distribute resources has withered to being no more than a rusty grid, cross-cut and intertwined by patrimonial networks. Within the Weberian and Hobbesian definitions of state, the state is effectively non-existent in Guinea-Bissau.[43] There is no monopoly on the legitimate use of violence and no state to guarantee the security and well-being of its citizens. In other words, the important political spaces that my informants seek to navigate form themselves around the state or its residue instead of in it, factionalism being, as Bayart clarifies, not epiphenomenal to the African state but its mainspring (Bayart 1993: 233, 240, 268).

Seen from 'below' or 'within', from the perspectives of youth in Bissau, there is no singular state, but rhizomatic structures and possibilities of movements cross-cutting ideological boundaries, state demarcations and national boundaries. My informants seek to navigate their way out of the social moratorium by manipulating these, rather than cultivating factional, ideological or traditional loyalties. And so, if the state in Africa is 'a plural space of interaction and enunciation [that] does not exist beyond the uses made of it by all social groups, including the most subordinated,' that is, 'a state of variable polarisation' (Bayart 1993: 252), then ought we not to start focusing even more on the rhizomatic or patrimonial aspects of 'politicking' in Africa? If we do exactly that in relation to Guinea-Bissau, we see ramifications of multiple overlapping networks, with people trying to navigate these states of variable polarisation, imagining new political trajectories and moving between interconnected networks, as they are engaged in the politics of survival and the quest of social becoming.

Focusing on the 'state' in Guinea-Bissau with rational–legal lenses thus allows us to see nothing but the dishonest and the pathological. It highlights the remains of a manner of societal organisation that is but a representation but obscures the actual social and political dynamics which people act in relation to. In a place such as Guinea-Bissau, the statist perspective amounts to looking at political processes through the wrong analytical optic, and as such our Weberian expectation – of bureaucracy as development – has compelled us to focus on people's actions through the lenses of a superimposed order that does not correspond to the foundation from which my informants make their choices and seek to realise their futures (see Dunn 2000).

Instead of being located in the state, the political space of youth in Bissau is factionally and patrimonially defined, as patrimonial networks and migration are the only available options for escaping the social moratorium and seeking to build a domain within the social terrain. The economy of affection, which may feed youth in the present, is most often not capable of granting them a future, but may yield a gatekeeper and thus an entrance into a patrimonial network. Yet even such access is considered a privilege, a rarity. The current state of affairs for youth in Bissau is such that gaining the possibility to navigate patrimonial networks is in itself deemed almost impossible, meaning that many of my informants, when between wars, are in fact searching for a possibility of gaining a patron but are unable to do so without the configuration of power changing or war opening patrimonial networks as patrons attempt to defend their networks. The act of engaging in war thus provides a possible entry into a patrimonial network, granting the agent a chance of increasing his life chances, escaping the social moratorium and embarking on a process of possible social becoming. In Bayart's words, commenting on a similar but not quite so aggravated (I would argue) process of social marginalisation in Cameroon: 'Recurrent unemployment prevents those without money from acquiring fashionable imported goods or from being able to choose a spouse – the *sine qua non* of social recognition. The social frustration caused by the economy of survival force many "little men" to make radical choices' (Bayart 1993: 240).

What we have seen in this chapter is thus how youth has become a space of confinement, as continuing economic decline has made it difficult for young people to set their lives along culturally prescribed life trajectories. Yet, be it in terms of symbolic, cultural or economic capital, agents will always try to secure an acceptable standard of life, and so we may broaden our current investigation by looking towards the 'radical choices' mentioned by Bayart, or in general at how youth seek to survive when networks have contracted to a bare minimum and resources are barricaded out of reach, when stuck in a social moratorium with very few possibilities of getting out of it. In Creole the answer is given via a term which is at the same time a cultural institution, a self-identity as well as a praxis. The answer is *dubriagem*.

Notes

1. The common Creole term for a circumcision ritual, male or female, which is a *rite de passage* into either youth, adulthood or seniority, depending on the ethnic and religious group. For the Papel the ritual is performed during adolescence and marks the move from youth to adulthood.

2. Even this is obviously a truth with severe limitations; since the bombing of Copenhagen by the British in 1807, which was the first recorded indiscriminate bombing of its kind, where the military tactic was directed towards civilian losses (*Gyldendals Leksikon*, Copenhagen 2002: 298), national military forces have regularly attacked civilians of the opposite side in the course of interstate warfare; within the last two centuries the Boer wars, the subordination of Ireland and the German and Russian campaigns during the Second World War stand as evident examples of the blurring of the divide even within interstate warfare.
3. Once again, as with the concept of 'community of experience', what is referred to is the process of shared experience instead of individual cognition.
4. Interestingly, the Mannheimian understanding of the phenomenon of generation is also related to warfare, as it is born out of the/his experiences of the First World War and the generational differences in perception and orientation in relation to it. Secondly, both the Mannheimian idea of generation and Schutz and Luckmann's (1995) idea of contemporaries and generations approximate my initial point of departure (although on different structural levels and thus with very different analytical possibilities) in seeing the Aguentas as a community of (shared) experience.
5. It is the fact that generation designates both cohort and time span (between parent and child) which grants it its synthesising abilities. Yet, rather than seeing this as analytically vague, it seems that Mannheim in fact directs our attention towards the experiential aspects of being young.
6. This school is rightly known as the Birmingham Centre for Contemporary Cultural Studies (the BCCS).
7. Especially so within the discipline of anthropology, due to its long-standing focus on kinship systems and family units as the traditional and primary fields of analysis.
8. Based on a Parsonian distinction (Parson 1966), Eisenstadt differentiated between the role of youth in universalistic and particularistic societies. Whereas in universalistic societies inclusive membership is based on universal criteria of citizenship (blood, birth, allegiance), in particularistic societies it is based on close affiliation and membership, such as ethnicity (Eisenstadt 1964: 160). This dichotomisation could account for the difference between youth as a cultural moratorium in the West and as a social moratorium in the South, yet, as Eisenstadt instead moves conceptually along an implicit, Weberian understanding of societal progress towards increasing bureaucratisation, the differentiation disregards the extent to which 'modern', universalistic societies, to use Eisenstadt's Parsonian concepts, are saturated by particularistic relations that cross-cut 'official' structures, evident in, for example, the phenomenon of nepotism.
9. But we must, in this perspective, be careful not to confuse suffering with constraint. Using lack of agency to define levels of suffering or violence (physical, structural or symbolic) seems problematic as it means that the mere constraint of being social constitutes suffering through a 'contextual domestication' of agency; it also seems to miss the point that, with few exceptions, we all move in, inhabit and manipulate numerous social structures at any given moment, with the implication that a non-agent is as abstract an entity as an absolute agent, or (after Bauman) that being completely dominant or completely dominated are both abstractions. In other words, even though we might be structurally limited in one aspect of our lives, we might not be in other coexisting and simultaneous aspects, even within the same relationship; moreover, not all limitations of agency are unpleasant or unwilled to the extent of constituting violations (physically, symbolically or structurally). Subjugation can be expedient, willed and pleasant (for some).

I do, however, agree with Kleinman et al. (1997) that there is a close correlation between impairment of agency and suffering, since at least in situations of

decline, conflict or war the social context becomes difficult to anticipate for several reasons and thus difficult to plan and implement strategy in, but we have to use the concept and experience of a degree of powerlessness as a stepping stone to an analytically constructive correlation between agency and suffering.
10. See Mead's work on Samoan youth for a classic discussion of cultural conceptualisations of youth (1969).
11. This dichotomisation could account for the difference between youth as a cultural moratorium in the West and as a social moratorium in the Third World, but the differentiation disregards the extent to which males are ideally expected to supply the money needed to feed the household, however, through the cultivation and trade of food items, women actually seem to provide the majority of the food needed. For the urban population the continuous decline thus affects gender relationships and roles, as urban males are dependent on finding work in order to provide for their families at the same time as jobs are increasingly difficult to find. 'You are who? ... Someone without two *pes* [coins]' my neighbour's wife once scolded her husband, indicating the influence that lack of employment and ability to provide has on male positions within the household. The changes within gender roles and relations within households and their effect on the general political process and mobilisation provide an interesting topic for further research.
12. Many of whom were in their thirties and fourties, and thus of relative maturity at the time of liberation. The liberation fighters who were still young when the war of liberation ended now constitute the large bulk of *antigo combatentes* (veterans of the liberation struggle), war veterans, who are equally impoverished and whose dissatisfaction with their social standing and lack of life chances was largely responsible for the influx of *antigo combatentes* to the Junta side.
13. The civil war in Guinea-Bissau can in this perspective be seen as a result of generational tension as the Aguentas were solely constituted of youth and the Junta Militar initially saw a large influx of *antigo combatentes*, thus creating a conflict scenario where a military force constituted largely of youth faced one which was initially largely comprised of their elders.
14. Except for three who have managed to leave for Europe.
15. *Lei preto* or *lei branku*. Both are juridically valid, yet *lei branku*, white law, is the most dominant in Bissau.
16. See Meyer Fortes for a wonderfully thorough description of parent-child relationships among the Tallensi as they progress along the generational trajectory (Fortes 1969).
17. In Creole this was *pape misti sedu riba di si fidjus*, literally 'a father wants to be on top of his sons', indicating the level of hierarchy that dominates the relationship.
18. *Misti sedu homi di nja cabeza,*
19. *Si abo i homi completo abo i poder di bu cabeza.*
20. Much like the use of 'boy'.
21. Getting a job – public or private – in Bissau being equally dependent on networks.
22. See Fortes (1984: 118) and Meillassoux (1981), who similarly argue that young men cannot fulfil themselves socially until they marry, but locates the power to decide who can marry and who cannot in the hands of powerful elders.
23. Although analytically precise, the concept of anomie is problematic as there will always be a relative distance between the ideal and the real, between the *culturally prescribed* and the *socially possible*. However, there is a difference between having a schism that can be socially and culturally incorporated, and one that is so significant that it leads to conflict.
24. It seems that people are rarely paid their full wages in Bissau, except perhaps for the political elite. A staggering number of people complain that their employer has not paid them, or just paid them a fragment of what they were due and the State seems to be the worst employer of all. In 2002 and the spring of 2003 there were numer-

ous strikes calling for the payment of civil servants, some of whom have not been paid for years, and nearly all of the state employees I know have been waiting for months for the government to pay their dues, or for the person who is supposed to redistribute the institution's funds to start distributing, but not daring to quit out of fear that then they would then not be paid at all. One primary school teacher I spoke to told me that he had not been paid for years but continued working because it was the only job he could get. So, despite the absurdity, from my Western point of view, of being employed if you are not getting paid, the teacher was looking after his future.

25. *Dal pa fera*. To give a woman (money) for the market is a normal transaction within relationships, before or after sexual encounters. *Dal pa fera* should, however, not be mistaken with actual payment, which is called x [*schish*] (referring to x amount of money) and which would means that the woman was a prostitute. The payment of x terminates a 'relationship', the payment of 'money for the market' consolidates it, underlining an obligation and a wish for its further existence. Although the amount in question might be identical, we are talking about two very different forms of transaction, with very different symbolic values and consequences.
26. Buba had been part of the platoon from the Presidença that was tied down behind the Bandim market at the final assault of the Junta.
27. Though the statistics on the Aguentas only record ethnicity on their fathers' side many were influenced by their mothers' Papel ethnicity in joining up, implying that the ethnic or kin connection plays a larger role than we may assume from the statistical data in themselves. It would be interesting to be able to see this 'shadow ethnicity' of the statistics as I believe it would raise the Papel affiliation considerably. As such Carlos and Buba are registered as Mandjako and Fula, respectively, though both joined after being influenced by their mothers' Papel family.
28. *Um tiro kada dia*, meaning 'one meal a day' (see also Lourenço-Lindell 2002: 71).
29. At a closer look, Hydén's economy of affection ought perhaps more correctly be termed an 'economy of affection, obligation and coercion', as it is based on relatedness rather than sentiment and often involves a degree of force.
30. The economy of affection is limited both in relation to whom it can afford to help in situations of scarcity, if the agents in it wish to maintain a minimum standard of life for its core agents, and in regard to the rules of obligations and distribution often being manipulated. My wife's field assistant thus took half his wage every month, leaving the other half for us to 'guard', seeing that he would be obliged to divide however much money he had within his close network; the obligation to share meant that he had to conceive of a way of saving up money without transgressing normative rules of conduct.
31. She builds on Williams Torry's work on famines.
32. 'Every human being passes through different ages within his lifetime, and at each age he attains uses different biological and intellectual capacities. Every stage in this progression constitutes an irreversible step in the unfolding of his life from its beginning to its end. At each stage he performs different tasks and roles in relation to other members of his society: from a child he becomes a father; from a pupil, a teacher; from a vigorous youth, a gradually aging adult ... in every human society this biological process of transition through different age stages, the process of growing up and of aging, is subject to cultural definitions. It becomes a basis for defining human beings, for the formation of mutual relationships and activities, and for the differential allocation of social roles' (Eisenstadt 1964: 21). What sets 'life trajectory' apart from age stages is, above all, that it is not a unidirectional singular process of maturation and that it is reversible. People can and do move between generational categories as well as 'inhabiting' multiple strands of transition at the same time, just as they move and are moved within them. Secondly, the concept differs in that it describes not only movement across the generational

order but also the imagined movement within this. The concept relates to an understanding of how one ought and can possibly move generationally and socially as well as to the tactics and strategies for this movement. Thirdly and finally a life trajectory relates to a process of becoming, which is constantly in the making. Where the idea of 'age stages' or 'life stages' gives an impression of lives automatically divided into four (childhood, adolescence, adulthood and old age), a focus on social becoming and life trajectories enables us to focus on the constant imaginaries and negotiations of meaning of people striving to be young, adults or old in certain ways and situations.

33. Within this spatial metaphor we can inhabit and navigate three different, concentrically ordered social spaces, moving from a domain, via a terrain, to a wilderness. In the current perspective one can fight for a social domain, in a social terrain, but against a social wilderness. A wilderness is, in other words, that which is not yet part of one's social world but borders it or otherwise lies beyond it (Jonathan Schwartz, personal communication, autumn 2002).

34. Mitchell differentiates between action sets and personal networks. An action set is, in this perspective, an instrumentally defined network actualised in relation to a short-term period of time. A personal network, in comparison, exists simultaneously on the basis of different interests and persists beyond the duration of a particular transaction (Mitchell 1969: 38). Mitchell's differentiation is applicable to the difference between networks based on the economy of affection and patrimonialism, yet the patron–client networks that are not directly patrimonial mediate the two extremes.

35. I do not want to imply that people only seek friendship from an economic perspective; however, the obligation to share is there if friendship is established, and is certainly the underlying motive for some.

36. As seen, for example, in the control of the cashew nut trade, fishing rights or telecommunication, which seem to be part of the political spoils passing from one patrimonial network to another.

37. Richards, in an earlier work (1995) which seems more to the point, talks about 'a crisis of youth'.

38. Patrimonialism is obviously not exploitative as a straightforward exchange of favours and obligation. However the interaction on which patron–client relationships are based is between the holder of capital and positions (symbolic, political or economic) and a person seeking the particular resource. The deeper the crisis or decline, the more the holder is able to define the terms of exchange in relation to the demand on the resource(s) s/he controls (see Eisenstadt and Roniger 1981). Currently in Bissau, the terms of exchange are extremely unfavourable for those seeking assistance and we are thus seeing youth running errands and showing servility for the mere possibility of patronage.

39. It is a Weberian idea of progress but interestingly without the dystopian vision of over-bureaucratisation.

40. The relation between the economy of affection, patrimonialism and state is thus one of gradation rather than division.

41. The reference to factions in this perspective derives from Bayart, but makes further sense in the present context as there are currently no revolutionary parties in Guinea-Bissau with alternative political views on the organisation of state affairs and the current societal order in general.

42. This is not to say that conflict and warfare are the only social option open to youth (in which case the percentage of mobilisation would have been far greater) but that they are among the few.

43. It resembles if anything the Marxian superstructure without the concomitant idea of easily defined and stable class formations, as the Western notion of class is not easily located in Bissau (see Chabal and Daloz 1999: 28).

Chapter 6

DUBRIAGEM AND SOCIAL NAVIGATION

CONSTRUCTING SOCIAL TRAJECTORIES THROUGH WAR

I now know that war gives me diarrhoea. As the shooting flared up in November so did my stomach and I spent the night on the toilet dehydrating to the rhythm of rifle shots and the hollow booms of RPGs.[1] *It is a thing of great amusement to my informants. When I met Vitór and Olivio after the shooting died down, Vitór asked me how I had passed the war. I answered truthfully that I spent most of the time on the toilet – a safe place to be. Vitór nearly choked on his beer, the aerated beverage muffling his laugh. Olivio, on the contrary – macho Aguenta that he is – gave me a sad, condescending look amply communicating his distaste for such an unmanly reaction to a bit of shooting. The look provoked me into asking if war did not scare him. 'I am not afraid of anything' he replied disdainfully. 'So will you go to war again?' I asked. 'Maybe I will do it. I will not go to war now, but maybe I will go. Everyone makes his own life',*[2] *he replied. Everyone makes his own life? Was going to war for Olivio a question of production, of shaping his life in the most expedient manner? No ideology, no enemy, just social navigation?*

As we have seen so far, patrimonial networks tend to contract and centre themselves around their core points or inner concentric circles in periods of decline. As resources dwindle young men often bear the brunt of retrenchment, as they are the first to be cut from the economy of affection and obligation as well as from patrimonial structures, since they constitute the outermost points within these systems of unequal exchange. However, during situations of war, political factions and their patrimonial structures, regardless of their reaction in the crisis normally leading up to it, will open up towards youth, as young men go from being secondary to their existence to being instead the prime agents in the defence of the faction and the position and resources of its distributive network. The value of the social category of youth changes from being marginal and redundant to being central and essential to the faction's survival.

War and conflict, in a terrain such as the Bissauian, thus opens up a navigational space as it provides young men with a chance to enter into a socio-political network by aligning themselves with a faction within a scenario of radicalised conflict. As war causes disruptions, from minor to massive, of the normal societal, though not necessarily social, order, it shakes loose hardened political configurations, bringing forth a terrain in which it is possible to socially and politically reposition oneself and be repositioned. For my informants, becoming soldiers not only entails an immediate move from dependent to independent, it also entails a move from socio-politically marginal to central and towards being possible, future providers through becoming part of a faction and thus of a patrimonial network. Mobilisation then, offers both short-term and long-term possibilities of escape from the social moratorium of youth.

A Multiplicity of Motives

Mobilising, in this perspective, becomes a means not only of navigating war, but equally of navigating the time after the war. It is informed by present and future orientations, a dual focus central to the very process of navigation in itself. Despite its immanent dangers, becoming a soldier or a militiaman grants one food, status, authority and protection in the here and now as well as opening up a field of possibilities to position oneself favourably in the future. However, although the factional aspect seems to saturate the Guinean political terrain, the process of mobilisation should not be seen as monocausal. Following Cairns's work on paramilitary youth in Northern Ireland we can, in general, see political mobilisation as motivated by socialisation, victimisation, status or reward (Cairns 1995: 132) and, I would like to add, the interrelation between them. Yet, when it comes to motives of actual recruitment into paramilitary organisations, that is, mobilisation into conflict rather than 'merely' politics, implying a commitment to violence, Cairns seems to come to a dead end, proposing a theory of gradual incorporation into the systematisation of violence. However, the view we get of the process of mobilisation in Bissau seems to indicate that he got it right the first time.

As we take a closer look at the political mobilisation of the Aguentas all of the above mentioned mobilising motives seem to apply. Even though I approached Guinea-Bissau with the idea that wars are fuelled by ideologies and ideologically defined enemies (a preconception I share with many Europeans, laymen, scientists, and politicians alike), I realised after a while that the variety of motives that made my informants join the government troops were linked to the politics of survival and the prospects of navigating networks and events. When asking into my interlocutors about their motives for mobilisation, I was presented with a number of, often amalgamated, explanations, as seen, for example, in the following conversation I had with Toto, quoted in length so as to give a picture of the multiplicity of motives involved:

What brought you to the Aguentas?
Well, the reason I joined the Aguentas is because we saw that what the Junta did was not good. It is not good for an elected president, because the law says that an elected president cannot be overthrown by arms, even if he does bad things then you must just suffer until the end of his mandate, so we can go to the elections again. If he loses the election he leaves. If he goes and succeeds in winning, then he must continue in power ... So he must continue in power and not be removed with arms. This is the only reason that brought me to join the armed forces.
Were there not other reasons?
There are many reasons.
Tell them to me.
Well, the second reason ... There was an uprising among all the troops ... The troops made a rebellion, and it was not just Balantas, or Papels or Mandinga. There were many people that rebelled, that went to support Asumané Mané, but these people, these troops, they went halfway and then they began to turn against the ethnic group of Papel.[3] They turned against the Papels. They started to treat the Papels in ways that did not please anyone. They even took me and I did not have anything to do with them, even though they were rebelling without us knowing. At that time I was a civilian – but I was taken by the Junta troops because like ... The Junta understood it like: Nino is Papel, I am also Papel, so they must start to treat [Papel] people badly. They said it was us who had chosen Nino, who had given him power here in this country. They took me twice. I did not obey them. And this is the reason that I said [to myself]: Well, if this is so [then] I must go and join the armed forces. [I must go] to take up arms and fire, to show them that I also ... That I can shoot [just] like them.
And what did they do when they grabbed you?
Well they took me, and I did not trust them to take me to the Base Area in their car.[4] I told them that I would not go, because I was a civilian. I had nothing to do with them. They told me to get in. I refused. They tried until they lost their will and they left for Mbila [a village near Saffim].

Were there other reasons?
What?
Were there other reasons?
Yes.
Which?
Also, when you talk about the respect of the uprising, they said that Asumané defended the rights of the troops, which does not correspond to the truth. It is not true because Asumané never rebelled to defend the rights of the troops. Asumané rebelled because they fired him from his job. He did something bad at his workplace and the President fired him, and he [Asumané] understood it like the president should not fire him from his job, and that caused him to[5]... He mobilised groups so as to be able to try to make a *coup d'état*. Because he lost that possibility he continued to mobilise troops to create a group, so that he could revolt. But it was not an uprising to assert the rights of troops. It was a *coup d'etat* because he had been fired, because he was Brigadier, head of the armed forces, and after he had problems the president fired him, and that is why he wanted to make a *coup d'état*.

The conversation demonstrates how different understandings of the motivation and legitimacy of mobilising coexist and become visible if one probes a bit. Toto touches upon the aspects of democracy, ethnicity, abuse and coercion, as well as configurations of power.

Ideology and Fighting for Democracy

The quote, however, equally points our attention towards the aspect of ideology, which I have so far argued is of minor importance in relation to warfare in Guinea-Bissau, and which Cairns omits altogether from his list of reasons for mobilisation mentioned above. Fieldwork shows us that constructions of opinion and interpretation are not smooth processes in which people reach agreement and follow the same lines of analysis, and social-scientific analyses should not portray them as such. However, the focus on democracy in Toto's quote leads us to an interesting phenomenon in situations of conflict and warfare, namely that the communication and function of ideology undergoes dramatic changes and radicalisations. In situations of collective violence, ideology seems to condense into discursive phrases (Gilliam 1998), positioning people in social categories and projecting social categories onto social maps.[6] In the fluid terrain of war, ideology is, in other words, often condensed into signs. It becomes emblematic, condensed into phrases, identifying Self and Other by way of narrative difference, worn and carried by discourse communities and used to differentiate friend from foe.

Few of my informants mentioned democracy as a reason for mobilisation; moreover, those who talked about it at all did so in a manner that was all but ideological in our normal understanding of the word.

As we see in the above quote, democracy is held to mean that the person holding the presidential office is granted four years to use his position with impunity: 'if he does bad things then you must just suffer until the end of his mandate', as Toto phrases it. Thus democracy is seen to grant the person holding office the freedom to do with it what he wants, a political immunity served in portions of four years at a time: four years of absolute rule rather than four years of democratic rule, the democratic process coming to a halt after presidential elections as patrimonial networks rather than political parties take office. In other words, references to democracy seem to have very little to do with ideology as a coherent system of ideas relating to the ideal movement and structuration of society in relation to the distribution of resources and power. It would seem that ideology, via the process of conflict and war, goes from being a system of ideas pertaining to an ordering of society, to being centred on a few contra-identificatory political slogans demarcating Self from Other via narrative and representation. Ideology, as it enters into warfare, thus becomes condensed into discursive phrases. Written on walls, carried on banners or screamed in the battlefield, it becomes the symbolic boundary separating one community from another, turning ideology into narrative politics. This is, of course, one of the main reasons that it is so difficult to propose alternative interpretations of, for example, political events within societies caught in warfare, as deviance from the dominant narratives or phrases will position one as a dissident, a subversive or a traitor.

If we look at the 'ideological' socialisation of children and youth in areas of conflict, that is, their socialisation into conflict, we equally see, from the existing research,[7] that what are comprehended by, for example Northern Irish children, in the process of making sense of and positioning themselves in relation to the tension in their society, are not the ideological statements and understandings that position differences of societal organisation and dynamics but rather contra-identificatory demarcations.[8] In Bissau the government side of the war attracted a considerable amount of international support by proclaiming the Junta aggression as being anti-democratic, constructing itself as the – pro forma – protector of Democracy. Democracy was, in other words, not only, as a discursive phrase, a source to the identification of friend and foe within Guinea-Bissau: it was equally a normative position portraying the Aguentas as championing a noble cause. Ideology, as sign and phrase, in this manner played an important role in the mobilisation of the Aguentas, but sadly, it did so by turning democracy into a factional label.[9]

Consequently, although references to democracy have the advantage of positioning the wartime activities of my informants positively by locating their acts and choices within a normatively, globally dominant political discourse – as well as positioning them positively in the present – the use of the concept seems to point our attention towards democracy as a discursive phrase rather than a political observance in itself. Or, in Bayart's somewhat cynical formulation: 'Wars great advantage over simple delinquency is that it legitimates in the name of justice and [/or] revolution the use of arms to get access to the resources of the state' (Bayart 1993: xiii).

Focusing on the ideological aspects of the conflict thus ought to make us ask the question why more people did not join the Aguentas if they were fighting for democracy and, not least, why it was exactly this specific group of people that did. If they were driven by political standpoints and ideological orientation, why then were the Aguentas predominantly Papels – are the Papels the key democrats in Guinea-Bissau? Furthermore, why were so many of the Aguentas from the city of Bissau? Toto himself partly answers the question in the above quote, as his second motive directs us towards ethnicity and victimisation as motives: that is, more specifically, a victimisation of the group of people that was to constitute the bulk of the Aguentas, namely the Papels. What must be made clear is that ethnicity is actualised in conflict in much the same way as ideology, as it is particularly clearly related to patrimonial political structures and distribution of authority and resources along networks (see Bayart 1993: 238); it is the logical meeting point between the economy of affection and patrimonial structures and thereby especially effectively mobilised. Equally, from the individual agent's perspective, ethnicity is especially effectively navigated as it supplies a ready-made entry into political networks. Yet patrimonialism was not the only factor that made ethnicity an issue during the war. Rather, ethnicity became an issue in relation to the specifics of the actual acts of war, as the drawing of the battle lines enforced the narrative of ethnic marginalisation.

Victimisation and Threat

As the majority of the Aguentas were from ex-President Nino Vieira's ethnic group, the 'Papels', it seems sensible to argue that the ease with which the *Governo* side were able to mobilise young Papels to join the Aguentas is closely related to the above-mentioned relation between classificatory kinship, social obligation and patrimonialism. Yet, if we look deeper into the ethnic aspect of the mobilisation of the Aguentas, we see that it was equally facilitated by the movement of the front line during the war. As the government side was denied influence in the countryside and encircled the area of Bissau and Prabis the front line of the war came to be drawn in the heart of Papel territory.[10] The government side was quick to point to this encirclement of Papel land and to propagate the ethno-political motives of the Junta. As mentioned earlier, the majority of the Aguentas from Bissau were from the *bairros* of Antula, Mpanctha, Cumtum, Kelélé, Bairro Militar, Plubá and Plack 1.[11] These areas, besides being some of the poorer areas of the city, are traditionally, and still predominantly, Papel, and were all close to the shifting front line of the war and negatively affected by it.[12] One of the reasons that a narrative of an ethnically motivated aggression made sense to these young Papels was thus related to the fact that they were inhabitants of 'Papel areas' being shelled and attacked by the Junta Militar making it possible to see the threat against the Papels as more than mere propaganda. The perceived ethnic prejudices of the Junta Militar came to resonate with the actual military advances of the Junta, and gained strength by fusing a narrative of ethnically motivated victimisation with experienced danger and ill-treatment. Aggression directed towards the Papels on the grounds of ethnic membership was in this fashion felt by many of the Papels joining the Aguentas, in effect showing that the government side was not alone in ethnicising the war as there was also a targeted harassment of the Papel community by the Junta soldiers. This is exemplified in Gutenberg's experience while in Saffim, which was described above, but also in the quote below, which is a fragment of an interview with Olivio, who joined the Aguentas while living close to the main barracks in inner Bissau, called QG:[13]

> [We were] primarily young people from Bissau. Young people who live in the area of Antula ... Young people who live in Antula, Luanda and things there. Barrio Militar, Plack 1 in Bissau, these areas where the front line is [was], there are mostly Papels There were conflicts. When the Junta went there [to the areas around the front line] they stayed in houses, and to these young people [who lived in the houses] they said: 'If you refuse to go, we will shoot and kill you, you are Nino's family, you see?' There are these Papel tribes that lives in those areas, and the majority of the young people they were ... The Junta troops would come to their homes, they would mistreat them, hit them. They would throw them out of their houses and others ... So other young people they became scared so they ran and entered the troops on Nino's side. This is how they started influencing their friends. When others started hearing that their friends had entered, they started entering the military, and then they follow them. They enter.

The narrative of ethnically motivated aggression against the Papel community coupled with actual experiences and, just as importantly, stories of experiences of ethnically motivated abuse led to the merging of ethnic, historical and conflict-related factors and gave meaning within a discourse of *tribalismo* – an amalgamation which greatly enhanced the narrative's interpretational strength for many Papels in the specific situation. Yet the reason behind the perceived or experienced victimisation was not exclusively ethnic as the experience and future prospect of Junta violence in itself could entice people to take up arms out of fear, anger or defence. In Carlos's words:

> Well, the war came as a surprise because ... I do not know. There are things that I do not know. I stayed [in Bissau] until the war started. I did not know anything about the war. I felt bad because it was a thing that had never happened in my life; since I was born I had never seen war. People ran, but I did not run, because I am not afraid of anything, because it is a thing that I have never experienced. I have never seen it. It was the first time I saw it in Guinea-Bissau. The war started and I felt bad, and afterwards I started seeing people die. A lot died. After that people ran; when I saw my mother die, I started being afraid. She was in her room and a bomb fell. It made me afraid and, because of my mother, I became angry with them, and that is why I became a soldier.

However, upon a closer look, the 'ethnification' of politics seems, as mentioned, more closely related to patrimonialism than to inter-ethnic hatred. Many of my informants were encouraged to join the Aguentas by their elders, who themselves stood in a patrimonial relationship to the president or his close political allies.

Part of the resilience of patrimonialism is that, contrary to popular belief, it is not centred on one primary patron but involves a network of patron–client relationships transcending the entire society. As such, ethnicity and patrimonialism strengthen each other, as ethnicity provides ready-made structures for the distribution of resources and invests it with moral obligation. Due to transactional facility and security patrimonial networks are thus likely to centre on family, lineage or ethnicity and thereby become effectuated along the entire continuum from the economy of affection and obligation to the patrimonial pinnacle. Yet there is nothing either novel or archaic about this. Resource-carrying networks have always been organised around kinship (Cohen 1969) as '[k]infolk have irresistible claims on one another's support and consideration' (Fortes 1969: 238), and in an ethnically diverse political situation ethnicity enters into the field of kinship by a process of concentric differentiation (Evans-Pritchard 1965).

Ethnicity thus serves as a platform for the allocation and distribution of resources and the call on obligation (Cohen 1969), enabling agents to strategically demarcate spheres of influence and authority, as well as facilitating the entry into, and tactical navigation of, these demarcations. Politicised ethnicity, as well as the ethnic tension we see in many situations of conflict and warfare, is a result of the politics of primary relationship and its concomitant loyalties and obligation infused into a macro-political context. As Cohen phrases it: 'People do not kill one another because their customs are different ... If men do actually quarrel seriously on the grounds of cultural difference it is because these cultural differences are associated with serious political cleavage' (ibid.: 200).

Day of Change

But despite their constructions of political legitimacy, articulated through a discourse of democracy and a narrative of ethnically motivated persecution, it should be specified that most of my informants seemed rather to have been motivated by the prospect of 'seeing one's future', *odja si futuro*, as the possibility of gaining a measure of control over ones life situation is called. Many Aguentas were pulled towards the government troops because of the prospect of increasing their life chances. What becomes clear, however, in the case of the Aguentas, is that, despite the fact that 'reward' was a primary motivating factor, there does not seem to have been talk of an economic focus per se.[14] In fact, the most striking feature of the aspect of reward, in the recruitment of the Aguentas, is that they were drawn into warfare by promises of future possibilities, rather than immediate gain. No money was ever paid my informants;[15] what were given instead were promises of possibilities: of being able to get a job after the war, of migration, or, for the ones with a second school diploma, of the possibility of studying abroad, all of which are normally linked with success in entering and manipulating patrimonial networks. In other words, my informants were recruited with promises implying escape from the social moratorium, rather than by actual money.

The *Governo* side's ability to recruit young males via mere promises of future possibilities thus indicates both the navigational orientation of my informants and the influence patrimonial networks have in Bissau, as the promises offered cohere with the possibilities embedded in entering a patrimonial network. Hence, from a social and political perspective, joining the Aguentas was seen as advantageous for ones life chances, as affiliation (for the Papels, ready-made) into a network of politico-economic relations and possibilities was what was on offer. When I asked Adilson why he wanted to join the government side of the war, he explained:

> Because I understood that they would be able to send me my day of change ...[16] After ... After the war, if all went well and we won, there was something ... If you had a good level you would get money to put in your pocket, or they would find you work.
> *Did they say what work, or just work?*
> Just work, abroad, in a place outside.
> *Okay, in other states. Where did you want to go?*

Whatever country they would send me to.
In Africa or Europe?
No, in Europe.

Mobilisation is, in this perspective, a road out of the social moratorium. At 34, Adilson was the oldest of my informants, yet without a household of his own, a job, a wife, or the ability to take care of himself economically, let alone a family; he was bitterly trapped in the category of youth. As he saw it, mobilising offered him the possibility of 'his day of change', that is, the decisive break from his current life position of social inertia. By becoming affiliated with a patrimonial network Adilson thought that he would be able to change his life and reposition himself socially by gaining what is most treasured in Bissau, absence: 'the empty space left by migration' (Pink 2001: 103; see also Gable 1995).

But mobilising was not only a way of connecting to a faction and becoming positioned in a patrimonial network; for many it was also a way of consolidating existing relations. Mobilisation in this manner becomes an act of maintaining or strengthening ones networks within the economy of affection and obligation by making it possible for agents to consolidate their relation with their seniors, as evident in the following excerpt from an interview with Vitór:

> My uncle said that I should enter. I said: 'No, I am not going.' And he said, 'Well, if you enter you do not have to go to war but it is easier, with a military card, you can continue service anywhere. If you go abroad with your military card, you can continue your service.' He came and bothered me, and that is what made me go. I went and I entered.
> *Why did your uncle want you to go to the Aguentas?*
> I cannot tell you what other people think in their heads ...

Vitór was honouring the wishes of his uncle, who, as the ex-president's former driver, was eager to demonstrate his loyalty to the patron of patrons by showing commitment to the political faction, thus strengthening his own position within the patrimonial network.

Acting in Peace through War

What both the above quotes show is that mobilisation is focused on either maintaining network relations or establishing them. For my informants the terrain of war opens up a space for alignment, be it under an ideological, ethnic or religious banner, in which they can tactically navigate the opportunities that emerge, as the terrain shifts and twists during the process of conflict. But, more importantly, what the connection between mobilisation and patrimonialism shows us is that the act of mobilising traverses the dichotomies between war, conflict and peace. My informants did not mobilise only to serve a military end but in order to gain a better life in times of peace as well. In other words, the relation between the three concepts forces us to notice that the political possibilities and forces at work in wartime are seen as directly related to a situation of peace, collapsing our otherwise guarded distinction between the two social states.

The narratives of fighting for democracy, ethnically motivated aggression and promises of future possibilities were, in other words, plausible and identifiable possibilities during both wartime and peace, though none of them are adequate frames of explanation in themselves. However, in the specific situation they merged to outline a road out of the social moratorium that was both socially grounded, feasible and justifiable. Taking my informants general social and societal position into consideration, we can explain all the above motives under the conceptual framework of bettering one's life chances. Thus, in the same interview as the above quote is from, Vitór continues:

Were there some things that the Aguentas from Bissau had in common? ...
These ...? If they had what?
If they had anything in common?
Well, living conditions. They thought that maybe it could become better if I went there, well you know, things like ... things like military they give you money. Others were [here in Bissau] until they stopped school. Others are still studying – 9., 10.1.[17] You see? They say: 'Well the day my studies end, and I finish school, I do not have anything to do, you see? If I stay here [in the Aguentas] maybe when the war ends I might have a possibility to get money to go abroad and study or to go to military academy or these things ...' Well others also say: '[When] the war has ended, I do not have conditions,' or 'If I leave it will be worse, because others they fled during the war, they fled and things went badly, they did not have money to buy anything, they did not have rice, they did not have anything and like this. So they had to return to Bissau, to stay here, and maybe get a hold of these things. If you do not have ...'[18] Others entered here because of that and because of food and things like this, do you see ...? If you do not have, you have to *dubria* with life, you see?

Focusing on motives for mobilising thus shows us how my informants are engaged in finding a way out of the social moratorium by tactically manipulating social and political structures to their advantage. 'If you do not have, you have to *dubria*' Vitór phrases it, the concept referring to the use of wit and tactics to get the best out of a difficult situation. In other words, rather than acting solely through an economic imperative, my informants seek to guide their lives through a difficult present terrain, while at the same time plotting and actualising social trajectories that can bring their lives adequately into the future. It is a complex process of moving and simultaneously planning movement in relation to both an unstable and fluctuating present and a distant and uncertain future: the process which in Creole is termed *dubriagem*.[19]

Dubriagem and Social Navigation

I first encountered the word *dubria* when talking to Pedro and Justino about their life possibilities in light of the country's continuous deterioration, and the gloomy predictability of further trouble. As Pedro and Justino were weaving a picture of the hardships that characterised their situation – of unemployment, conflict and retrenchment – I consequently asked them what they then did to survive. How did they get by, let alone get money for food, wine and amusement? A word surfaced which did not hang long enough in the air for me to get a proper grasp of it, but was immediately transmuted into a listing of acts and relationships that could secure you a meal. As I interrupted, asking about this unfamiliar word, surprised at not having heard it before, Pedro and Justino responded in unison: '*Dubria, dubria.*' Pedro was moving his upper body in a disjointed yet rhythmical sway, looking somewhat as if he were shadow-boxing: arms along his side, weaving and bobbing his torso back and forth as though dodging invisible pulls and pushes. Pedro repeated: '*Bu ta dubria, dubria. Dubria!,*' 'You dubria ... it's movement, dynamism'. '*Dynamismo,*' Justino added. 'You *dubria* ... so that you can see your life,' he continued:

> Guineans are *dubriado*. Like during the war ... It was dangerous during the war, but there were these generous people and they would give you. You could go to the harbour and they would give you fish ... one kilo, two kilos. And you could get rice, you know, Guineans they are *dubriado*. They would say, how many are you in your house, and people would say, Ten, even though they were six, and people would bring their neighbour's children.[20]

Dubriagem thus describes the use of shrewdness and craftiness to navigate dangerous or difficult terrains. 'You *dubria* in order to see your life' is a commonly used phrase, bringing us back to navigation as motion within motion, that is, as action in a terrain that is not a stable field or surface but changeable as well as opaque, in which the impermanence of the socio-political configurations means that one cannot take the future shape of the terrain for granted and in which overviews are not given but constantly have to be gained.

Navigating the Socially Opaque

The words *dubria* and *dubriagem* apparently do not exist in Portuguese, or at least not any longer, but translate instead into *disenrascar*, that is, to disentangle or to free of difficulty.[21] As I was unable to find it in the Portuguese language, I initially thought that the concept was unique to Creole; however, I was to find out that it has a parallel in the French phrase *se débrouiller*,[22] meaning, to get by or get the best out of a situation (Reed-Danahay 1996: 63–64; see also Waage 2002),[23] related to the substantive *débrouillardise*, referring to the ability to get by. Etymologically the word is related to *brouillard*, or fog,[24] and interestingly the word has a maritime use, meaning to clear up as the cloud or fog drifts away;[25] this is expressive of the use of *dubriagem* in gaining clarity in ones life, as shown above. So 'we *dubria* so that we can see our lives,' as my informants say, means to gain a perspective on which way the unstable terrain is moving them and how they are able to move across the terrain. *Dubria* in this perspective is the ability that enables one to navigate one's way through murky socio-political circumstances as well as being the actual praxis of doing so.

Dual Temporality

Few social-scientific works have dealt specifically with actual praxis in situations of instability, conflict and turmoil. Trond Waage's description of how youth *se débrouille* in Ngaoundéré, Cameroun, explains in detail how, through improvisation, they seek to survive and gain the foundations for their existence in an opaque and uncertain context (Waage 2002). Equally, both the concepts of *dubriagem* and *se débrouille* bear resemblance to the Brazilian praxis of *jeitinho* as 'a way of accomplishing a goal ... by using ... ones informal social and personal resources' (Barbosa 1995: 36). Common to all three terms is an emphasis on flexibility and tactics: that is, rather than denoting demarcative and constitutive strategic action, all three concepts direct our attention towards the tactical praxis of navigating networks and events within a social environment in motion. *Dubriagem* and social navigation are thus akin to the embodied, practical knowledge of *metis*, so excellently described by James Scott. Yet, rather than designating 'a knack' or 'cunnning', *dubriagem* is directed towards both immediate and future survival as the praxis of navigating lives along an envisioned trajectory in an unstable environment.

Social navigation thus emphasises intermorphology and flexibility as key aspects of praxis (see Waage 2002: 388), and this ability to elucidate the relationship between the way we move and the movement of social environments is exactly what sets it apart from our normal conceptualisations of praxis and what distinguishes it as an analytical optic. Social navigation designates praxis imbued with the 'flexibility and "preadaptation" necessary for unpredictable change' (Bateson 1972: 495): the praxis of moving across a terrain in movement that, due to the multitude of factors influencing it, is always unfolding and requires of us the capacity to 'adapt' and 'read' 'capricious environments' (Scott 1998: 331).

Dubriagem is thus both a process of disentanglement from confining structures and relations, of escaping and moving around the hurdles immediately in front of you or coming towards you, and the beginnings of a line of flight into the future. It is, importantly, directly related to practice, and there is nothing metaphysical about it. As *dynamismo*, that is, as a dynamic quality, it is either a present or future advantageous movement into position, opportunity or even mere survival, indicating that *dubria* – as navigation – encompasses both the assessment of the dangers and possibilities of one's present position and plotting and attempting to actualise lines of flight into the future.

That *dubria* encompasses both immediate survival and the drawing of trajectories into the future becomes even clearer when delving into its ramifications, as issues of making ends meet and gaining points of view are emphasised. 'You *dubria* to survive' is the most common description of the concept, indicating the acts needed to take care of your immediate needs and to deal with immediate dangers. Yet it should be noted that *dubriagem* is more than an act of survival. Survival in Creole is *sobrevivi*, designating a continuum of life through the immediate. *Dubriagem* is related to movement through both the present and future, the socially immediate and the social imaginary. *Dubria* therefore also designates the complex of actions that enables you to see your life,[26] that is, gain an idea of the possible course and unfolding of your life trajectory. In *dubriagem*, then, one seeks to act in and through difficult and changeable circumstances, as well as to gain a position of orientation and interpretation. One seeks to direct and control the movement of ones life rather than having it be directed and moved by the shifting of the unstable social environment it is immersed in. As such, *dubriagem* is an effort to gain directionality and expediency of movement. It is to plot, to actualise the trajectory plotted and to relate one's action and plot to a constantly shifting terrain. *Dubriagem* is to simultaneously keep oneself free of immediate social dangers and direct ones life towards better possible futures.

Motion within Motion

In a social-scientific perspective, the term navigation gains strength from being capable of encompassing some of the more dense, yet analytically elusive, dimensions of social action by addressing the praxis of moving through social environments in motion. *Dubriagem* is processuality squared and as an underlying precondition for my informants' action this implies that they do not presume stability in their social terrain and that they must constantly be attentive of its possible shifts and slides.[27] Social navigation is thus attuned simultaneously to the immediate configurations of the social terrain and to its imagined reconfigurations, which in the present context of conflict and war, means that my informants must simultaneously address both the immediacy of finding their bearings in a turbulent situation and the drawing of possible lines of flight into the future. Navigation designates both praxis and planning: being able to anticipate a route across a terrain as well as actually executing the imagined trajectory, moving towards possible clearings and along possible routes emerging in the social options or embedded in the social ties of the given context. However, this also entails that the agent, in social navigation, is engaged in the process of realigning his plot as he goes along (Ingold 2002: Chapter 13). The concept therefore moves us away from the faulty image of plotting and action as being discrete sequences along a line of movement towards a picture of plotting and action in constant dialogue as the agent seeks to move within a social environment which is itself in motion and moving the agent.

Navigation in this perspective resembles the de Certeauian 'walk' centred on both the near and the far, a here and a there (de Certeau 1988: 99). Within the context of the immediate, navigating terrains of war is thus to guide and direct oneself through a perilous present. It is action related to the immediacy of survival as the agent is attentive of and deals with actual dangers, oncoming obstacles or imperceptible hazards. The immediacy of navigation refers to gaining a picture of how one is currently positioned in the given terrain and what short-term possibilities surround ones body in the murky waters of societal conflict and instability; it also designates the act of actually moving within it, simultaneously drawing trajectories into the future, locating navigational points or positions in the yet-to-come. To paraphrase Deleuze and Guattari, we can say that navigating means imagining, plotting and actualising 'a smooth space' through dangerous waters (2002: 380–81).

In fact, navigation, when used to account for social action covers exactly the duality of action as related to both present and future orientation, as it is to draw a course as well to keep a course along an imagined trajectory; it is simultaneously navigating the immediate obstacles in front of you, plotting and getting ready to navigate the next and keeping an eye on one's imagined trajectory. Navigation in this perspective places demands on the complexity of our analysis as it removes the opposition between the diachronic and synchronic aspects of social praxis, meaning that we need to position our informants' actions both within their experience of their 'being' as part of a historical process, of their individual lives as process and of their lives as immediacy: that is, as both position and process.

Strategy and Tactics

'*Dubria* with life. That is what Guineans do,' Jon Manuel said with pride. Yet, having no money, job or home, Jon Manuel cannot be said to be a very good *dubriadur*. However, as a birth gift, given to him by virtue of his identity as a Guinean subject, he seems to feel blessed by the quality. My interlocutors thus referred to *dubriagem* with a certain respect and pride – as a national characteristic similar in form to, for example, the Finnish idea of *sisu*, the English stiff upper lip or German thoroughness. But *dubriagem* is not an assertive or aggressive quality. It is rather a quality characterised by astuteness and slyness. It is not a process of constitution, formation or construction but, as indicated by Pedro's body language, one of manipulation, flexibility and movement. It is, in other words, not a question of assertion and crystallisation but of dynamism and fluidity.

Coupling the idea of navigation with a conceptual dichotomy from de Certeau (1984), we can say that strategy is the process of demarcating and constituting space and tactics the process of navigating them. The difference between tactics and strategy, as sketched by de Certeau, was initially theorised by Clausewitz, who sees tactics as the military praxis created and actualised in relation to a specific battle – that is, the ordering of action in actual situations of combat – and strategy as the ordering of the relation between battles directed towards the primary goal of winning the war. Or, in his own words, 'tactics is the theory of the use of military forces in combat. Strategy is the theory of the use of combats for the object of the war ... or the employment of the battle as the means towards the attainment of the object of the war' (Clausewitz 1997: 75, 141).

In de Certeau's less militaristic perspective the distinction lends itself expediently to illuminating political praxis. Conceptually differentiating strategy from tactics enables us to illuminate two different actualisations of political agency. We can act politically either by trying to establish a space in which we seek to impose and institutionalise our understanding or structuration of the world, a sedentary act of creating a domain, or by navigating the spaces of others to our advantage, a migratory act of creating trajectories. Most often both types of political agency will obviously be in use but it is important to understand that both are acts that in effect work to enhance the position of the agent, as their points of departure are identical, that is, the access to resources, be they symbolic, cultural or economic. We can in this perspective thus say that tactical action, such as *dubriagem*, is used both to secure ones immediate survival and to gain strategic possibilities, with the movement between them being what defines navigation.

In a historical perspective, the fact that *dubriagem* – as slyness and the manipulation of the force field of others – comes to be seen as a positive essence of 'the Guinean' is understandable in regard to the structural conditions under which the Guinean citizen – or (historically) subject – has had to survive. From 500 years of colonisation, exploitation and enslavement, through one of the longest independence wars in Africa, to three decades of political repression and a currently bleak and unpromising place in the global capitalist system, the Guinean subject has had to make do in a societal space defined and controlled by the strategy of others. Being Guinean has for so long been identical to not having control over the societal configuration, shifts and movements defining the terrain on which they seek to build and live their lives that Guineans have been forced into making the best of their tactical rather than strategic abilities and have come to see it as a national characteristic. But *dubriagem* is not restricted to a mythical national characteristic of underlying resistance – or making ends meet – in the face of repression. Rather, *dubriagem* is lived.

On Domains and Terrains

Asking directly about ways of *dubria* gives one an infinite number of seemingly incompatible acts, covering everything from constructive to destructive behaviour. *Dubria* thus encompasses such different acts as finding or procuring the odd bits and pieces of work, running errands in the hope of a later return, using your body to get what you need (in Guinea-Bissau primarily a female tactic), persuading someone to give you something, cheating on your wife or husband, or stealing. The concept is, as such, not solely a positive one. However, what the tremendous differences between the types of acts that can be categorised as *dubriagem* show us is that the concept does not categorise a certain type of normative praxis but rather designates a category of praxis which is carried out beneath or beside dominant rules and regulations. Having an affair with another man's wife is in this perspective to *dubria*, as it entails operating beneath – or manipulating – the accepted rules of conduct between a married woman and another man.

Once again infusing de Certeau into the context of Bissau, we can thus say that, whereas strategy would be used to create and define a terrain of action, *dubria*, as tactic, is rather used to navigate a given, already constructed, terrain, and can be seen as the 'makeshift creativity of groups and individuals', manipulating and acting between and across the rules defined by others (de Certeau 1988: xiv). In other words, whereas strategy is the process of creating and consolidating space, *dubriagem* is tactical praxis as it describes the process of manoeuvring within space demarcated by others. Strategy is used to create localised spaces of action defined by their relations to an important Other (ibid.: xix): 'Every strategic rationalisation seeks first of all to distinguish its "own" place, that is, the place of its own power and will, from an environment' (ibid.: 36). Strategy thus defined is an act, or set of acts, leading to the creation of a space, an institutional or sedentary demarcation, by subjects with influence to exercise their will; for those who lack the power to demarcate a space of their will the option is not passivity or resignation, but is instead tactical manoeuvring or navigation. Navigating the space of others is one of the defining traits of young men in Bissau as they are without control over the movement of their societal terrain. In other words, rather than trying to shape societal processes, they try to grab on to the possibilities and chances that arise in the shadow of the strategic acts of those in power.

In a de Certeauian perspective, tactics can thus be seen to be the process of survival or bettering one's life chances by navigating the space organised and defined by others. Operating in the force field of others, the agent turns events into possibilities by manipulating rules, systems or structures. Consequently, in contrast to the use of strategy, the agent does not produce spatialised or institutionalised localisations through tactics, but navigates the social terrains and spaces of possibility constituted by others' strategy (ibid.: xix). In other words, where strategic action produces the sedentary space of a domain by anchoring, demarcations and localisations, tactical actions produces trajectories of moving space. So, where strategy produces sedentary space, configurations of enclosures, of walls and boundaries (Deleuze and Guattari 2002: 381), the moving space of tactics operates between and across these, manipulating the pathways between them, penetrating their fissures and taking advantage of the continuous destruction and rebuilding of social and political demarcations. A tactic 'remains dependent on the possibilities offered by circumstance' (de Certeau 1988: 29), yet, being unlocalised, I see it as the trait of the migrant or the seaman rather than the nomad (see Deleuze and Guattari 2002) as its space becomes a trail of constant movement cutting through and between the space of others and moving between uncertain, unforeseen points in the social terrain created around it or on it (ibid.: 380):[28]

> Thus it [a tactic] must play on and with a terrain imposed on it and organised by the law of foreign power ... it takes advantage of 'opportunities' and depends on them, being without any base where it could stockpile its winnings, build up its own position and plan raids ... in short, a tactic is the art of the weak. (de Certeau 1988: 36–37)

Tactics and strategy in this manner enter into a variable of power defined by the degree of influence one has in ordering and regulating the social terrain one is part of. The movement between strategy and tactics can be explained by its relation to rules. Following Bourdieu, we can say that the movement between strategy and rule is a matter of time – a causality (1992: 9), while the relationship between tactics and rule is rather one of manipulation, or, I would contend, navigation. Strategy is action directed at defining, actualising or consolidating rules; tactics are actions directed at making the best of them, using and bending them.

Yet it is also within the issue of power that the conceptual pair has its major limitation as it is a generalisation providing a simplified picture of the complexities of social navigation and terrains. Seeing strategy as acts of the powerful and tactics as acts of the weak disregards the fact that a terrain is an intrinsically multilayered phenomenon containing a multitude of negotiations of power, and instead leads us into the traditional social-scientific mistake of defining people or groups as consistently either powerful or powerless in our effort to make the social world understandable by way of simplification, thus blinding ourselves to the fact that what we define, from the outside, as a powerful majority may in fact be seeking, for instance, to act tactically as a minority.[29] In other words, in praxis, the alignment of the concepts of strategy and tactics along a variable of power becomes diffuse and unclear. If, for example, we try to define who has the capacity to produce space via the use of strategy, the dichotomy between the tactician and the strategist gets blurred as it becomes difficult to imagine people so devoid of power that they do not possess the ability to demarcate their 'own' space. The agent is, in other words, tied up in a range of power configurations in which he may be dominant in one yet weak in another, depending on which position and point of view one is seeing the world from.

My interlocutors are far from incapable of strategically producing and demarcating a space of their will, defining rules and demarcating the space of their authority; in fact, they do so on a daily basis, for example, among their peers, within romantic relationships and so on. Yet, the difference between strategy and tactics nonetheless becomes clear in their position within the larger social field as they are unable to make use of strategy to gain the space that they need in order to acquire social status, that is, within the socially institutionalised realms of authority, which, as shown earlier, is the defining trait of the social moratorium. Hence, in the lives of my informants, their lack of social mobility derives from difficulty in positioning and demarcating themselves socially, exemplified by their inability to set up a household – the primary layer of a socially prescribed terrain, and the fundamental layer of sedentary space, the domain – and thus squarely locate an initial demarcation of their will and power. Power in this perspective is the ability to create space, social or physical, to impose one's will on a (discursively and socially) demarcated centre of organisation delineated from the surrounding environment. In other words, my informants are unable to create the social space needed for their positive social demarcation and identification.

Tactical Navigation

Not being able to make use of strategy in the public sphere is one of the defining traits of the social moratorium of youth, which becomes instead characterised by the tactical praxis of navigating networks and events. However, as decline and instability continue even tactical manoeuvring is becoming more and more difficult as the possibilities of using, or just relying upon, traditional networks of support and survival are contracting. With the retrenchment of both the economy of affection and the patrimonial networks the tactical possibilities of making ends meet are being reduced. Most urban youth are therefore experiencing a continuous deterioration of their social possibilities with more and more youth searching for an affiliation with even a distant possibility of accessing resources and becoming increasingly easily exploited. As Durham comments: 'while youth themselves are used to sustain the power of those in positions of power they feel increasingly unable to attain economic or symbolic capital' (Durham 2000: 113).

Thus, despite the fact that it is becoming increasingly clear, following the period of decline, that the return rate of the tactics of patrimonial alliance is poor, it is still highly treasured as youth in Bissau seem to be on the constant lookout for a patron. However, exactly this tactic testifies to the fact that their actions need to be seen in the light of both the immediate and the imagined, as the agent sketches possible trajectories into the future by letting himself be exploited in the present. In other words, the current situation of urbanised youth is so dire that they try to survive and even plan their way into adulthood, by running errands and doing favours that apparently lead them nowhere, except down the road of exploitation, yet in the hope that it might lead to future opportunities. They seek to gain the liaisons needed to manage and possibly accumulate sufficient resources to plan a line of flight that will make it possible to escape from the dependency of a junior status (see O'Brien 1996: 58). Yet, even when entering patrimonial networks, the relationship is obviously non-contractual and the possible gain minimal.

Attaining entry into a patrimonial network in Bissau thus most often means letting others use you as a resource rather than being able to gain access to the resources of others. Yet, with the ongoing retrenchment, my informants are in a situation where even being exploited by (the right) patron is becoming difficult as they find the networks they are trying to manipulate increasingly hard to open, map or predict, in effect making a situation of exploitation one to be longed for. Nonetheless there is an event which reopens closed social spaces in Bissau: a situation in which networks, instead of being constricted and congested become approachable and encompassing.

Mobilisation as Dubriagem

> When the war started we were in Prabis ... Many people went to Prabis; many people went there ... Like we sat there [and] we could hear how they shot at each other, we could hear how there was war. Since we sat there we thought like:[30] 'We are clever, we can go and join the troops. We can quickly become someone big, quickly.'

My initial reaction to Paulo was that he had a close to nauseating faith in his own intelligence. Constantly reminding people of his intellectual ability I found him tedious company. However, as I got close enough to the day-to-day life of the Aguentas to experience the constant bantering they received for having chosen the wrong side of the conflict, the constant ridicule of disastrous tactics, I learnt that 'stupid'[31] must have been the adjective that Paulo has heard most often in connection with his name since the end of the war. In this perspective, his constant references to his intellectual ability seemed like sad attempts at convincing people that he was not as stupid as his failed tactics would lead people to believe.

Yet we can read so much more from the above quote than the unsuccessful attempts at escaping the stigma of failed tactics. It emphasises how joining the army in a situation of warfare can be an act of *dubriagem*, pointing our attention towards my informants' tactical evaluation of their possibilities in relation to the onset of war. Entering the army in order to 'see ones life', that is, to take control of it and be able to guide it in the right direction, was a common description of the motivating factor behind joining the Aguentas. My informants, exemplified by Paulo's quote, thus navigated the space opened by others' strategy of warfare, which in Guinea-Bissau is literally 'to *dubria* with one's life',[32] that is, to attempt to define, reposition and boost one's life chances.

So, despite the fact that Paulo's tactics failed so ungracefully, his quote is nonetheless a good description of how he and his friend Julio sought to navigate the possibilities which arose as the war set in.

Hence the quote shows how mobilising can have tactical implications. Navigating the space of warfare in this manner becomes an act of seeking the potentially advantageous, as the event of war provides a possibility (as both hope and quest) of escape from the social moratorium of youth. Thus, when the terrain is right, mobilisation into warfare is a way of acquiring economic advancement, independence and social position; the tragic paradox is obviously that it might very well get you killed, which in itself bears testimony to the sad state of possibilities for youth in the country. Rather than seeing hatred, war or violence as motives in themselves, *dubriagem* points our attention towards life chances (Dahrendorf 1979) when looking for mobilising motives. Understanding why my informants went to war brings forth once again the realisation that they were not fighting against an enemy but rather for a possibility. Mobilisation into 'new wars', then, is not necessarily only motivated by the desire for self-enrichment or accumulation of wealth by looting and theft but rather the accommodation of needs in relation to both short-term and long-term social and physical survival and social becoming.

Furthermore, my informants were not fooled into warfare or driven by naked economic interest. The radical aspect of mobilisation, that it is likely to get you killed, did not come as a surprise to them. In fact, seeing that they entered in the middle of the war, with violent deaths dominating the picture and a rosy ideal of heroism being difficult to maintain, they were more than acutely aware of the dangers. So the question still beckons: why did they not just wait and see what would happen after the war? Would it not be far more 'rational' to try to navigate the reconfigured post-war terrain to one's advantage, instead of joining a militia on the unpopular, decimated side of the war? Why did they act in circumstances of war rather than wait for the post-war change in circumstances?

In order to answer the question, we need to look closer at the cultural understandings of social structure, agency and possibility that underlie my informants' perspectives and anticipations of peace, conflict and war. We need to look at their understandings of their society, its overall movement, and their possibilities within its perceived flow of (mis)dynamics. To make sense of people's navigation we need to illuminate their perspectives within the terrain they see themselves as having to traverse. In Bissau we need words other than the usual 'heroism' or 'bloodlust' or 'self-enrichment' to understand how my informants perceive the movement and characteristics of the general terrain that underlies situations of war, conflict and peace. We need especially to look at the movement of this social terrain in order to understand how they envision their social horizons. How we see our ability to act in relation to our social horizons greatly influences our tactics, plotting and actual social navigation. What I shall therefore turn my attention towards is my informants' perspective on the terrain in which the social category of 'youth' is positioned and in which the smouldering factional conflicts and patrimonial political structures are drawn – in peace or in war – so as to be able to illuminate their social horizons and thus their imagined action and enacted imaginaries.

Notes

1. Rocket-propelled Grenades.
2. *Kada kin na fassi si vida*, a commonly heard statement in Creole.
3. *É bin volta contra etinia Papel.*
4. The headquarters of the Junta Militar.
5. *Puil.*
6. The concept of discursive phrases will be further elaborated later in the chapter. It is borrowed from Laura Gilliam's work on children's understandings of the Other in paramilitary areas in north and east Belfast (Gilliam 1998 and forthcoming).
7. It is the smallest of fields, Cairns (1996) and Gilliam (1998, 2004) being some of the few scholars to have worked intensely with the problem of the political socialisation of children into conflict.
8. As Gilliam (1998) has shown, this is so even for perceived character traits such as 'nice' and 'nasty', 'good' and 'bad'.
9. This use of ideology as a discursive phrase is not restricted to the former government, or to Guinea-Bissau for that matter. However, when I contacted the political parties in Bissau after the election in 1999, not one was able to show a political manifesto explaining their ideology and vision for Guinean society, although the Partido Renovação Social (PRS) was alleged to have had one. Equally, when I would ask my interlocutors for their point of view, they would unanimously tell me that democracy was good, but most often be unable to specify why it was better than other political orientations.
10. Prabis is a town and peninsula north of Bissau.
11. Aimé et al. (1999b: 43).
12. Typically these areas were targeted for heavy shelling, or, being close to the Junta front line, in the prime 'looting zone' of the Junta soldiers.
13. QG is an abbreviation of Quartel Geral, the 'head' barracks, but has come to designate the surrounding residential area.
14. According to my informants, no money was given to them upon joining, and the only material benefits they reaped from their commitment was limited to half a bag of rice during the entire duration of the war.
15. There is some uncertainty about this fact, yet all of my informants emphasise the occasional distribution of rice as the only payment they received. Since fighting for money is not considered laudable, the denial may be related to not wanting to represent oneself as a mercenary.
16. 'They' refers both to the 'big men' on the government side and to government recruitment officers who were sent to Papel *bairros* and other areas to persuade able-bodied males to join the Aguentas.

17. Secondary school grade: 10.1 is the equivalent of A levels.
18. The silence saying 'then, one has to do what one can.'
19. *Dubria* is the active form of the infinitive *dubriagem*; *dubriado* and *dubriadur* (further along in the text) are the adjective form and noun, respectively.
20. Justino is specifically referring to the distribution and appropriation of relief aid during the 1998–1999 war, in which the amount of relief aid received depended on the size of ones household, which consequently meant that people would bring as many children as possible and thus receive more rice than they were otherwise entitled to.
21. *Portuguese–English Dictionary*, George G. Harrap, London, 1963.
22. Susan R. Whyte, personal communication.
23. Reed-Danahay interestingly relates the French concept to social fluidity, which brings its meaning back to the present concept of social navigation.
24. Even here there does not seem to be a link with Portuguese, as 'fog' translates to *nevoeiro* and 'foggy' to *nevoento*.
25. *Fransk–Dansk Ordbog*, H. Hagerup, Copenhagen (1964), Reed-Danahay (1996: 64).
26. *Bu ta dubria pa pudi odja bu vida.*
27. Navigation is in this manner defined as motion within motion rather than by dependency on maps (Ingold 2000). Navigation as process and praxis combines map-making and way-finding (ibid.) as we simultaneously navigate the immediate and the imagined, i.e. the next hurdle as well as the many imagined to come, in our movement towards a distant goal. The fact that Ingold, in an otherwise sublime chapter, needs to add the adjective 'terrestrial' when talking about navigation on land further indicates the problems inherent in his definition.
28. According to Deleuze and Guattari the space of the nomad is smooth, moving between defined points, whereas the space of the migrant traverses the striated space of others (Deleuze and Guattari 2002).
29. This is a common scenario seen, for example, with the Protestants in Northern Ireland and the Serbs in ex-Yugoslavia who, as globally discursively demonised, seek to create positive representations of their actions and perceived needs while constantly having to stay attentive to and protect themselves from what they see as a historically proved and constituted aggression directed towards them.
30. *Suma.*
31. *Burro.*
32. *Dubria ku vida.*

PART IV

ON SHIFTING GROUND

Chapter 7

INHABITING UNSTABLE TERRAINS

THE EVERYDAY OF DECLINE AND CONFLICT

The everyday in Bissau swings in tune with its perceived proximity to disorder. Its most minute rhythms are overlapped by larger temporal rhythms. Morning rituals, afternoon chats, greetings, sayings and telling expressions merge with predictabilities within larger frameworks, with the specific mode of intense discussions at signs of trouble, the fact that cigarettes are the first things to be sold out if smokers anticipate problems, the constant underlying adjustment of possible escape routes out of town, or just that our neighbour's foster daughter, as she told my wife in an interview,[1] always made sure to keep a reserve of clean clothes so that she would be neatly dressed during any future flight to a refuge.[2]

As shown in the previous chapter navigating the immediate and the imagined is what led my informants to the Aguentas. Their mobilisation was a result of their evaluation of the politically possible and the politically imaginable (Bourdieu 1984: 101; Bayart 1993: 248); that is, of their perceived positions and possible movement as agents within the current and future Guinean social terrain. However, in order to better understand the motives and actions of my informants we need a deeper insight into the way they interpret the social terrain they see themselves as having to move in. As social navigation entails a constant interaction and intermorphological relation between the agent and the terrain, it is necessary for us to understand how the Aguentas see the characteristics of their terrain if we wish to gain an insight into their conflict engagement.

Stable Instability and Ordered Disorder

Bissau is falling apart, '*i na darna-darna tudo*', the locals say, drawing out the 'u' to signify the magnitude of the dilapidation. The physicality of the process is iconic of a deeper sense of crisis and decline: that is, of political, institutional, economic and even identificatory deterioration. The decay and destruction of conflict are constant reminders of the perilous position of current Guinean society as well as the longstanding period of time it has been in it.

As in many sub-Saharan African countries, the persistence of decline in Bissau is clearly visible in the socio-economic statistics.[3] Yet, despite the clarity of the figures, it is still difficult to perceive the hardness of life from GDP and columns of numbers. Were we instead to situate the fact that, for example, 36 per cent of the population in Guinea-Bissau does not have access to health services, the continuous political instability and economic decline become somewhat more tangible, as illness and treatment are more familiar constraints. If we further add the aspect that, even if within the proximity of health services, most of my informants cannot afford to pay for the medical consultations, or if they can, the medicine is out of reach, the sting of decline becomes yet clearer. Approximately a fourth of the Guinean population live within walking distance of the country's main hospital, yet people jokingly say that if one enters through the front door of the central hospital of Simão Mendes, one inevitably leaves through the back door – leading to the cemetery – as the facility is most often without even the most basic requirements, such as medicine and electricity. The processes of decline and turmoil might thus be clearly visible in the statistics but the picture they paint is not nearly as explicit as experiencing the situation. To gain a detailed perspective one has to live there, to see the way people inhabit decline and turmoil and the way that decline and turmoil come to inhabit people.

The continued processes of decline and turmoil thus pervade the most basic aspects of my interlocutors' lives, affecting their very existential and societal security. Decline and turmoil are not only visible in individual lives but equally in the social – in the social moratorium of youth and in the diminished life chances and social possibilities available to the Guinean agents in general. More specifically, I have till now shown that the prolonged period of decline and turmoil has resulted in my informants having difficulties in realising their desired life trajectories; they feel impaired in their social becoming, unable to become an *adulto completto*, a complete man. The consequences of prolonged instability and decline have a generally destabilising effect on Guineans' lives as social beings and their possibilities of social navigation: from seeking to live ones life through pervasive societal (mis)dynamics to being attentive to the frailty of socio-political structures.

Socio-politics

Although we have seen that patrimonial political structures are the stable element of Guinean politics, it is nonetheless important that we understand that these networks are in almost constant configuration and that patrimonial politics have social consequences that are different from those we expect to see emerging from within a bureaucratic state setting. Focusing on the Aguentas, we thus see that, if one's patrimonial network is disempowered, as a result of elections, conflict or war, the result is radical social change that affects the entire network in question from the top positions within the state to the outermost link of the larger network.[4] A small minority within the 'declassed' network will most probably have secured themselves an relatively strong economic foundation, yet for most the resources gained will already have been redistributed, through social and political networks, meaning that political changes entail entire networks and societal groups becoming without means, losing positions and possibilities that dramatically affect their everyday existence.

This is not to say that all is in constant turmoil, as many cultural and social understandings and practices are relatively enduring in Bissau. However, contrary to the West, where social mobility is relatively slow and positions within social strata relatively static, upward mobility in Bissau is as rapid as becoming déclassé, as the socio-political environment is in almost constant flux. Political change, as such, has widespread social consequences, and, as the *Governo* lost the war, every branch within the entirety of the patrimonial network lost. The top politicians were deprived of their positions, their property and their fortunes. The officers were expelled from the army, equally deprived of property and wealth. The civil servants, holding paid jobs, were replaced.[5] Wives were deprived of economic support from their husbands who were formerly within the patrimonial network's food chain. And the Aguentas, at the bottom of the network, were left as stigmatised losers, as poor *dubriadurs* left to depend on the economy of affection and obligation and waiting for the next possibility to navigate the socio-political terrain.

It is thus not only the physical hardness of life, the mortality and the morbidity which have become constants in Guinea-Bissau but equally the knowledge of the frailty and infirmity of social standing and political configurations. For my interlocutors there is no expectation of stability. Guinean society is seen as being in a state of continuous decline, conflict and turmoil, encompassing a constant possibility of war. In Dó's words:

Do you think that there will be another war?
If there will be another war [said in disbelief]? You know Guinea-Bissau poorly. Tearing each others asses apart that is our meal of the day.[6] We will have war again ... Before a year has gone. Mark my words, before a year.

Coming to Bissau at a period of presumed consolidation of a durable peace after the termination of the civil war in 1999, I was not expecting an answer emphasising the normality of tearing each other's backsides to pieces. Obviously there would be tension in Bissau but I was not anticipating such negative forecasts. I was hoping, perhaps naively, to be able to analyse a process of positive societal transformation: from the construction of fences, borders and institutions of war to the emergence of a society rising up from the ashes. However, the people I encountered in Bissau did not seem to feel the optimism of new beginnings, but rather the nostalgia for those that were long gone. They did not see themselves as inhabiting a world of evolving possibilities but one of slow but constant deterioration. The war had not encompassed the possibility of a new beginning but seemed rather to have been a manifestation of the strength of the existing decline and conflict. Instead of doing an ethnography of emergence, I was left doing one of decline (see Ferguson 1999).[7]

The Parliament of the Poor

Yet, in doing so, allow me first of all to present a *collegason* which amply illustrates some of the aspects of inhabiting decline and conflict, that is, the 'parliament of the poor', a small demarcation of friendship, solidarity and determination constituted by a group of young people at their regular meeting-place on a low, porous wall in Bissau.

The Parliament as Collegason

Despite its name, the Parliament is not a political institution but a social one, a compound of social categories, hierarchies and networks symbolically located between irony and a very non-humorous reality. It is a *collegason*, a relatively loosely organised peer group of about twenty friends of roughly the same age.

As a *collegason*, the Parliament of the Poor is not a place but a social space. It is central to the lives of many of my interlocutors not as a physical location but as a social arrangement,[8] and falls into an urbanised variant of social organisation that is as old as it is common in West Africa, namely an age group.[9] However, in a multi-ethnic urban setting such as the Bissauian the traditional ethnic, religious and age demarcations of age groups have given way to a more loosely organised structure of solidarity. In this perspective the Parliament is both a social network supporting its members in times of distress and a site of interpretation and evaluation of rumours and political change in which tactics are constructed and debated. It is a communicative forum through which people seek to identify social patterns and construct feasible navigational courses through the turbulent societal processes they are caught and participate in.

> Look at this place. Look at it, all the holes, all the rubbish, everything is falling apart ... Rubbish all over the place. It stinks. Look at the street and the pavement – it has not been fixed since the Portuguese. Nothing has been done since the Portuguese. You do not want foreigners to see this. You will be ashamed.

When Roberto said this he was agitated, pointing to different parts of the area surrounding the Parliament of the Poor. Although some of the destruction and disrepair surrounding the Parliament was caused by the war Roberto must nonetheless have been born into most of it, pointing our attention to the fact that decline and instability have become the stable societal expression: 'Nothing has been done since the Portuguese,' as he says, decay being constant.

The Parliament is an undifferentiated part of the general decay. Yet, despite collecting on top of a collapsing, porous wall outside Maria's even more porous house, the Parliament has by name a touch of the grandiose and youth who spend their time there jokingly give each other titles – the *collegason* being the seat of a president, ministers, non-titled members and multitudes of intricate networks, alliances and groupings – the irony highlighting its marginality.[10] However, being a social rather than a political institution, the Parliament is not a site of political action but rather of political marginalisation. In fact, it is integrally connected to the social moratorium of youth, mirroring its premises in a number of ways. You do not, for example, really do anything there, nothing physical anyway; for that you walk over to the stadium and its worn-out football field and basketball and tennis courts. At the Parliament, you just hang out. Quite literally, like hanging a coat on a chair, people place their bodies on the crumbling wall. Most of the time you just sit there, maybe content enough, but alert, ready for something to do or something to happen. Ready for work, entertainment, possibilities, but not anticipating any, you debate the state of affairs – politics, music, football and, not least, societal change – while overlooking the street with its open sewers, cracked pavement, broken water pipe, chronic puddles, leg-breaking holes, looking at the same traces of decline and destruction day after day until you gradually stop noticing them. After having spent sufficient time at the Parliament, the decay and destruction start to merge into a landscape in which you know how to move, what to look out for, where to step and not to step, what to do and what not to do. It becomes routinised and everyday, its detail most often avoiding speculation and articulation except when it is changing, tumbling down or falling in or coming into focus through the presence of a visitor. And so, discursively, practically and physically, the Parliament of the Poor serves as an example of how decline and conflict becomes the everyday and enters social institutions, routines and, not least, praxis. In short, the sad dynamics of the position of youth within the Guinean society seems articulated through the very existence of the Parliament as, situated in the midst of decline and dilapidation, it is a meeting-place for a number of unemployed youth caught in the social moratorium.

Conflict and Warfare: The Prosaic and the Event

The Parliament became one of my prime windows and fields of entry into Guinean society. As the members of the *collegason* sat on the small wall they would flirt, fight, laugh and complain. They would remark upon the people going by – positioning them in relation to their networks, in relation to rumours, romance, prospects, possibilities, dislike and not least in relation to the political situation, allegiances, social bonds and conflict. Equally they would spend lengths of time debating the general societal situation, the political state of affairs, the who's who of Guinean society, past, present and future. However, the Parliament also gave a good insight into which situations would spur narrative production and which would not: that is, into which event the people at the Parliament would need to make sense of and which apparently fell into an already established interpretation. We would sit and watch the build-up of trouble, registering the movement of people and commenting on it in such a calm way that it seemed almost like indifference to me. Yet, as soon as shots were fired, briefly during the night or more seriously as in November 2000, the debate would continue endlessly, twisting and turning the picture in dialogue until all aspects had been uncovered and all scenarios sketched within a detailed social imaginary. It was a differentiation between the ordinary and the specific, which was made even further evident to me when I started doing small, informal, life story interviews.

Combined with the interpretative praxis I was able to observe from my daily presence at the Parliament, these life stories showed a consolidation of societal instability as terrain in Bissau, as turmoil and instability, via overlapping stages of improvisation and routinisation, seem to have entered into the very way in which people see and describe the characteristics and possibilities of the social terrain they seek to navigate.[11] This was indicated through the different peaks in interpretative praxis by the people at the Parliament but became consolidated through the 'foregrounding' and 'backgrounding' of events in the telling of life stories,[12] in which societal instability became background and the radicalisation of conflict foreground. The construction of life stories being both an interpretative and positional praxis, they direct our attention to how the individual sees his or her flow through life but also to the terrain being navigated, indicating that decline and conflict have become the background against which events and novelty are made sense of. In other words, the fact that life stories are saturated with decline and instability emphasises the normalisation (quantitative, not qualitative)[13] of what, for others, would be considered ruptures in the societal fabric. My informants have been in the thick of social and political turmoil, conflict and decline for so long that it has become the expected terrain of action.

That decline, instability and conflict have become background could furthermore be seen when asking about the future. As my friend Vitór put it shortly after the outbreak of fighting in November 2000:

What will happen now, will things change?
No, here in Bissau ... War in Bissau is like this. It is like the rainy season. It darkens, and then everything falls down. Then it darkens again and it falls down. Here, war is like this.

In this manner conflict and decline are experienced as the constants of the social terrain and thus come to define it as a navigational space, with no envisaged utopias but dystopic possibilities secreting from the present into the near future.

The persistence of decline and conflict in Bissau has thus brought about a routinisation of instability, dilapidation and destruction. They have become the expected manifestations of the movement of Guinean society written into the city; in people's understanding of their society's movement through time; and in the possibilities embedded in them as social agents. This does not, however, entail a reduction of social-political turmoil and instability. It does not signify a reduction but rather an accommodation of disorder; as Mbembe has put it, the '[decline becomes] so etched into the urban landscape that it no longer creates a spectacle. It ceases to surprise' (Mbembe 1995: 330).[14]

In this manner Bissau exemplifies the absurdity of thinking of peace, conflict and war as separate societal states. Peace in Bissau means an absence of actual fighting; yet, even in the most peaceful periods I have witnessed in the country, there is nonetheless a very 'unpeaceful' constant alertness of socio-political movements as outbreaks of fighting always seem possible, if not imminent. What we see when looking at Bissau is an oscillation not so much between war and peace but rather between conflict and war, the country being caught in a series of coups, coup attempts and purges. So what stands out as extraordinary is not decline or conflict, which is placed, heavily surveyed, in the realm of the everyday, but rather actual warfare. And, although every bout of fighting or serious tension implies another period of heterodoxy, of reflection and awareness of other possible interpretations and actions (see Bourdieu 1992: 164), the existing decay – bombed buildings, bullet and shrapnel marks on doors and walls – settles into a crumbling physical and social context in which change is located.

Thus, the variety of everyday events might be quite noticeable, but the actual physical and societal decay, albeit so apparent to a visitor, recedes to the background, highlighted only by conscious reflection or action – when changing it, wondering how it used to function or physically manipulating it by, for example, kicking off loose bits of asphalt overhanging a caved-in sewer or pulling open the heavy metal door to the stadium by grabbing on to the holes cut by shrapnel. It is a situation in which decline and conflict become societal states from which change is, in itself, made sense of and evaluated, inscribing 'the devastation in the everydayness of life' (Mbembe 1995: 331). In Bissau, the war-inflicted damage blends into the general decomposition of the city and has over time been gently covered over by moss and softened by opportunistic plants, giving it the appearance of addition rather than infliction – a process analogous to the interpretative endeavour whereby the jagged-edged destruction becomes blunted by 'routinisation'. The scars on the urban landscape do not register as signs of crisis (the destructive signs of the ignition of decline), but rather as signs of its recurrent radicalisation. What is analysed locally is, in this manner, not the dilapidation, decline and conflict, which seem to merge into a general and predictable 'hardness of life', but rather the movements of the social terrain as it moves towards or away from radicalisations of conflict, and as change opens possibilities of tactical manoeuvring and provides the signs telling one what to expect. What becomes clear when doing fieldwork in Bissau is, in other words, just as much the process of routinisation as that of conflict or decline.

The Routinisation of Decline and Conflict

I was walking through the stadium complex with Pedro. As we had been talking about the war, he started pointing out all the traces of the conflict that were visible within the interior of the compound. 'Look, over there are bullet holes'; 'these are holes cut by shrapnel'; 'see, where the grenade fell?' Walking by the wall separating the tennis courts from the football grounds he stopped, touched the holes with his fingers and then walked on. As we moved towards the outer metal door of the compound, the unordered holes, cut by shrapnel, seemed to be shining at us as the sun shone through – the outside gently oozing through into what, turning around, suddenly protruded as a landscape of destruction. I had walked here a million times before, unreflectively letting the signs of war become part of the terrain. The walk with Pedro had unpacked them, stripped them of their gentle wrapping of routinisation.

At its most abstract level one can see routinisation as a multifaceted construction and constitution of contingent relations working on three interrelated and inseparable levels, making it analytically possible to speak about the (interwoven) construction of routines of organisation (social order), routines of interpretation (narrative and discourse) and routines of action (praxis). Routinisation, in this perspective, designates the process of relating action to perceived terrains (interpretative, organisational or practical) and routine ways of acting in perceived terrains. However, routines are related to expediency; in fact, the very potency of routines comes from the need to make sense of events, to order them and find modes of action through them.[15] In situations of warfare the initial entropy ceases – via this threefold routinisation – to be a source of paralysis as the context of immediacy becomes dotted with conceptualised terrains of contingent understandings, relations and actions. Routinisation is a fundamental act in the construction of social terrains and all human experience can in this perspective be routinised, which – contrary to what many believe – accounts for the existence of social and cultural order in, for example, warfare, which many believe to be entropic.[16]

Getting the Prepositions Right: Coping With, or In, Crisis?

As the merging of different, primary constructions of order, routinisations are the last to be destroyed and the first to emerge in the onset of war. As conflict or war becomes a constant, people debate and create routines allowing them to live their lives as well as possible despite the difficult terrain. In warfare as a perceived short-lived situation, agents thus construct routines so as to cope with conflict; yet a second scenario also exists as conflict or warfare can become the expected social terrain that the agents act in and on thereby laying the foundation for the routines of the everyday. The routinisation of crisis into the everyday, however, is not a sign of coping with crisis but rather of coping in crisis, and it does not instigate change but routinises it, turning crisis into an anticipated period of decline, decay or turmoil. In other words, coping in crisis refers to crisis as a terrain of action and interpretation rather than a chaotic transitory hurdle. Routinising decline or turmoil is equivalent to an internalisation of rot, where the initial condition of crisis pervades the physical, social and societal bodies of the community under focus, making it the rough matter embracing lives, making it 'everyday'.

Although this differentiation between prepositions might seem trivial it is of major importance in relation to the way we investigate crises, decline or conflict as societal, social or individual phenomena. In the situation in question, the concept of 'routinisation' allows us to research the Guinean conflict as context rather than in context.[17] This is not to say that we do not get a good understanding of crises, decline and conflicts by situating them in their complex contextual settings – that is equally an essential analytical endeavour. But by viewing these types of social situations as context, as chronicity (Estroff 1993),[18] we become able to analytically approach and illuminate the actual social dynamics of these situations of prolonged conflict and decline, making it possible for us to see how conflicts influence lives lived, shade understandings of social realities, come to constitute a framework for social interpretation and action, and thus become grounds of becoming. The chronicity and routinisation of crisis make it possible for us to shift the focus from brutality and immediacy to decline or conflict as everyday. Focusing on routinisation thus allows us to illuminate how prolonged decline and turmoil enter into social life, as Ferguson has noted in his work on the Zambian copper belt: 'the circumstances of economic decline have affected not only national income figures and infant mortality but also urban cultural forms, modes of social interaction, configurations of identity and solidarity, and even the very meanings people are able to give their own lives and fortunes' (Ferguson 1999: 12).

Actions, constructions of meaning, social relationships and identities are not temporarily remodelled or hibernating in situations of prolonged social turmoil, decline or conflict; they are not passing through, but located, created and recreated in it. So we really do need to get the prepositions right, since our regular, European, understanding of crisis, conflict and war sees them as intermediary moments of chaos where social processes collapse upon themselves, only to come to life after the crisis is overcome. Bissau shows us the opposite. It flaunts a process of 'routinisation' whereby crisis becomes decline, making it impossible for us to locate it as a fleeting social state. Looking at decline, social turmoil and conflict as context enables us to see these situations as social terrains instead of constructing them as social or societal vacuums. It means that we can, following Bhabha, see states of emergency as situations of emergence (1994: 41).[19] In the current Bissau, we are, in other words, facing a scenario where the everyday and changes in the everyday are constructed out of what seems to be chronic decline, social turmoil and conflict.

Turning Weber in His Grave

The 'routinisation' of decline, social turmoil and conflict thus entails an 'everydaying' of these states of instability as anticipated social reality, constituting the foundation for prediction and interpretation of societal change as well as the subsequent pattern of interaction, relations and action. It is this process of contingency, related to action and strategy, which I have thus far analytically approached by borrowing the concept of routinisation from, primarily, Weber (1965: 363–73; 1982: 98), bending his influential work to fit my needs,[20] by talking about the 'routinisation' of decline and conflict.[21]

However, it would seem that I am not doing justice to Weber's theory of change within the institutionalisations of different types of authority.[22] The present context highlights instead a process whereby crisis becomes expected prolonged decline and instability by way of the threefold routinisation of the social negotiation of meaning, action and organisation, which are needed for, and essential in, the constitution of everyday survival. Yet I might perhaps be closer to the concept's Weberian use than first meets the eye, since the process transforms crisis from the unusual and noticeable to the unremarkable (Gerth and Mills 1958: 54) that is, from the exceptional to the imponderable. This is further emphasised if we look at the German term actually used by Weber, *Veralltäglichung* – making something everyday or 'everydaying' (Tilly 1978: 37).

Routinisation in Bissau is the first step in the process of establishing conflict and instability as social terrain through a process of everydaying that makes conflict and turmoil the anticipated social movement and context. The chaos of conflict actually stands alone only in the instant before its identification, after which it becomes encased in meaning and acted upon, and the more chronic the crisis, the more it becomes background, thus avoiding a fixed stare and rather becoming the subject of passing glances. To paraphrase Weber once more, one could say that the routinisation of crisis, in quite essential respects, is identical to adjustment to the initial conditions of chaos (see Gerth and Mills 1958: 54).

In any case, what is being described is the emergence of the knowledge of, and actions in, a field of crisis whereby the agent tries to manage in a very difficult situation by routinising social change. But routinisation is not just adjustment to change. Rather, it is the social metamorphosis of change into perceived continuity, and the concept is, in this manner, equally close to its use by Berger and Luckmann on the subject of the constitution of social institutions.[23] From somewhere between Weber and Berger and Luckmann we can thus say that the routinisation of conflict is a solidification of points of view and spaces of action built on instability and danger in a fluid and uncertain world. In the present context it can be seen as the process of creating lines of order in disorder (see Taussig 1992), meaning that we can talk about the routinisation of crisis and conflict when decay and destruction become (perceived as) the normal state of things, saturating smaller-scale social formations of, for example, identity constructions and micro-histories, as well as large-scale organisation, categorisation and institutionalisation (Berger and Luckmann 1967: 53–61). What must be made clear, however, is that routinisation does not change the initial condition of turbulence but indicates a process of adaption to it which is necessary for being able to act in situations of conflict and turmoil. It does not, in other words, change the unstable character of the Guinean society but instead sets instability as the terrain of action.

Routinisation or Habituation?

We could, in a longer time perspective, also talk about the 'habituation' of conflict, indicating a process whereby the everyday routines and action in fields of crisis are solidified into the emergence of, for example, 'habitus' (see Bourdieu 1992), where crisis becomes a primary condition of experience with its consequent influence on the definitions of the possible, impossible and probable and thereby directly located in praxis (ibid.: 72, 78). But, where routinisation points our attention towards how people shape their social organisations, interpretations and actions according to manifestations of violence and disarray, the concept of habitus seems more useful at illuminating reproduction – for instance, the social reproduction of violent social formations or institutions rather than emergent production and change such as of new social processes, acts and understandings. If we look at the difference between the two concepts with a more narrow focus, we equally see that the phenomenon of 'habit' connotes unconsciously repeated actions, 'so polished and smooth that they seem to unreel almost without the actor's participation and conscious planning' (Schutz and Luckmann 1995: 27). In contrast, routine is related to an evaluated expedience of action, to an interpretation of perceived future context and possibility. Habit, in this perspective, works behind our cognitive grasp, while routines work through it. The difference between routinisation and habituation is, in other words, that where the construction of habit is an unreflected social sediment, routinisation is contingent; moreover, in war habits are a luxury – or idiocy – that one can barely afford.[24]

In other words, it seems that we can say that a major difference in relation to socially navigating stable and unstable societies is that navigational habits disappear and give way to navigational routines, which, rather than being imponderable sets of action and interpretation, are constantly evaluated and related to new movements of the socio-political environment so that routines are never durable enough to become habitual. Terrains of conflict corrupt social habits of both thought and action.

'*No ta djubi situason so*' – we just look at the situation – is one of the remarks I have heard most often from my informants, yet it is not as passive as it sounds because what they are doing is following the socio-political movements in order to anticipate probable terrains of action, constantly aware of the relationship between their reading of the terrain and its oncoming movement. Here habit is what we do independently of context, while routinisation is action ordered in relation to context. Yet habits and habitual action are an important part of our everyday life, constituting the humdrum and taken-for-granted aspect of it, and, as social habits become problematic and challenged by the radicalisation of conflict into warfare, we need to turn our attention towards how we constitute an everyday life when its habitual aspect is being undermined.

Immediacy and an Everyday of Decline and Conflict

As the Junta entered Bissau, Vitór's company was tied down in combat by the Bandim market. Being some 500 metres from home, he made a run for it. Becoming aware that the war had de facto ended, that his platoon from Delta Force II, the second Company at the Presidença, were most probably fighting the last battle of the old regime, he gave up hope, managed to escape and sneaked home. When he arrived, he slipped into the backyard, into his room in the annexe, took off his uniform and hid his weapons. Late the next evening he ventured out onto the street to see what was happening, saw that the war had stopped, went back inside, stayed in for a few days, and then started picking up his life where he had left it: hanging out with his friends in their collegason, looking for a job, occasionally partying, but most of the time without anything to do except hope for the goodwill of his uncle for food and shelter.

Two years after the war had ended, his weapons were still hidden away in his room. When I asked him why he wanted to keep them he said: 'You do not understand. This is not Europe. Bissau is not like the rest of the world. Here no one knows what will happen, no one. We just sit here and look at the situation but if the place starts smelling badly [i.e. if war breaks out],[25] *or if someone wants to hurt me, I will be ready. No one has more arms than me.' From somewhere between boastfulness and paranoia, war is a constant possibility.*

Vitór provides a good example of how the social terrain can become characterised by stable instability in situations of prolonged conflict, as he is ever alert to the shifting terrain while trying to plot, modify and actualise action. His everyday life is in this manner a ceaseless attentiveness to the possibly volatile, the social terrain never being left unaccompanied and taken for granted, as he, like everybody else in Bissau, is focused on predicting arising possibilities and dangers. In other words, whereas we normally think of a concept such as 'everyday life' to be absent, or at least the first to disappear in situations of conflict and war, Vitór is a good example of how the everyday is transformed in situations of prolonged conflict, and yet still constitutes the terrain which is modified by our action and which modifies our acts (Schutz and Luckmann 1995: 6).[26] Vitór shows us that there is indeed a production of the everyday in Bissau but he also points our attention to some poorly illuminated aspects of our understanding of the phenomenon, as he turns our attention towards an everyday that is not necessarily unconscious and beyond our awareness.

Normality and the Everyday

At its most evident the 'everyday' is seen as that which we take for granted; as the imponderable background of our lives, our orientation and our efforts at making sense of the social worlds we produce and inhabit (Schutz and Luckmann 1995; Schutz 1996). Our everyday, as an experiential quality, leads a silent life behind our awareness, only to come to light when we are confronted with that which it is not.[26] At its simplest, this could be the registering of our normal, everyday bodily states through the experience of imbalance, such as when catching a cold; at a more complex and abstract level it can be becoming aware of our interpretations of the world through encountering interpretations that are foreign to our cultural understanding of the world. The everyday thus appears to us in comparison, that is, when juxtaposed with the unusual or the extraordinary. It is the 'matter-of-fact' reality of our existence, which we only become aware of when it is challenged or confronted (Schutz and Luckmann 1995: 128). Yet taking this line of reasoning a step further we are also able to grasp the everyday from a perspective that is not strictly contra-identificational: that is, where we do not only conceptualise the everyday by what it is not. If we recognise the everyday through encountering novelty or change, is our experience of the everyday not that of an expected continuance (of a bodily state, a social order, praxis and so on) through time? Do we, for example, not experience the everyday when we expect to have a generalised similar tomorrow? In other words, we encounter our everyday whenever we presume continuity. As such, the everyday is what frees us from constantly having to assess our social, societal, political or physical world as we engage with it; yet, in relation to the lives of my informants, this conceptualisation does not address the issue of how we are to designate the experience of constant social awareness which characterises their lives.

A Bissauian Everyday

What we currently witness in Bissau thus both challenges and supports the concept of the everyday. As social decline, turmoil and conflict have been prevalent long enough to be 'routinised', we see that the social terrain of my informants has changed from being characterised by an expectation of the continuance of societal order to an expectation of societal disorder.

In Bissau it is warfare that shatters the everyday, not conflict or turmoil. Situations of prolonged decline and conflict thus come to entail the emergence of a radically different everydayness from what is seen in 'stable' societies by substituting the crystallisation of social, political and societal order with that of disorder. The social processes of routinisation have, in Bissau, grounded/established a radical state of what Taussig, following Brecht, has called 'ordered disorder' (Taussig 1992), as turmoil and conflict have become the expected dynamics of the Guinean society. That is, instead of inheriting a stable and enduring societal order young Guineans are born into a world of experienced and expected instability. In Guinea-Bissau, the societal constants are currently conflict and turmoil, rather than law and order. The outcome is the paradox of having instability become stable social fact.

Dangerously Close to a 'Native's' Point of View

This paradox, however, is one that affects not just our informants, but also affects us as researchers, although coming from one of the continents of plenty. Researchers, aid workers and other outsiders go through the same process of 'routinisation' of social turmoil and decline as their interlocutors, with only the 'slight' difference of having external sources of money, health insurance, contact with the outside world, abundances of future possibilities and, underlying all these, the option to stay or leave. Yet, despite our privileged position, the process whereby decline and turmoil come to orientate our praxis is, interestingly, the same process of necessary interpretative reduction of entropy, enabling us to sketch a terrain in which we are able to make decisions and act.

Ethnographic fieldwork is in itself a process of socialisation and the consequence of actively researching decline and conflict for long periods of time is that one enters into the exact same process of living in and constructing an everyday of disorder, resulting in one becoming increasingly analytically blind to it. 'Violent acts do not show up well against a background of violence,' Malcolm Deas has noted (1997: 366), and we need to be aware that, when turmoil and conflict come to constitute essential parts of our socio-political environment, then they become more difficult to notice and analytically isolate as we become accustomed to the same uncertainty and moved by the same shifting terrain as our interlocutors, which may explain why we so often focus on the blood-and-guts events rather than the humdrum events of everyday conflict as lived. In Lutz' eloquent critique of the narrow focus on war as battle:

> [It] discounts the extent of war's remnants in structuring life as lived. It prevents an ethnography of agrarian life with landmines as the fallowing principle, kinship systems with rape and missing men at their centre, political discussions in the midst of national security states' barbed wire limits on discourse, and the invention of the identity civilian. (Lutz 1999: 615)

Lutz's observations are important as they lead us to the social dynamics of such situations of mis-dynamics. Rather than focusing on violence in itself I believe, accordingly, that a better understanding of the way that instability becomes experienced as an everyday societal condition will dramatically improve our knowledge of some of the general social processes in zones of prolonged conflict, enabling us to position the understandings and motives influencing our informants' actions and interpretation. If we concentrate on the extraordinary, the massacres, rapes and crimes against humanity, we are very likely to overlook people's construct of the everyday and the effects this has on the experience of conflict and warfare, on the generation of tactics and strategy and the continuation and (even) instigation of war. We need, in other words, to examine not only destructive praxis, trauma and healing processes, but also how conflict and war become socially incorporated into the everyday, how they become dominant aspects of the political and societal terrain that give rise to the possibilities and constraints people (soldiers and civilians alike) envision as surrounding their lives.[27] We must, in other words, keep our analytical eye not only on the social production of conflict and warfare but also on how situations of conflict and warfare shape what is socially produced. As decline and conflict become everyday, people become aware and act according to a social terrain that is fluid and in motion, with instability as its prime characteristic. What we see is that the presumed continuity of a social order, which otherwise underlies our experience of having an everyday life, has been replaced with a consolidation and normalisation of disorder.

From Stable Fields to Shifting Terrains

Vitór often indulged in over-explicit descriptions of his nightly escapades. I was uninterested, but my attempts at communicating my reserve for the intimate details of his coital endeavours seemed only to trigger a descent into even more exhaustive descriptions. This morning, after having been served yet another explicit narrative of his conquest and subsequent 'fuck',[28] sound effects included, I opted for a moral stance and said: 'I hope you protect yourself, you know with AIDS and all.' Vitór answered disapprovingly: 'You mean use a condom? No, I do not do that. Us here we do not do that. If you are not killed by AIDS you are killed by something else.' It sounded almost reasonable: living in a society that claims one of the lowest average life expectancies in the world, which leads in terms of poverty and epidemics and is stuck in a process of progressive and persistent conflict and decline, why would one worry about sexually transmitted diseases?

Stagnation and Agentive Limitation

Vitór's attitude demonstrates the influence that inhabiting an unstable social world can have on our social navigation and plotting of trajectories; it touches on the way people feel that they can control and plan their lives and directs our attention towards the diminishing importance given to the distant future in such a situation. It points our attention towards an understanding of the social terrain as so fluctuating that it is futile to plan far ahead within it, as well as towards a feeling of lacking the ability to control even the most basic grounds for action. As Justino commented in relation to the outbreak of fighting in November 2000:

> *How do you see the current situation?*
> How can you see it? This is crisis – is it not? They said that when we get democracy things will get better but nothing, nothing goes forward, [things change] only for the worse.[29] But there is nothing to do about it, nothing to do about it.
> *Can people not do anything to make the situation better?*
> It is like people can do nothing, nothing. Guinea-Bissau is tired, the state is already dead. We have nothing. People have no money. No money to buy rice or anything. We can do nothing, nothing.

Justino's answer shows us that from the point of view of my interlocutors, caught in the middle of the current period of conflict and decline, the situation is characterised by a relative reduction of their agency.[30] They see themselves as caught up in a flow of events that is somehow beyond their reach and feel powerless to change the situation they are in. As such Justino's quote points our attention to a defining trait of crisis, personal or social, namely that we feel unable to control the exterior forces influencing our possibilities and choices (see Jackson 2002). Or in Habermas's words:

> ... crisis cannot be separated from the viewpoint of the one who is undergoing it – the patient experiences his powerlessness *vis-à-vis* the objectivity of the illness only because he is a subject condemned to passivity and temporarily deprived of the possibility of being a subject in full possession of his powers.
>
> We therefore associate with crisis the idea of an objective force that deprives a subject of some part of his normal sovereignty. To conceive of a process as a crisis is tacitly to give it a normative meaning – the resolution of the crisis effects a liberation of the subject caught up in it. (1992: 1)

Crisis in this perspective is similar to many of the ways in which the experience of violence and social suffering has been conceptualised, and constitutes an interesting foundation for its conceptualisation, however, when addressing issues of crisis, suffering and violence it becomes important to emphasise that we are never, in situations of peace and stability as well as conflict and war, left to do exactly as we please.

As shown in an earlier chapter, the social moratorium is a multiple marginalisation in which the continued scarcity of economic, social or cultural capital makes it difficult for youth to define themselves in praxis and locate themselves socially, and which thus results in difficulties in actualising life trajectories and realising social becoming, thereby finding voice and status. However, overemphasising lack of agency would be misleading. We are all capable of changing structure and acting strategically within structures, but whether we are in a position to use our agency as we want, in relation to a given relationship or within a given context, is a different matter. The concept of agent and agency implied in such an overarching discussion brings to mind Iris Murdoch's critique of the concept of 'the agent' in existentialism, who 'freely chooses his reasons ... [as] a highly conscious, self-contained being' (Murdoch 1970: 35). In many of the approaches to suffering and violence, our current usage of the concept of agency is in this manner starting to bear many similarities to the notion of an unconditioned agent, and we should perhaps try to consolidate the fact that one can clearly talk of agents and agency without accepting an idea of an autonomous and absolute subject (Bevir 1999).

Habermas further comments on the concept of crisis, saying that, in a more social perspective, it 'assumes the form of a disintegration of social institutions' (1992: 3). What we have seen in relation to the lives of my informants is that they live their lives in a context where social institutions and configurations of power are constantly being not just disintegrated but also rebuilt and that this reconstruction offers a possibility of using ones agentive potential to a larger degree than usual. In fact, as decline and conflict have been routinised in Bissau, my informants make their lack of possibilities and life chances explicit by hanging around passing time, feeling unable to change the state of affairs but being acutely aware of any movements in the terrain that could grant them the chance to engage in it. It is a general stagnation and awareness of social possibilities which is exemplified no better than in the life of Septimo.

Septimo the Persistent

Septimo could sit on the small wall overlooking the street for ages. At times in solitude and at times in company, he would doggedly sit on the small wall till late in the evening. Most times he would come early in the morning. I would pass him on my way to Guiné Telecom's internet 'cafe' and have an early morning chat. I would often see him in the afternoon when spending a few hours on the wall myself. Also I would pass him in the evening, eventually say goodnight and head for bed. This specific day I had spent most of my day on the wall with him, with only a few hours' break when we went to the stadium in the late afternoon. Having spent so much time together we had run out of things to say, when the growing tediousness of the situation compelled me to break the silence and ask him yet another question:

> *What are things like for you as youth here?*
> You know what it is like. That is why we sit here every day. This is being young in Bissau. I sit here in the morning, in the afternoon, then I go and play basket[ball], and I sit here again. If I get a bit of money,[31] I go to Capital [a nightclub] at the weekends ... I am tired of my life; it is shit. A shit life. [It is a] life without progress without a guaranteed future.[32] The day I leave [Guinea-Bissau] that is when I will see my future.

Our attention is once again directed towards the social moratorium of youth, with migration as one of the idealised exits, as well as towards some general aspects of agents' positions in situations of prolonged decline. His statement indicates a problem of agency, with his life being described as motionless and directionless, and himself as powerless to change his situation, that is, with a minimised agentive potential. Septimo is in a situation where he has no ability to actualise a social trajectory, his life being without 'progress'. The reference to migration, as the point where he will be able to realise his future, points both to a feeling of being structurally constrained by his position in Guinean society to a related problem of being unable to positively inscribe his life into a Guinean societal context, unable to actualise the socially expected life trajectory, as the current societal situation is too dire for him to envisage a way out of the social moratorium and into a positive future. It is an agentive constriction once again made clear to me by Justino, as I was asking him about his life and social position in Bissau: 'You, you know who you are because you have chosen your life. Me I do not know yet because I do not have possibilities to choose. I do not have a future yet. I know that I have a name, but I do not know who I am.' The quote clearly demonstrates the interconnectedness between the experience of 'youth' and the lack of possibilities, which, coupled with the context of prolonged decline, crystallises into agentive stagnation, with youth confined in a social moratorium without the possibility of realising their social becoming.

Uncertain Futures

Generally, in situations that are not characterised by manifest societal disruption, the social world we inhabit is seen as relatively stable, a relatively ordered universe of possibilities where one can roughly anticipate the outcomes (negative or positive) of ones strategies or tactics, which are in themselves oriented towards the future realisation of a set of actions related to an anticipated set of conditions and limitations. Conversely, in situations of heightened conflict and war the first thing to crumble is the ordered universe of anticipatory processes and possibilities constituting our everyday, making one's pursuit of information and possible implementation of strategy or tactics dependent on a delicate balancing of a relatively indeterminable terrain and an uncertain set of outcomes. The social fabric is, in such situations, an emergent property, a developing reality (Kapferer 1976: 3). The logical consequence of this is a reduction in the temporal and spatial depth of ones horizon affecting the interplay between action and telos, trapping the agent in the immediate and near future and reducing the temporal potency of his actions and strategies, making it difficult for the agent to plan towards a distant future. As Justino continued when I asked him how he saw his future:

> My future ... There is nothing here for us, nothing. When I get up in the morning I pray for something to eat, if I see it I am happy, before I go to bed I pray and say thanks. The next day I get up and I pray that I will find something to eat. You see?

The statement emphasises the feeling of agentive reduction exactly because 'agency' is dependent on possibility before strategy or tactics. Given the instability of the socio-political circumstances and the confining boundaries of the social moratorium, my informants find it hard to make long-term predictions other than those built on instability itself. Instability and scarcity become the foundation from where they imagine the oncoming and the future movements of the terrain and thus from which they plan and actualise their trajectories. Being the aspect that the agent can least afford to miscalculate, it becomes the defining element of the socio-political environment.

Routinisation and the ordering of disorder do not, in other words, imply that the socio-political environment stops being fluid but that my interlocutors' interpretation of their social terrain and plotting of action has become attuned to its fluidity. My interlocutors all have visions of how they want their lives to be and all seek to navigate them towards a distant telos, but the shifts of the terrain and the way the terrain shifts them as they seek to navigate it mean that they are unable to take for granted the socio-political continuity needed to draw a course into a distant future. Inhabiting shifting terrains means, in other words, that the future remains uncertain and opaque and therefore relatively inaccessible, consequently making the drawing of paths into the future provisional and unsettled.

Locked into Conflict

What distinguishes situations characterised by prolonged social turmoil such as Bissau, from other scenarios, is that the consecutive troublesome events in Bissau, with their societal eruptions and ramifications, continuously challenge readings and understanding of the social terrain before they can be presumed to be enduring – that is, before routinisations gain the hardness and constancy of habit and become sedimentations. Crisis gains an oxymoronic permanence, dissolves itself in the process and leaves us with a continuous state of social instability. In Bissau instability and uncertainty are omnipresent social facts and many of the inhabitants' acts are tactically directed towards decline and conflict as the norm, as the routinised social reality of the everyday.

The concept of routinisation is thus essential if we want to understand areas of societal turmoil as social terrains, since it enables agents to act in the uncertain terrains of conflict by reducing social unpredictability through the creation of patterns of organisation and interpretation. We are, in this perspective, dealing with the construction of points of view and terrains of action with points of view being actual perspectives, positions and lines of interpretation of movement (individual or collective) and terrains of action being spaces of perceived social relations, imagined possibilities of transformations and consequences of acts. In other words, the routinisation of conflict is, as said, what allows us to navigate terrains in a situation where overviews have to be gained rather than being products of socialisation,[33] which is in effect where the concept of terrain differs from that of field and the concept of navigation from that of praxis: that is, in being directed towards the shifting, uncertain and reflexively routinised instead of the stable, sedimented and habitual.

From Chessboard to Choppy Sea

It is when focusing on my informants' endeavour of sketching and actualising social trajectories in a political terrain as uncertain as the Bissauian that the concept of navigation reveals itself as an especially useful analytical tool, gaining an edge over its related counterparts as it illuminates movement in and across an environment that is itself in motion. Within the shifting and fluid circumstances of warfare and social turmoil, navigation thus provides us with an image of socio-political action as having to be attentive to the constant currents, shifts, pulls and undertows of societal (mis)dynamics: that is, attention towards the immediate terrain, to where one is moved by the terrain as well as where one is moving towards. Navigation thus designates a complex actualisation of will as it is moving within movement contrary to the usual conceptualisation of action as being performed on, and out from, unwavering ground; that is, a relatively stable sociocultural field as seen, for example, in the use of the analogy of games to designate socio-political action (Bourdieu 1984, 1994; cf. Shore 1996; Bourdieu and Wacquant 2001).[34] I shall be discussing below the relative heuristic merits of the concepts of social navigation, praxis and fields so as to clarify the choice of the one over the other.

Socio-political action is often made sense of via the imagery of games.[35] In relation to game metaphors, a field is a demarcated space, identified by the forms of stakes (or capital) being played for, the rules being played by, and the demarcation being played on – the spatial image conveyed being one of a demarcated, solidified surface or structure. So, for the game analogy to work, we need to see the field as a defined and clearly demarcated social space, we must have defined and constant players and we must have transparency of rules. In other words, even though the structures of relations within social fields differ from games, as they are not consciously constructed and pre-arranged with explicit rules (Bourdieu and Wacquant 2001: 85),[36] there are nonetheless stable fields, strategies and trophies to be fought for within the 'game' in question (see also Barth 1959, 1981). The (playing) field, as a relatively stable demarcated arena, is the foundation that enables us to talk of a game at all, as it is both what demarcates the game, where the game is actualised, and what is moved through within the process of the game.[37]

In relation to our current focus on the lives of a group of youth caught in a very unstable social environment, the difficulty with the notion of field is that it indicates a stability and demarcation of social structure. People may move and act vertically in the social topography of a field, competing for position and capital,[38] and thus act strategically in relation to each other as competitors (Barth 1959, 1981), but they do so without having to worry about the movement of the field itself, which is so clearly a prime focus of my informants.[39] The game metaphor brings forth an image of people interacting with each other on a field rather than having to interact with each other and the field. It thus conveys a picture of 'field' as stable social structure constituting the ground on which the game is actualised and enacted. The metaphors of 'game' and 'field' build on an idea of underlying permanence or very slow socio-political change rather than that of, for example, speed, flux or turbulence (see Armitage and Virilio 1999; Virilio 2001). This is not to imply that social fields, in the Bourdieuesque perspective, are static entities. Yet the concept generally conveys a constitution through slow processes of sedimentation and habituation, thus differing from the Guinea-Bissauian example in relation to the speed and volatility of change.

In relation to the analytical endeavour in focus within this book, this vision of stability and foundational passiveness corresponds very poorly to the empirical context of Bissau,[40] where, rather than implying slow and unnoticeable transformation, socio-political change implies continuous turmoil. Within this, the concept of navigation opens up a broader understanding of action, as it has the capacity of describing movement within and through an environment that is in itself in motion, that is, in a social terrain more similar to a choppy sea than to a chessboard.[41] Like the field, then, a social terrain has a certain topography,[42] yet its topographicality is not a relatively static or transparent structural grid but rather a murky and constantly emergent one. A social environment such as the Guinean is constantly shifting, meaning that the terrain moves the agent just as much as the agent seeks to move through the terrain. Furthermore, it is non-transparent, meaning that the agent is able to imagine what comes after the next wave but never really has certainty, which is the underlying reason for the previously described general limitation of prospective orientation to the near future.[43]

The concept of navigation thus makes it possible to analytically encompass the fact that social terrains, in situations of turmoil and conflict – and increasingly in general, given the increasing speed and breadth (if not depth) of social change and information – are often fluid and unstable, and that in acting the agent is attentive both to the shifting terrain and its immediate and future configurations and to his own movement. The point is, in other words, that we need to be aware of and able to illuminate the fact that we engage the terrain as well as the terrain engages us, without it predetermining our action. We navigate in relation to how we perceive the terrain and interpret its movement, to how we perceive our positions and possibilities within it and how we perceive the limitations and possibilities that unfold through the shifts of the terrain and the manner in which its shifts move us.[44]

The fact that our social environments are in movement is, importantly, not unique to Bissau or, for that matter, to areas of conflict or decline. All social environments are constantly in motion, yet some move at a slower pace than others, so people have time to internalise change and sediment it as part of their knowledge of the world, which is exactly where societies of ongoing turmoil differ from the relatively stable. Yet what happens if social change is so rapid that these configurations of power do not have time to settle into our unconscious? When our internalisation of change does not have time to sediment itself into 'social fact' before new change starts to wash the emergent fact away? When history is not constructed from smooth chains of internalisations and improvisations, but from crisis and tentative routinisations? When the players are constantly changing (both affiliations and configurations), and the demarcated space for the game is constantly in flux, expanding and contracting in relation to shifts and pulls that move between the local, regional and global – that is, when the terrain is in motion rather than being solid and stable?

Reflexive Routinisation

The answer, I believe, lies in increased social reflexivity, that is, an increased interpretation of social terrain, perspective and horizon in which one is, if not 'conscious of the eye through which one looks' (Benedict 1989: 14),[45] then at least conscious of the constructed character of routines of discourse and action. Social reflexivity thus means that people become aware of how they interpret the social terrain, plot tactics and go about realising their social trajectories, simply because the speed of change within the social world they inhabit is so rapid that the agent must constantly check the efficacy of his interpretation in relation to the changing environment he seeks to move in. Reflexive routinisation thus means that interpretations are never allowed to sediment and harden, and must constantly be assessed anew.

Generally we are made aware of our social routines when they are challenged, lose expediency or create novel results. In situations of turmoil, it therefore becomes necessary for the agent to reflect upon the tactics to adopt and how to act in relation to the shifting terrain (see Giddens 1984).[46] Importantly for the present discussion, reflexivity, in Giddens's perspective, is not confined to the realm of the social-scientific observer and praxis, but is part of all social praxis as humans seek to live their lives as best they can.[47] An agent has, he holds, 'reasons for his or her activities' and is 'able to elaborate discursively upon those reasons'. In fact, 'Continuity of practices presumes reflexivity, but reflexivity in turn is possible only because of the continuity of practises that make them distinctively 'the same' across space and time. 'Reflexivity' hence should be understood not merely as 'self-consciousness' but as the monitored character of the ongoing flow of social life. (Giddens 1984: 3).

Equally, in Bissau, the 'ongoing flow of social life' is monitored due to the constant motion of the socio-political terrain. What constitutes the expected order of the everyday in Bissau is the disorder of conflict, which has become context by its manifestations being routinised. In fact, it is qua routinisation that we can talk about the everyday at all, but where routinisation will normally lead to sedimentation,[48] quite literally describing the process of constructing solid terrain, in Bissau it is never granted the chance to do so. Reflexive routinisation thus provides an appropriate concluding note to this chapter as it illuminates one of the main consequences of rapid social change. In other words, in both scenarios an everyday exists with people trying to establish routines, seeking to reduce entropy and make the social terrain navigational, but the imponderability or taken-for-granted quality of the process of routinisation varies. In situations of relative stability, the sedimentation of social interpretations as enduring truths and routinised action makes them almost invisible, whereas they become more brittle and reflected upon in situations of rapid social change.

However, despite the above detour into theory, my point is not just a theoretical one. Looking at a situation such as the Bissauian, we see that my informants must, when acting in and interpreting the socio-political contexts, keep an eye on the movement of the social terrain and be aware not only of the shifting terrain but also of shifting interpretations of 'social order' if they do not wish to be caught off guard. 'You speak with one eye and look out with the other,' a Protestant friend of mine in Belfast said, neatly emphasising the fact that agents in such situations act towards what is visible and presented and yet constantly focus on eventual movement.

So, although conflict and instability have become routinised in Bissau they have not settled as an unconsciously or subconsciously existing matrix beyond the cognitive grasp of my informants, that is, they are not yet internalised and sedimented to the state of 'imponderabilia'. Rather, as decline, turmoil and conflict become routinised their every change and movement are simultaneously scrutinised. Whereas changes in the immediate usually relate, for most people, to personal relationships, work possibilities and so on, in Bissau they touch upon close social relationships (the economy of affection) and larger scale social relations (patrimonial networks), and thus upon the complete range of the agents' possibilities. The movement of the social terrain and the instability of political configurations therefore have severe ramifications that agents cannot afford to neglect. The volatility of the socio-political environment is constantly present in their rationalisations, from the most mundane to the most exceptional, from fulfilling social obligations to going to war. It is a constant awareness of instability that has entered into the way many of my informants see their social possibilities and futures, and not least into their everyday actions and tactics.

Living with the Possibility of Noise

Néné cooked food for most of the young men who did not have a household of their own, in inner Bissau. Her food was excellent, with generous helpings of good quality, and, not least, inexpensive. This day, as ordinary as any, just before the fighting in November, I was sitting in her courtyard trying to digest the enormous portion of rice, before moving on, when a street vendor approached Néné asking her if she would be interested in buying some glasses. Néné studied the glasses, seemingly interested, asked their price and then thought for a moment before saying: 'No, I do not want them, we do not know if there is more noise on its way.'[49] In other words, before making the investment Néné wanted more knowledge of the movement of the terrain. Estimations of the favourable nature of an act, a non-act or an idea are, in Bissau, often related to the movement of the social terrain by assessing the immediate and the imagined, expediency constantly drawing us back to the concept of navigation.

The estimation and evaluation of an act or non-act in relation to the shifting and moving social terrain not only saturates the political or societal level of Guinean society but also influences personal relationships. I overheard Raul turn down Joaquim, with whom he had served in the Aguentas, when he asked for a small loan: 'We do not know if the place will smell rotten.'[50] Joaquim, who apparently really needed the money, spent the next half-hour trying to get Raul to part with an amount as small as the cost of a meal, but to no avail, Raul seeing the terrain as moving towards trouble and thus not wanting to part with his money. Hence, at the same time as instability is becoming routinised, my informants are monitoring it, keeping it in the realm of the ponderable rather than imponderable; what complicates matters, however, is that, at the same time as the crisis becomes a field of emergence of subjectivities (Mbembe 1995: 324), it also becomes a field of emergence of (constructed and constantly shifting) objectivities,[51] as well as both becoming targets of a constant awareness.

Decline and conflicts in Guinea-Bissau are constantly observed and analysed as people follow and monitor their eternal changes and reconfigurations, and shape their actions to fit the given movement. At the same time as meaningfully constructing and strategically, acting in response to the shifting articulations and configurations of instability they act with alertness and doubt towards already interpreted configurations of crisis. What we see is, in other words, a situation of being aware of what has already shaped your awareness making societal turmoil simultaneously the social fabric that shapes interpretation and action and that which is interpreted and acted upon. We can thus position my informants, and not least their actions, in a terrain of anticipated fluidity.

What we have seen till now is that, given the social position of my informants and the political networks controlling the movement of resources, engaging in war, besides providing food and immediate empowerment, also entails a possibility of commencing one's process of social becoming, of attaining adulthood. Equally, we have seen that decline and conflict have become socially routinised and instability has been the defining trait of Guinean society in war or peace. People are often – and I believe this phenomenon can be generalised beyond the Guinean borders – trying to survive and plan their lives while taking into consideration that the terrains they are navigating within are in motion, and therefore act and choose their tactics in relation to this. But to state that my informants see and act through an understanding of their social terrain as in motion is not enough. We need also to illuminate how they see and imagine its movement if we wish to understand their acts and motives during the war.

To understand why my informants chose to navigate the terrain of war we thus need to investigate their perspectives on the general movement of their society as it informs how they seek to act and plot their trajectories. In other words, from looking at the movement of the social terrain in a synchronic perspective – that is focusing on the uncertain terrains in which my informants seek to survive – I shall now shift my attention towards their diachronic perspective of the social terrain. Thus, in the next chapter I shall discuss how the perceived societal movement through time shapes my informants' understanding of their imagined futures and possible movement through time.

Notes

1. Also a social anthropologist, my wife was involved in researching the practice of fostering in Guinea-Bissau.
2. See Flanding (2002) for a further analysis of refuge, refugees and internally displaced persons (IDPs) in relation to the civil war in Bissau.
3. If we compare GDP per capita figures from 1975 to 1998, there is a clear fall in the twenty-year period as well as a further deterioration through to the year 2001 (Human Development Report 2000, 2001).

4. One fundamental change is in the spread of its redistributive ability.
5. In a bureaucratic state, civil servants occupy a position in the state which in Bissau they own until removed by changes in the networks in power.
6. *Findi um utru cadera.*
7. It should be said that doing an ethnography of decline obviously does not entail only being confronted with despair and deterioration. One of the most respectworthy aspects of the people I know in Guinea-Bissau is their strength and ability to be gentle, giving and considerate in a situation where these are the last qualities one expects to have survived.
8. Although it is mostly found in the same location it sometimes moves across the road or into someone's yard, without this having a noticeable effect on its social 'function'.
9. See Eisenstadt (1964), Gable (1995).
10. A *collegason*, as explained earlier, is a peer group built on an age group foundation.
11. On the process of routinising uncertainty and fear, see also Green (1994).
12. On the theory and method of life stories, see, for example, Bourdieu (1988), Agger and Jensen (1990), Roy Schafer (1992), Charlotte Linde (1993).
13. Although what is normal in the quantitative sense has a tendency to also become normal in the qualitative sense, the distinction between the two is nonetheless important. My interlocutors do not see conflict and decline as normal in the sense that this is how it ought to be but rather in the sense that this is how it has shown itself to be.
14. I have been inspired by much of Mbembe's work, as he presents fascinating reflections on the social and cultural consequences of persistent decline. However, I am puzzled as to the position and genesis of his data as he constantly speaks on behalf of 'Africa', though the only African we encounter through much of his work is himself. Are there agents, fieldwork and methodologies in Mbembe's empirical studies, or is Mbembe's work the result of an internal dialogue shaped and emergent from within his own horizon?
15. We must therefore distinguish between routines and habit, as one is consciously created and reflected action and the other unreflective.
16. See Kelman and Hamilton (1989) for an analysis of the routinisation of extreme acts and situations of warfare and persecution.
17. K. Hastrup, personal communication, June 2001.
18. By using the concept of chronicity I do not want to imply that crisis or 'hardship' is imagined as being without finality, but rather that there is an acknowledgement of its lack of clear endings – a certainty of its uncertainty, so to speak.
19. Bhabha, following Walter Benjamin, sees the state of emergency as the normal state of affairs. The observation is forceful in that it underlines the futility of expecting stability and permanence, yet we still have to differentiate between the speed of change that societies move with.
20. See Weber, *Makt og Byråkrati* (1982).
21. Weber obviously talks about the 'routinisation of charismatically based political power' as a process whereby the charismatic movement becomes routinised into the traditional or bureaucratic (ibid.).
22. Weber's work is on a different level of description, working with ideal types rather than lived life, and located in very different social and historical circumstances, dealing specifically with the political existence and transformation of archetypical modes of authority.
23. On further and different usage of the concept, see, for example, Kelman and Hamilton (1989) on crimes of obedience; Leidner (1993) on the routinisation of work tasks; and Green (1994) on fear.

24. Habit designates an unconsciously repeated 'empty' action, while routine is related to expediency.
25. *Si kau na bin chiera fedi.*
26. A point of view that is interestingly close to Bourdieu´s generative structuralism.
27. As Löfgren points out, the concept has mainly been influential in interdisciplinary positioning, demarcating a sphere of analysis focused on the overlooked, marginal and powerless (Löfgren 1990: 10), thereby broadening the scope of anthropology by allowing us to look at social life as more than myths, ceremonies and ritualisation and instead engage analytically in social praxis. Similarly Gullestad has also argued that 'in anthropology, studying everyday life means studying the apparently trivial and the humdrum rather than the solemn and the sacred, the thoughts and words of ordinary people rather than the interpretations of local experts' (Gullestad 1992: 35).

    The concept thus acquires its meaning in juxtaposition with situations such as ceremonies, rituals, war or other similar social phenomena indicating a realm of research that does not overemphasise and generalise 'the exceptional'. It is a perspective which is directly relevant to the study of war and conflict as it enables us to situate acts of violence within their social and cultural terrain instead of isolating them as events.
28. Apologies for the language, but the word *mocca* has only one translation.
29. *So pa pior.*
30. Though not of their agentive potential. Our potential to act cannot be taken away from us but our possibility of action can be reduced or increased.
31. *Na odja dinhiero.*
32. *Sin progresso sin vida garantido.*
33. Importantly, that is, not as an 'autopoietic phenomenon', but rather as a dialogically constructed, loudly debated, negotiated and heterogeneous process.
34. For Bourdieu, the field is a space of competition and struggle defined by its configuration of objective relations between different positions; that is, by being a specific constellation of agents holding and competing for different positions defined by different forms of power (Bourdieu and Wacquant 2001: 84–85). However, whereas these configurations might change as people compete for capital, the positions – the structural grid – seem invested with a foundational status and hardness, constituting the stability of the model.
35. For Bourdieu, this means that we can conceive of agents, within fields, as creating and using strategies to compete for positions. In fact, a given field is defined by competition, as it is demarcated by relations between capital and position and movement between positions.
36. As Brad Shore illuminates in his book *Culture in Mind*, it is the very existence of rules that distinguishes games from play (1996: 105). But an even more elementary difference is, in my view, the fact that 'play' is directed towards exploration whereas 'game' is directed towards competition.
37. This is the process whereby we define habitus as 'history turned into nature' (Bourdieu 1992: 78–79). Here habitus bears remarkable similarities to the concept of sedimentation. In fact the consistent use of habit(us) seems to refer to sediment as both verb and noun, that is, being simultaneously sediment and sedimentation.
38. Vertical competition being a struggle after capital and positions of capital involving strategies, subjugation and domination, as, for example, via symbolic violence.
39. Bourdieu has made a contribution to our understanding of social action that differs from, for example, that of Giddens, by emphasising the concept of field over that of institution, leading us towards a more dynamic picture of praxis via a picture of the quest for capital – of following strategy rather than rules (Harker et al. 1990: 202). However, what we see in and via the position of the field in the game

model (Bourdieu notwithstanding) is that the movements of agents are enacted on a field perceived as stable, which is my point of contestation in relation to the Aguentas in Guinea-Bissau.
40. The underlying stability on which Bourdieu seems to see people as trying to actualise their action is thus very similar to an idea of the everyday. His understanding of the practice of agents relates to the idea of action seemingly mirrored in constancy, privileging reproduction rather than production, order rather than chaos, settled social fields rather than shifting terrains.
41. Susan R. Whyte, personal communication, January 2002.
42. Topography is not only a spatial description but also concerns the specific relationship between elevations and descents. What separates the Guinean socio-political environment from a field is that it is in constant motion in relation both to the space it occupies and to its topography. Where fields are static and earthbound my use of the concept of terrain and environment emphasises motion and opacity.
43. Equally, when my informants do plan into the distant future, it is nearly always in relation to migration and a return to Guinea-Bissau after a period of migration.
44. The point I am trying to make is that in the complex scenario there are more aspects to the actualisation of trajectories than the wishes of the agent or the determinacy of structural possibilities, as both agent and terrain are in motion. The moving agent is not the sole motion/fluidity and the 'objective' positions and relations are not the sole determinant.
45. I must here apologise for a deliberate omission. Ruth Benedict actually states that '*it is hard to be conscious* of the eye through which one looks (1989: 14), a point I have echoed earlier, yet the fact is not whether it is hard or not, but rather that it is necessary. Reflexivity has in this perspective, been the trademark of modern anthropology, logically arising from within a discipline in which one is confronted with an array of descriptions of social perspectives and facts. Yet much the same multitude of encounters with other social realities constitutes the horizon for many youth today, as they are constantly made aware of 'alterities' that challenge their own norms, positions and perspectives.
46. Through the concepts of routinisation and reflexivity, Giddens develops an approach to social structuration that implies that agents continuously recreate the social praxis they enter into and thereby express themselves as agents (1984: 2).
47. Giddens, however, sees certain types of knowledge as more accessible to reflection than others, such as practical knowledge. He differentiates between the unconscious and the discursively conscious, but nonetheless criticises the psychoanalytical understanding of unconscious forces as foundations for social action for their failure to take into account the level of autonomy agents are able to sustain reflexively over their own conduct.
48. On the process of sedimentation see also Berger and Luckmann (1967), Laclau (1990), Lyotard (1991), Ricoeur (1991). An interesting divergence occurs in the present usage of the concept, within a context of instability, as sedimentation is normally thought of in the manner of solidification or petrifaction. In a social-scientific perspective sedimentation thus comes to connote the temporally hardened quality of, for example, social structure, though it is, within a given terrain, constantly in process.
49. *No ka ta sibi si barrulho ka na bin ten.*
50. *No ka sibi si kau na bin chiera fedi.*
51. Most socio-political objectivities being so short-lived in Guinea-Bissau that they seem recognised as only passing truths.

Chapter 8

FROM NEGRITUDE TO INEPTITUDE

ON HORIZONS AND BROKEN IMAGINARIES

> We lean on nature but we are steered by the social imaginary ... Within the folds of a social imaginary, we see ourselves as agents who traverse a social space and inhabit a temporal horizon, entertaining certain beliefs and norms, engage in and make sense of our practices in terms of purpose, timing and appropriateness, and exist among other agents. The social imaginary is something more than an immediate practical understanding of how to do particular things ... It involves a form of understanding that has a wider grasp of our history and social existence. (Goankar 2002: 7, 10)

So far, the book has had a pragmatic edge to it. Seeking to socially situate the actions and motives of my informants, I have accounted for their possibilities of social navigation, and thereby tried to show that meaning does not only reside in discourse but is equally embedded in pragmatic action. Moreover, I have sought to show that conflict and decline have become context in Bissau and that my informants' actions must be seen as part of the underlying series of operations 'through which people weave their existence in incoherence, uncertainty, instability and discontinuity' (Mbembe 1995: 325), as well as part of the way they seek to steer their lives into the future. Whereas in the last chapter I focussed on the characteristics of the Bissauian social terrain from the viewpoint of my informants and their possibilities of moving within it, in this I shall focus on their perceptions of its movement and on how this influences their conceptualisation of their social becoming and navigational possibilities; that is, on their perceived and anticipated movement in relevant time.

That conflict and decline have been routinised in Bissau is not only visible in the immediate as my informants engage the current social terrain, but is also, via narrativisation, inscribed into their spatial and temporal horizons. Conflict and decline have for my informants become part of the Guinean social imaginary (see Castoriadis 1997), of what Taylor has defined as the way 'people "imagine" their social surroundings', or more specifically of 'how we stand in relation to one another, how we got to where we are, [and] how we relate to other groups' (Taylor 2002: 106, 107; see also Taylor 2004).[1] Taylor's definition goes a long way towards making the otherwise elusive concept of the social imaginary analytically useful. Yet, despite the broad strokes it is painted in, the definition lacks an important aspect of the social imaginary, namely its relation to imagined futures, to prospects.[2]

The social imaginary, I hold, can be defined and analysed as the sum of our social horizons. Imaginaries are, within the framework of social navigation, related to perspectives and horizons, where perspectives are the processes of orientation by which we seek to gain an interpretative grasp of our social terrain, and horizons are the demarcations – or limits – of our perspectives, that is, the social terrain of which we have gained an overview. Our horizons are thus defined by four different perspectives: the retrospective, introspective, extrospective and prospective. These four spheres of orientation define our position and possibilities within the world as they inform agents of where they come from, what they have become, where they stand in relation to others and, not least, where and how they can move. All four spheres of orientation are social constructions, created through dialogue, representation and praxis and constituting, in unison, our social imaginaries.[3]

Yet, importantly, our social imaginaries also designate the expected continuations of our horizons (see Nordstrom 1997: Chapters 6–7).[4] The imaginary is related, though not identical, to the Husserlian concept of protention (Husserl 1964: 76) as a pre-perceptive premonition, a logical induction building on social experience and knowledge (Bourdieu 1998: 80). Furthermore, Bourdieu's own notion of *illusio* as 'a feel for the game' is related to the social imaginary as 'a future in the making' meaning that 'one positions oneself not where the ball is but where it will be [and that] one invests oneself not where the profit is, but where it will be' (ibid.: 76–78). What is important is that the social imaginary, as I see it, is not to be equated with the fictitious or with fantasy[5] or to be seen as merely an image or a representation. Rather, the social imaginary builds on our action in and experience of our social terrain and is an integral part of our praxis. It is, I contend, the sphere of our existence which we have not yet experienced but which we nonetheless act towards in anticipation.[6]

Making Sense of Conflict and Decline

What we shall see in the following is that the social imaginary in Bissau has become defined by an unhappy marriage between perspectives, in which the *retrospective* paints a picture of constant societal erosion, unkept promises and abuse of power; the *introspective* locates the decay and regression in the population, the latter seen as constitutive of the state of affairs; and the *extrospective* solidifies the merging of the two former points of view by contra-identification, together creating a *prospect* of societal dysfunctionality as the expected social terrain and its development. Decline and conflict have been routinised in interpretation to such an extent that they have come to colour my informants' ideas of their shared social becoming, of social possibilities and ultimately of their social identity as Guineans: a routinisation of instability in perspectives and social interpretation, which is no clearer than in the constructions of histories.

Retrospection and Historical Trajectories

The way we, as social categories, inscribe ourselves in the world is dialectically related to our social horizons and thus our conceptualisation and demarcation of our physical and social terrains and our possibilities of action within them. Historical memory and the perceived congruent movement through time of individual and group is part of what shapes the agent's sense of what is normal and possible, leading us, as social scientists, away from focusing on the factuality of history and towards investigating its actuality;[7] it is exactly towards the construction and consequences of my informants' understanding of their collective flow through time that I turn my attention.

Collective histories – that is, constructions of contingent relations between an identified community and the past and the present – are politically salient narratives because of their construction of the relation between social entity, becoming and terrain.[8] It is via our perceived movement through time that we anchor social entities and socio-political orders within a given terrain. By being selective constructions of the past, interpreted from the present and thus inseparable from contemporary influences, needs and requirements, histories are political resources in the construction and articulation of rights and demands. They connect communities to a given place through primordial ties, through a logic of integral becoming between terrain and social entity, thereby either sanctioning or delegitimising allocations of authority and resources. Even when historical interpretations are culturally, socially and/or politically institutionalised as (for example) histories of state, group or lineage, they are, despite their institutional armour, often in the centre of conflicts because they legitimise or delegitimise present configurations of power. It is via this retrospective construction of primordiality that collective histories are inseparably related to politics as they come to constitute a foundation for claims to resources and authority and subsequently become mythico-histories (see Mallki 1995; Daniel 1996) lodged in ideology and drawn into the future. Agents, groups, communities or societies will, in other words, legitimise or delegitimise their position in a given field via history, that is, via myths of creation that anchor the community and its relation to the social and physical terrain securely in the past and thereby legitimise their present position and/or delegitimise that of others.

As we shall see, this accurately describes the situation in Guinea-Bissau although with one important difference: historical narratives are often integral parts of conflicts as they are used to discursively defend and legitimise an existing advantageous position or a claim to an advantageous position and yet in Bissau histories somehow seem directed less towards claims to privileged social positions than towards explaining underprivilege. They are, in other words, used to make sense of the general hardness of life and to get an idea of what to expect of the unstable social terrain.

Negritude and Inversionary Discourse

As shown earlier, my informants use adjectives such as 'broken' and 'tired' when describing the city they live in.[9] That this refers to actual destruction and decline seems evident, but it equally connotes an inertness of social movement. The city has become, from the perspective of my interlocutors, a worn-out entity that has lost its dynamics. That Bissau is 'tired' thus means that the city is seen as no longer moving down a defined or anticipated road to progress but has been halted in its movement and left fighting an uphill struggle instead.[10]

As collective social trajectories histories are not just limited to points in the past or demarcations in the present, but constitute the 'roads' or 'rivers' that communities see themselves cutting and having cut through time.[11] What is happening in Bissau is that history, as a trajectory of social space, is seen as having lost its forward orientation and directionality to the point of collapsing. This is not to say that Guinean history is no longer directed towards the future or that it does not inform people's understandings of their possible futures. Yet my interlocutors' understandings of their collective history no longer includes a defined telos that the Guinean society is seen as moving towards, but is instead directed towards a generalised near future. It is no longer towards specific points in the future – be it a socialist state of equality or a capitalist state of affluence – but nonetheless encompasses an idea of their common, future predicament. From a Bissauian perspective, the dream of progress has, as such, gone out of reach and is made increasingly inaccessible by the incessant decline, conflict and turmoil. However, we need not go far back in time to find a very different collective history being promulgated in Bissau. In fact, Bissau has within the last thirty years gone through a number of official collective historical interpretations, each encompassing very different social positions, interpretations of social becoming and future scenarios, which I describe in subsequent sections.

Colonialism and Social Darwinism

As institutionalised collective histories, the first one we encounter in Bissau, is a European idea of civilisation and the process of becoming civilised set in the colonial period: namely that of social Darwinism. Fundamentally an evolutionist paradigm, social Darwinism placed different coexisting races, and their civilisatory manifestations at different levels of the evolutionary process in a movement from savagery to (European-style) civilisation.[12] Different social bodies and expressions, located along a parameter of techno-rationality, could be placed on an evolutionary line moving from hunter-gatherer communities to societies and states, with the complexity of the social 'organism' determining its position on the evolutionary ladder (see Banton 1977). Social Darwinism was thus the creation of a teleology of progress, which meant that Africans had the misfortune of setting off along the unidirectional line of progress at a later stage than their colonisers and therefore of having 'reached' a level of societal development below that of the latter, thereby legitimising European colonial praxis. Through the fusion of social Darwinism and ethnocentrism, colonialism came to be seen as a modernising praxis, a developmental movement by which the 'indigenous' peoples were, paradoxically, granted the opportunity to acquire the level of civilisation of the West through forced exploitation, assimilation and, ultimately, acceptance of their inferiority, making it possible, as Chabal states, for colonisation to become a civilising mission:[13]

> In social and cultural terms, the Africans were deemed to be near the bottom of the evolutionary scale. In terms of economic development, they were thought to occupy a slot a shade above hunting and gathering societies but well below feudal ones. For this reason, the colonial 'mission' was justified and underpinned by a belief in the simple causality of development which European imperial rule would undoubtedly create and sustain. (Chabal 1996: 48)

The social Darwinist view of the world thus made it possible to represent exploitation and coercion as positive social factors that civilised the uncivilised; or, in Fanon's harsher phrasing, commenting on the colonisers representation of their dominance as: 'a mother who unceasingly restrains her fundamentally perverse offspring from managing to commit suicide and from free rein to its evil instincts' (Fanon 1990: 169–70).

Evolutionism and social Darwinism were integral narratives to the shaping of colonialism as well as to the legitimation of colonial praxis. The historical understanding was institutionalised and propagated through the state apparatus, state praxis and the educational system, taught to the lucky few who attended school in Portuguese Guiné, as the country was then called. However, people do not accept their exploitation passively and the social Darwinist understanding of difference, inseparably connected to the actual physical exploitation and denigration of the colonised, was to be the point of contestation which led to the construction of an inversionary interpretation of history and which was to fuel the coming waves of liberation movements. It was, in other words, the discursive construction of African social inferiority which was first to come under attack by the Negritudinists and which was to be the point of departure for the very ideology of Negritude (Kemedjio 1998).

From Negritude to Cabralian Marxism

Having thus far looked at such disheartening subjects as decline, war and the vanquished, Negritude, as an influential liberation teleology in West Africa, ought to be an uplifting addition to the book. Aimé Césairé coined the term in 1933 (Vaillant 1990: 244) in an attempt to construct and unfold a 'black point of view' and to assert the positive racial character of the *nègre* (Lambert 1993: 254, 256). Working within the French literary tradition, Césaire's ambition was to rework the myth of African societal and intellectual inferiority towards a positive repositioning of blacks within the history of civilisation.[14] Césaire's work was to inspire a range of young francophone intellectuals,[15] and his friendship with the Senegalese academic and politician Senghor was to be influential in further proliferating the idea of Negritude.[16]

Senghor was to give the concept a central place in the liberation of Senegal from the French.[17] In fact, he was to build his liberation claims around a Negritudinist liberation narrative positioning 'Africans' positively in the movement of the world and delegitimising European colonisation and the contemporary inclusion of Senegal into French West Africa. The Negritude movement was in this manner able to challenge the legitimacy of the global hegemony of the West by attacking the dominant historical construction of the contemporary world order. In Apter's words: 'Insofar as a dominant history has erased their's, [sic] [the history of the marginalised], what is recounted is an anti-history, a history obliterated by victors, the retrieval of which is itself a way of legitimating violence. The retrieving of revelatory past events provides authenticity and a certain resonance to present ones' (Apter 1997: 17).

The concept of Negritude brought to the fore a social imaginary developed in the shadows of the general dissatisfaction towards colonial domination. It brought forth an alternative history of civilisation, providing different identificatory possibilities and prospects from those of the earlier social Darwinism. The dawn of Negritude was an agentive moment, contesting the dominant social Darwinist teleology, social hierarchies and political configurations.[18] For West Africa this was, in other words, to be the period where the colonised started to bare their own historicities, to claim equal humanity *vis-à-vis* that of their colonisers, and to frame the imaginaries for future liberation struggles (see Fanon 1990; Schmidt and Schröder 2001).

On African Departures

Seeing that the understandings of socio-racial differences were based on a difference of civilisatory points of departure, most of the liberation theorists, both first and second wave, worked through a reinterpretation of the sociocultural history premised on the 'complexity' of the colonised societies prior to colonisation. By retracing and revalorising their 'beginnings', the liberation movements were able to re-plot their history and to reposition the indigenous population and their place in the world.

Yet Negritude was to become more than merely a historical construction of positive racial characteristics, as it was theoretically developed in, for example, Senghorian Negritude into a *Weltanschauung* and *Neger-Sein* (Senghor 1972: 82, 84), that is, an African perspective of the world and being-in-the-world.[19] Negritude, as the forerunner of later liberation ideologies and movements, was thus simultaneously, the creation of being, voice and view, enabling the creation of a history of civilisations, positively constructing and positioning African civilisation (formerly an oxymoron) alongside the world's other imagined civilisations as distinct and yet equal.[20] 'African' was to become a civilisatory label in its own right and of equal worth, to be understood on its own terms and via its own history.

From the First- to the Second-generation Liberationists

The African liberationists generally identified themselves as socialists, identifying colonialism (rightly, I would contend) as a manifestation of capitalism. However, despite being proclaimed socialists, the Negritudinists seem in retrospect to have been more focused on ethnology and archaeology than historical materialism and scientific Marxism. Termed 'populist socialism' or 'African socialism', the ideology was open to interpretation and symbolically anchored in 'traditional' African cultural values, political systems and social organisation, emphasising 'Africanness' over historical materialism (Keller 1987: 1–3). However, as the ideological landscape hardened at the end of the 1960s with the bitterly fought second-wave liberation wars, the first-generation 'African socialists' were followed by the more dogmatic or, depending on one's point of view, scientific Afro-Marxist movements, such as PAIGC in Guinea-Bissau and Cape Verde, FRELIMO in Mozambique and MPLA in Angola.[21] Common to both first- and second-generation liberationists was the fact that they questioned the earlier notions of the racial and societal inferiority of the colonised people and, via a symbolic reversal, repositioned and revalued what they saw as the 'indigenous' populations and their progress through time.[22] They were, however, to do this in very different ways.[23]

If we take Senghor and Cabral as examples of first- and second-generation liberationists, we see that they both symbolically anchor and legitimate their ideologies in history. For both, precolonial society was seen as having already embarked on an autonomous line of civilisation prior to the period of conquest, which was subsequently to be thwarted by European colonisation (McCulloch 1983: 113, 115). Thus both periods of liberation theorisation took their point of departure in the 'African' past, identifying former civilisations, drawing connections into the present,[24] and building their ideologies on what they identified as positive African social and cultural traits. However, for the second wave of liberationists, such as Cabral, African civilisation was not something that had to be (re)discovered, but rather an existing socio-structurally defined reality, leading a marginal existence under the repressive colonial societal form (Cabral 1973: 40–44).[25] In other words, where the Senghorian view of African Civilisation was anchored in the ethnological and archaeological analyses of African cultures and in the universe of legends and metaphysicality (Kemedjio 1998: 193), Cabral took instead an approach that focused on social structure rather than on myths and symbols, finding African civilisations in the egalitarian, acephalous societies of the continent.[26] Rather than focusing on the essential African being, the second-generation liberationists, such as Cabral, were more concerned with the precolonial and indigenous society's position within a Marxist perspective of societal evolution. Where the Negritudinists emphasise the cultural richness of the past, refuting the idea of Africans as savages, the second-generation liberationists emphasise the development of African civilisation on a socio-structural level, positioning it closer to the socialist organisation of society than that of their European colonisers and identifying it as a more evolved societal state. Ironically, however, both directions of the rediscovery of black civilisation based their ideology in Western science, in ethnology and Marxism.[27]

Yet what both the first- and second-generation liberation movements have in common is the clear use of the past and historical revisions to designate corrective futures. Both the first and second generation liberationists are exemplary in showing the function of history and historical constructions in a political context, that is, of putting history to political use,[28] and, in incorporating the struggle for independence within a Marxist teleology, the 'new' history of 'the Guineans' was able to become positively intertwined within modernity's grand narrative of progress.[29]

Cabralian Marxism and a Return to the Source

In this theory of societal development and history of civilisation, African cultures were no longer viewed as lagging behind their European counterparts, as they so evidently were in social Darwinism,[30] but were instead positioned ahead of them, with colonialism being identified as the regressive agent that had spoiled their societal trajectory and was keeping them from realising their future. Cabral, the leader of the dominant Guinean liberation movement, the PAIGC, thus followed a Negritudinist point of departure, stating that colonisation had halted the historical development of the 'indigenous' civilisation, rendering it dormant, but not destroying it (Cabral 1972: 4). Combining ideas of civilisatory revival with a Marxist political philosophy and teleology, the precolonial sociocultural scenario could, in Cabral's perspective, be revived or reintroduced from the more rural areas, where the colonial power, due to lack of interest and influence, had not succeeded in radically changing it (Cabral 1973: 43):

> Already we are seeing in our own case how the various peoples of Guinea are finding cooperation increasingly possible and useful as they free themselves from attitudes of tribal strife – attitudes that were encouraged, directly or indirectly by colonial rule and its consequences. My own point of view is that this process of integration had in fact begun before the Portuguese conquest, and that the imposition of colonial rule stopped it. (Cabral in Lyon 1980: 157)

As such, it was the Portuguese conquest and its subsequent imposition of the colonial system of production, hierarchy and divisions that halted the process of integration whereby the masses were beginning to unite into an egalitarian social form. Colonisation had, according to Cabral, paralysed the progressive horizontal, non-hierarchical social structure of the peoples of Guinea-Bissau and changed it towards a regressive, hierarchical social structure intrinsic to the colonising European societies. The Guinean goal of liberation, according to Cabral, was therefore to be able to revitalise their original, horizontal social structure and thus to realign the modes of production appropriate to 'the evolution of the liberated people' within the 'general framework of history' (Cabral 1973: 43, 56). It was a step towards the classless society of the past, represented by the acephalous Balanta social structure,[31] and as soon as the masses united in battle against colonialism and attained their freedom,[32] an independent Marxist state would be able to lead the Guineans back to their advanced position within the line of progress described in historical materialism. Only socialism would be able to take Guinea-Bissau forwards – or *leba Guiné pa diante*, as they say in Creole, the increasingly hollow rallying call of every government and politician since independence.

From Socialism to Capitalism

As in many formerly socialist countries, the Marxist teleology was institutionalised into and propagated by the one-party state as soon as the country gained independence. Guinean youth were taught the doctrine of inevitable progress of the Guinean society towards socialism and eventually communism for the best part of twenty years, as the Cabralian-Marxist version of Guinean progress was incorporated into school curricula via the subject *Formação Militante*.[33] But, despite its official institutionalisation and the scientific packaging of the PAIGC ideology within historical materialism, progress did not materialise with the flow of time. As Mendy states:

> The imperative to exercise effective control over society and the economy [in Guinea-Bissau] led to new rulers to be guided by what they constantly referred to as 'realism' and 'pragmatism'. Consequently, deviations from the radical agenda were inevitable, resulting in, among other things, accelerated institutional erosion, more factional struggles, greater political instability and increasing pressure for the democratisation of the political space ... Obssessed [sic] with exercising effective control over youth, labour, women and society in general, an over-zealous national security force intimidated and silenced almost all dissenting voices ... This situation reinforced disillusionment with independence and, in the context of a deteriorating economic crisis, withdrawal from participation in politics and the economy. (Mendy 1999: 22)

Thus, according to Mendy the schism between the official ideology of progress and the actual experience of repression and regression led to disillusionment. However, Bissau was not the only socialist country to be caught in such a profound discrepancy between the political ideal and the real, as obvious from the worldwide collapse of communist regimes in the late 1980s. And so, due to the changing climate within the global political situation,[34] as the political movements changed the constellation of beneficiaries as well as the scientific status of Marxism and historical materialism, the regime in Bissau was forced to start making the structural changes necessary for the alliance between free market forces and multiparty democracy if it was to attract aid from sources other than formerly socialist countries.

With the fall of the Wall and of communist ideology, Guinea-Bissau was once again in the middle of not only an ideological but also a teleological shift. The end of the cold war and the delegitimisation of historical materialism entailed an official revision of the perceived historical trajectory of the Guineans. The downfall of the communist block and the emerging global disrepute of Marxist politics and theories left Guineans with the ruins of a positive historical anchorage and constructive social imaginary, as well as with a political elite that for twenty years had accumulated resources (material and symbolic) under the canopy of a centralised one-party state and patrimonial networks. As seen in numerous formerly socialist states, the consequences of Marxist policy were an extreme centralisation of state resources, corruption and factionalism. However, it was with the delegitimisation of the socialist teleology that the poverty and (mis)dynamics of the Guinean society were thrown in relief as more than a transitory setback in the progress towards communism. It was with the fall of the Wall and the subsequent demonisation of Marxism that it became unquestionably clear that Guinea-Bissau had not followed the road towards the construction of socialism, but, rather, had led itself towards extreme poverty and the increasing marginalisation of large parts of the population.

Though communism and capitalism alike essentially work through an idea of unidirectional progress, they do so in very different ways. In the Marxist teleology, there is a specific end goal, that is, a socialist/communist society. The story of historical materialism is in other words finalistic.[35] In capitalist teleology, on the contrary, the end goal is left undecided, seeing that it is constructed and perceived as a constant movement towards further enrichment, making the enrichment in question unspecified continuous growth in wealth. In other words, with the shift from Marxism to capitalism, and the concomitant cold embrace of structural adjustment programmes and its celebration of free market forces,[36] the underlying movement towards progress changed from a perceived movement towards a final ideal state of societal harmony, towards an open-ended idea of non-finite economic enrichment. Yet this equally entailed a re-emergence of the former social Darwinistic evolutionistic parameter – often euphemised as development – with the slight difference that a society's level of progress is currently crudely measured by its level of wealth and placed within a scheme of differentiation of societal evolution holding rich and poor as its outer points. The Guineans went, in other words, from being able to classify themselves as progressive to being reclassified as regressive, an interpretative shift which is consequential for their social identity and hence their understanding of their social position and possibilities of social movement.

Negritude Gone Sour

In a Marxist teleology the Guineans were seen as occupying a privileged historical position. The acephalous social organisation of the Balantas was generalised as representative of the Senegambians, and thus of 'the Guineans', and its non-hierarchical configurations of power were seen as closer to communism than to capitalistic modes of production. Guinea-Bissau was thus positioned positively within the general flow of history.

In a capitalist teleology, however, 'progress' is seen as defined by enrichment, and enrichment as possible through the free movement of capital, goods and people. After it became clear that the socialist means to a better society had failed, the capitalist road to progress was the remaining hope for the increasingly impoverished country. As Guinea-Bissau entered into capitalism and a market economy, abandoning its currency to become part of the ECOWAS – enabling the free movement of people and goods, implementing the prescribed structural adjustment programmes and officially changing its political system to multiparty democracy – the expectations were that progress would materialise. However, due to a multitude of factors,[37] the economic situation did not improve, leaving Guineans not only struggling to make ends meet, but with a massive discrepancy between their actual situation and their officially projected historical trajectory – in an acute state of anomie, striving to make sense of their apparent inability to lead themselves to progress.

The move from colonialism to socialism had failed and yet the move from socialism to capitalism had shown itself to be equally negative, as the normative end goal of enrichment was intact but the script was somehow ineffectual in a Guinean context. According to a capitalist perception of differences between states levels of wealth are normative indicators, as advanced is directly related to affluent and underdeveloped to poor.[38] The capitalist perspective thus often disregards the history and contingency of poverty and creates evolutionist differentiations on economic foundations. Within this perspective Guinea-Bissau is no longer poor because it is undesirably placed within a global capitalist system; it is poor because it somehow fails to appropriate the benefits of the system, because it is poorly developed. Still having a dominant economy of '*naturalia*', suffering the consequences of deflation because of the lack of economic impetus in the country, and with 88 per cent of the population surviving on less than one dollar a day,[39] the turn towards capitalism implied a return of Guinea-Bissau to the position of the dunce of progress. It has, in other words, gone from Negritude back to ineptitude.

In short, it would seem that the fall of the Marxist teleology, embedded in the liberation theory of Cabral, has to a large degree – and this seems to be a general phenomenon in many of the former socialist countries – left the Guineans with an unpleasant view of their collective past and future. It has left them with broken imaginaries. Where it was formerly possible to gain direction and meaning in fighting for a better society of equality and liberty, Guinea-Bissau has with the ideological shift, the structural adjustment programme and the entrance into ECOWAS, been placed politically, economically and teleologically on the road to growth within the world of capitalist societies, and yet is apparently unable to grab onto progress itself.

So, despite the fact that the world 'after the fall of the Wall' is depicted as one where there is but one force of progress, capitalism (Hinkelammert 1993: 106), and where all supposedly have the possibility of roaring down the road of 'growth', none of this seems to be happening in Guinea-Bissau. It is clear for my informants, as for most people in Bissau, that progress does occur, that new advances, despite occasional crises and cut backs, are constantly being made in one area or another and yet it is equally clear that it for some reason evades Guinea-Bissau. In fact, trying to muscle in on the capitalist road to prosperity as prescribed by the World Bank by engaging in over ten years of structural adjustment programmes,[40] has mainly led to the social moratorium of youth, persistent instability and increasing urban impoverishment and retrenchment (see Lourenço-Lindell 1996: 163; Aguilar and Stenman 1997: 78; Ferguson 1999).[41]

The Death of Progress

The broken communist and capitalist imaginaries have had profoundly negative effects on my interlocutors' understandings of the social possibilities and movement of Guinean subjects and society. In general, the historical understanding of the Guinean movement through time is seen as having been profoundly negative, and the societal understanding of many Guineans bear similarities to the state of 'abjection' described by Ferguson in relation to the experience of prolonged decline in the Zambian copper belt (see Ferguson 1999). My interlocutors are, however, starting to see themselves not only as the 'inhabitants' of a history of decline but also as its 'bearers' and, instead of having been bowed down, dejected and rejected by external forces they seem to have re-hierarchised and repositioned themselves as inferior, internalising their precarious social, political and economic position as an essential trait located in their bodies rather than stemming from their disadvantaged economic and political localisation in relation to global capitalism.

'Progress has died,' people say in Bissau, seemingly having lost faith in the possibility of entering into a positive societal and historical movement. The anomie, the demise of Marxism and the negative identificatory consequences of the drift towards free market capitalism have in unison entailed a growing disbelief in the promise, or even possibility, of development as a local Guinean phenomenon. Taking the former intensity of the institutionalisation of the Marxist doctrine and the current intensity and global propagation and proliferation of capitalism into consideration and coupling it with the present context of decline, crisis and war, we acquire a picture where Bissau has, within the lifetime of my informants, been ripe with positive political ideals but void of positive political praxis, making painfully clear the discrepancy between historical representation of one's society's dynamics and the actual experience of its mis-dynamics (Hastrup 1992). In fact, my informants epitomise the demise of positive imaginaries. Many of them, being old enough to have attended school in the period of transition in the late 1980s and early 1990s,[42] have been schooled in both the Marxist and the capitalist versions of progress, and been disappointed by both, including by the present situation, characterised by a lack of congruence between the experience of everyday life and the official rhetoric proclaiming imminent progress as usual (Mbembe 1995: 324). Such a discrepancy obviously does not go unnoticed and is constantly reflected and commented upon by my interlocutors. In the following quote I was asking Pam about his recollection of *Formação Militante*, the teaching of the Marxist teleology:

> *What would they tell you?*
> They told you things about the liberation war. They told you that they would build the land. That they would take Guinea-Bissau forwards. I thought ... when I was a child I thought, like: When I grow up it will be delicious. Bissau will be delicious, I will have a delicious life. But nothing is delicious. They have not built anything, nothing.

The quote testifies to Pam's view on progress as being merely a broken promise or worn-out rhetoric. Furthermore, the phrase 'I thought, like: When I grow up ...' is an exact articulation of a broken imaginary. Returning to the educational system, and the interpretation of collective history communicated within it, the change in ideology but lack of positive change is also commented on by Fransisco:

> It [*Formação Militante*] changed when I was in the 7th grade. Afterwards it changed to *Educação Social*. In *Educação Social* they taught you how to be respectable in society, how to comport yourself in relation to the state ... about democracy ... But in *Formação Militante* you would talk about the war, when it started, and why it started. They would talk about the past ... [about] what happened during the war of independence.
> *What would they say?*
> They said, like, that they started the war of independence because whites were treating the blacks poorly. They said that the people of Guinea-Bissau are united and that when we are united we can take Guinea-Bissau forwards. If we unite we will build the land ... but they did not build it ... we thought they would! They were sons of the land.[43] If a son of the land tells you he will build the land you really think that he will build it, is it not so? If I go to my father's house and say that I will build it[44] you will believe me. That is why people went to [fight in the liberation] war, so that we could go forward.

The quote shows the teleological dimension of *Formação Militante*, as it sought to the move towards a better society as envisioned by Marx and Engels, and applied by Cabral, drawing a line from the war of liberation into the future better society. 'Building the land' and 'going forwards' are obvious metaphors for progress.

What clearly emerges from the above quotes, however, is the fact that progress was not achieved, and that what has been experienced instead is anomie. Both quotes, thus, focus squarely on promises or possibilities of better futures that have not materialised. Furthermore, although seeing that Guinea-Bissau is not going forward, the transition from Marxism to capitalism is not evaluated in relation to societal or ideological changes but to the continuation of the lack of honouring ideologically imagined futures. The discrepancy between the ideal and the real has thus meant that the ideological imaginaries have crumbled, leaving behind empty promises and a growing disbelief in progress. The point is also made by Arno as he comments on the former school lessons on progress:

> They said that it is a green and rich land, that we still do not know what riches Guinea-Bissau has, that there will be development, and that after school I will have a future ... for our land, for our children. But even the teachers who taught us don't have jobs now. There are some that have succeeded but most have not. And for us, we finished school but there is no

work. You see? Since I was born I have not seen development, you see? During the Portuguese there was electricity, oil, factories. We had an automobile plant. It is like ... all the things we had then have all died.

In other words, the time elapsed since independence has not been one of historical realisation, as anticipated by Cabral, or of the inevitable economic progress more recently promised by the neo-liberalists, but rather of historical disintegration, in which both the anchorage and the expected future for the Guineans have changed for the worse, so much so that according to Arno the colonial period, the time of the Portuguese, stands not as a time of oppression, denigration and enslavement, but stability, order and plenty. My informants seem, as Bourdieu harshly phrases it, to be in a situation where 'the best they can expect from the future is the return to the old order' (1984: 111).

It would seem that the ideas of both historical materialism and perpetual capitalist progress are too removed from my informants' experiences of their individual and collective movement through time to gain dominance, meaning instead that history is increasingly being seen as an externally induced and uncontrollable succession of changes (see Hastrup 1992) and leading my informants to shed the last traces of the belief in the inevitability of modernisation (Marxist as well as capitalist) (Chabal 1996: 48). Yet their crumbled imaginaries have not been replaced by a localised idea of historical progress towards a defined normative state. Instead, Bissau is seen as somehow abandoned. As progress has shown itself to be too elusive for people to believe in the ability of Guinea-Bissau to move towards it, local history has come to a dead end of decline and conflict, resulting in the social trajectory of my informants, as Guineans, losing its directionality. Instead of collective history being a river or a road, it has in Bissau become an amputee imparting only pathology. Taking a Massumi quote out of context, one could say that: 'Time is no longer a progression to and from privileged points – beginnings, climaxes, and ends – that give a priori order and a depth of personal or historical meaning to the course of things' (Massumi 1997: 746).

What makes this process of decline even worse is that it is perceived as internally localised and generated. In other words, progress is evident in the constant developments in the West within the fields of medicine, information technology, transportation and so on, and yet it evades Bissau, making every innovation and advancement around them proof of the fact that progress applies to the rest of the world but somehow not to them. Guinea-Bissau is seen as stuck while the rest of the world is moving forwards; the belief in national societal progress has withered, though the belief in global progress has not. Global development is a process that Guinea-Bissau is – temporarily – placed outside of, with no date or workable scripts of action for its re-entry. This reveals the saturation of the routinisation of decline and conflict with feelings of crisis, signifying 'stagnation, decline, and decay, the opposite of correct and desirable progress' (Lindquist 1996: 58).

The consequences of this process are catastrophic. In relation to youth in Bissau, everyday history fits into a continuity – not a linearity – of abuse, corruption and war, so that my informants do not see political violence as unusual or illegitimate but rather as an ever present political modality integral to themselves as agents and constantly made manifest in the movement of their social terrain.

Absurd Nostalgia and Nostalgia for the Absurd

I was sitting in the courtyard of Vitór's uncle's house with Vitór, Tony and Jon. It was late afternoon, the best part of the day, and we were sitting, comfortably out of reach of the sun, discussing politics. I had initially started the discussion by asking why Guinea-Bissau was so worn-out,[45] why things were going so bad. Jon thought a bit, and then said: 'Whites want us to fight, they sell arms so we can go to war. When Africa unites, excuse me, we will not need you any more ... Whites bring war. It is the whites who brought hardship to Africa.'[46] He looked down, apparently embarrassed by having criticised people of my 'colour'. I protested vaguely at being implicated saying that I had never brought war, but my mumbling was interrupted by Tony, who yelled at Jon: 'What! What was here before the Portuguese? Nothing! There was nothing before the Portuguese came. People had nothing, not even clothes ... What were people wearing when the Portuguese came?' he asked and answered his own question, 'Nothing, nothing, there was nothing here,' ending with: 'better during the Portuguese.'[47] Jon stayed quiet, not pursuing the line of argument, Vitór was as usual uninterested, and I was as usual somewhere between confusion and trying to memorise what had been said while grabbing for my notebook.

It did not strike me until later that what I had witnessed was a clash of collective histories. It was a disagreement of historicity, Negritude facing ineptitude; the Cabralian Marxist perspective of colonialism as the destructive agent opposing a (re)current understanding of African societal 'retardedness'; an interpretative disagreement with the poles of the collective's movement through time being under debate. However, much as I had expected to encounter the historical interpretation expressed by Jon, of the present trouble originating in colonialism or imperialism, I was not expecting to hear a historical understanding depicting colonialism in positive terms. Tony's statement portrays the social category of Guineans as societally inept, pointing towards a historical understanding I had thought belonged to former colonisers rather than to a young Guinean. Yet it is only one among a great many similar remarks about the positive aspects of colonisation that I was to hear during my fifteen months of fieldwork. Many among my informants saw the colonial period as a time of plenty and, not least, of order, in comparison to the postcolonial period. *Mindjor na tempo di Tugas* is the expression used, meaning literally 'better during the Portuguese'; yet, obviously, what was better was not the inequalities, conferred inferiority and mistreatment addressed by the Marxist liberation movement, but rather the relative stability, wealth and social order. In other words, we are currently seeing a very different 'return to the source' from what was envisioned by Cabral. The Portuguese presence in Guinean history has completed an interpretative loop, and, with Fanon probably turning in his grave, is once again being seen as having been a civilising influence.

Double Inversion

Instead of seeing the rich, precolonial culture and society evoked by both the Negritudinists and Cabral as both the anchorage and future which were destroyed by Portuguese colonialism, we are now seeing a longing for the prosperity and stability of colonial times (rather than for colonial times themselves), a refutation of the historical narrative of liberation in favour of a historical narrative that re-emphasises the perceived incompatibility between Guinea-Bissau and development. Thus societal progress came and is perceived as necessarily coming from the outside. It is an understanding that is not unique to my informants but is rather a perspective on social difference that is constantly communicated, implicitly or explicitly, through media, organisations and institutions, a communication my informants are very much aware of as they relate the African continent to war, atrocities, starvation and AIDS, and the West to aid, development, power and progress. *Mindjor na tempo di Tugas*, better during the Portuguese, makes sense because Whites are seen, from Bissau, to have 'greater mastery over the world than Blacks' (Jackson 1998: 114). They are seen as being better able to take advantage of its productive and constructive forces, and at controlling the destructive. Moreover, the idea of progress as external to Africa is not only persistent in Guinea-Bissau, but is, although academically discredited, still communicated via Western representations of African social-political mis-dynamics and Afro-pessimism (Okumo 2001, see also Duffield 1998: 76; Ferguson 1999: 17). The experience of growing decline and dilapidation combined with a broad range of media communication, local as well as French and Portuguese television and radio, about social and political problems, has led to a historical reinterpretation marking a return to an almost social Darwinist understanding.

The following quote is from a conversation I had with Arno, who despite being terribly patriotic, was equally terribly pessimistic about his country's future:

> *What was here before the Portuguese?*
> The society was backward ... it was not developed. But we had this deep Creole, pure ... people lived in villages. They had nothing.
> *Did they tell you about this in school?*
> At school they only told us about colonisation. The Portuguese came and they showed us that we could work better. Then Bissau was called Osau.[48] We didn't say Bissau ... Osau. They sold them land in Bissau and the Portuguese continued their work. But then they came with arms, and we didn't know arms well so they tricked us. But then they started showing people how to work again.
> *So, if the Portuguese had not come, how would it have been?*
> It was no good if the Portuguese had not come. We had to have colonisation, but it is not good to use force. If the Portuguese had not come to Guinea-Bissau, if they had not come to Africa, it would have been a delay for all people. If people join together they will grow, because there are those differences between those who are more ... those who are better. So you have to join together.

Arno clearly sees Guinean history as part of a larger evolutionary scheme from which Guinea-Bissau has been left out from the onset. The quote clearly shows an evolutionary, social Darwinist understanding at work, in which the idea of the 'less able' having to acquire progress from the 'more able' is the epitome of 'colonialism as a civilising mission'. Creole *puru* – a pure, original Creole – is a reference to a pre-Portuguese language,[49] but, as the quote shows, this precolonial Guinea-Bissau does not resemble that envisioned by Cabral, but rather a period of unenlightenment and backwardness from which Guinea-Bissau crossed into the civilised world through being colonised.

Let my informant Fransisco sum up for me. Sitting on my porch one afternoon, talking of the war, Fransisco said: 'In Guinea-Bissau it is like this, people start wars so we can go forwards.' I asked: 'Well, do you go forward?' He started laughing. Like many other Guineans, Fransisco laughs when something is sad, miserable or disturbing.[50] Often our conversations will cross straight into the realm of the absurd because of his inability to stop laughing as he addresses a subject that he finds particularly disturbing. Talking of war, the death of his kin who were Aguentas or the general poverty of his society, Fransisco will be drying his eyes from incessant giggling, and yet he always regains control, centres himself and gives a serious answer. This time he replied:

> Like ... After the War of Independence there was Luís Cabral ... When he entered power he started killing people. He killed people a lot. [He killed] students – more than Nino – students. Even if you were abroad, when you entered the airport they would take you and kill you ... But he also worked. He built more than Nino. But people started hating him because he killed people a lot. So they said: 'Well, we have to make another war' and like Luís Cabral is Capo-Verdean, like Amilcar Cabral ... he [Amilcar Cabral] was born in Bafata ... he [Luís Cabral] was also born here, but he is not from here and people thought: Nino, that one is really, really a son of the land, purely, purely ...[51] He is Papel. So they started a war and when Nino entered power people thought that he would build it ... So when he entered power everyone was happy ... but then he started dressing deliciously, many cars, women, and after him, Kumba Yala and ... It is like, this is what we have till now ... only dirty bellies.[52]

Introspection and Embodied Instability

As shown, what we are seeing in Bissau is a routinisation of social decline and conflict, which has been so prevalent that it has come to influence my informants' anticipation of the movement of their social terrain and of their own possibilities of movement. What I shall now focus on, however, is how decline and conflict – via their centrality in the perceived 'Guinean' process of becoming – become part of how the individual agent is able to envision his possibilities of action. It is a movement from the retrospective to the introspective, which was made clear to me by my informants' comments on the outbreak of fighting in November 2000, and later emphasised as I sought to further explore their interpretations of the conflict and warfare. The relation between decline and introspection has forged a perspective in which the evasiveness of progress has become internally rather than externally derived: that is, lacking progress, decline and turmoil are seen not as induced but as immanent – tied to Guinea-Bissau as a social entity and to my interlocutors as Guineans, as those who constitute society.

War and the Bleakness of Blackness

On the evening of the 22nd of November war broke out again. Tension had been building for what seemed like ages, and a general feeling of nervousness and apprehension had become pronounced. During the afternoon, Arno, Olivio and Dó were at the Parliament of the Poor eagerly debating possible scenarios, outcomes and navigations of the oncoming turmoil. Arno said: 'If anything happens today it will be during the night; the hyena only eats at night,' the hyena representing the soldiers. Olivio, who did not seem to have quite recovered from the last war, grabbed my arms and said: 'If war breaks out again you must stay here and experience it.'[53] I told him that if it was a skirmish, I would not leave, but if it broke out and it was nasty,[54] I would most certainly try to get out of Guinea-Bissau. Olivio laughed, slightly hysterically, and said: 'Do you think a boat will come for you? Who will send a boat for you? You cannot get out, you will die, we will all die,' he said, still laughing. Annoyed at his ridicule I asked him if he would not leave if he could. He replied: 'No, I am not going anywhere. Blacks are made for this ... We are made for war, for hardship.' He took a step out on the pavement, puffed up his chest, grinned and repeated, 'We are made for hardship.'

Shortly after our conversation – as night fell – the hyenas did indeed come out. I was sitting at Baiana,[55] waiting for the Champions League game between Leeds and Real Madrid to start, when the first shots were fired close by,[56] a few of the bullets drawing lines of light over the sky. Half the people at the cafe got up and started running in different directions. Yet for some reason the other half of the customers just stayed seated, calmly finishing their drinks in absurd contrast. The man next to me, an officer, on whose conversation I had been eavesdropping with great interest, since he had been talking about Asumané Mané retaking control of the military, said angrily, as the first shots rang out: 'That is the problem, blacks do not respect blacks – whites maybe but other blacks, never!' He finished his coffee, got up, said, 'Work calls' and proceeded to walk slowly towards the barracks at Amura or Marinha, apparently in no real hurry. I moved away from the window. Confused by the unevenness of reactions and not knowing which option to pick – run or pretend I was not worried – I settled for illogical logic. I went home and put on my boots, not wanting to have to make a run for it in sandals, packed the things necessary for my work in a small backpack, and went back and saw the game. Real Madrid won 2–0, unfortunately.

The next morning I woke at 5.45 to what I presume were the hollow thumps of mortar grenades or RPGs,[57] followed by explosions, the staccato cracks of automatic weapons and the equally aggressive morning call of our neighbour's battle-hardened rooster. Not wanting to be visible through the window, I crawled across the floor, put on my clothes, went downstairs and spent the rest of the morning with the Guinean family in whose house I was renting a room. The main fighting was quickly over and after a few days the troops loyal to the president announced their imminent victory, and so Bissau calmed down, with only occasional gunfire being heard after that.[58]

A few days after there was a full crowd at the Parliament of the Poor. None of the regulars had opted to follow the endless lines of people leaving the city, but a few had cleaned the *palettas* (storm drains) so immaculately that they could take cover without getting their clothes dirty. The Parliamentarians were talking loudly, debating the events of the last couple of days. Luízinho, especially, who generally gets aggressive when the topic falls on politics or war, was debating in a deafening mode, yelling: 'I don't care! My father is not there [in the military], my uncle is not there. Let them kill each other, let them all kill each other.' He then calmed down a bit, turned his back and said, from somewhere between distaste and resignation: '*Pretos pa!*'[59] meaning, 'Blacks!' It was said in an aggressive whisper, something between a curse and an insult.

Being caught in the skirmish opened a space of resonance as a point of empathic understanding (Wikan 1992), so important in ethnographic fieldwork, enabling me to gain a glimpse of the uncertainty that warfare carries with it.[60] Yet even more strikingly the event emphasised the apparent interconnectedness, from a Bissauian point of view, between societal dysfunctionality, war and 'blackness', as exemplified in the above quotes. However, blackness is not a universally negative social category. As in the above quotes, the negative aspect of blackness is situated in political contexts, and seen as a characteristic of the interrelationship between powerful and less powerful blacks. Blackness in a political context thus connotes a lack of respect, defined as a transgression of the rules of transaction. In this fashion, 'lack of respect' is generally mentioned as the main cause for the outbreak of the war in 1998, as well as in connection with the last war, and is related to greed, deception or other transgressions of the economies of affection, obligation or patrimonialism.[61]

This understanding became further clarified as I was talking to one of my neighbours, André. Like most of my informants, André is caught in the social moratorium of youth. He is unemployed, living off the food and money he can scrounge from his family. André was talking about the situation of youth, about his life chances and the difficulty he has in getting a job and making ends meet, and about the social strain of being a dependant at the age of 26. When I asked why the situation was as it was, André said:

> Blacks do not respect each other. Blacks are like this, they all want to be full but they do not want others to be full. They want everything for themselves. If I am unemployed and this person [he points towards his neighbour's house] has a job, and I ask for a job at the place where he works, he will go and tell the boss that I am lazy and [that] I am no good. But it is not true. He will tell him this, just so I cannot get the job.
> *But why does he not want you to get the job?*
> So, that he can have everything to himself. So that if I have no money I have to ask him; if I have no food I have to ask him, and he will say, 'Ohh

you. You always ask for things, give me this, give me this ... Take this then (he makes a throwing motion towards the ground).' Blacks are like this!

At first glance, the quote borders on banal jealousy. However, what distinguishes it from jealousy is that the reference to André's neighbour was exemplary rather than factual. André was giving an example of the relationship between blacks rather than describing an actual occurrence and thus communicating what he saw as the general connection between exchange, reciprocity, status and authority. In this manner, the quote equally clearly shows how the context of power is able to enter the picture as the economy of affection and obligation is played out. All of my informants entered into quite elaborate and expanded obligations of helping each other and sharing to the point that it is difficult to pass people eating without them inviting you to partake in their meal by calling '*bin no kume*', 'come we eat', no matter how little food they seem to have. Whatever food, money or other goods there are are most often shared – through networks or within families or *collegasons*, contradicting the general idea of greed and lack of respect for one's fellow (Black) man. Hence, what André shows us is the underlying factor that makes it meaningful to talk about the negative aspects of Blackness, namely politics, greed and power. 'Negative blackness' is related to the degrading actions of powerful individuals in asymmetric social relationships as well as to competition for power, and so 'blackness' is not often used in explaining interaction between friends, colleagues or family, but is articulated in relation to destruction or overt expressions of power.

Yet, despite being related to the realm of politics, this negative concept of blackness is nonetheless seen as an immanent personality trait of Blacks underlying acts of greed, aggression and violence. That is, negative blackness has gained centrality in relation to my informants' praxis as it has come to define the expected mode of action within political contexts. The destruction, greed and decline associated with blackness is thus seen as constantly lurking beneath the surface, as 'pervasive internal failings' (Briggs 2001: 683), constantly materialising as decline, turmoil and conflict.

Black Politics: From a Sweet Mouth to a Dirty Belly

Blackness in this perspective becomes the defined essence of Guinean political man and thus traceable through Guinean history. It becomes the perceived spoiler turning Negritude sour and making the Guinean flow through time one of continuous decline and conflict. The destructive and conflictual aspect of the Guinean political scene has come to be seen as the very essence of Guinean politics. To understand this process better, we need to illuminate what this essence implies and in doing that, probing a bit further into the negative meanings of blackness, we see that its negative traits become manifest in situations of power. The negative understanding of blackness is thus a clearly situated discourse, applicable in the context of political distribution of resources and often articulated through the twin concepts of *sabi boca* (sweet mouth) and *suso barriga* (dirty belly), or, in Septimo's words:

> Blacks cannot rule,[62] they cannot rule. In the land of the whites,[63] if you are in power you might eat a little, but you will build as well, but here ... people do not think for tomorrow. They just want to be full, all of them, just eat.
> *How do they eat ... what do they do so they can eat?*
> They just eat. Look at Kumba Yala, what does he do? He just eats. He said that he would build the land, but he does not do anything, sweet mouth but only a dirty belly.

In fact, Kumba Yala, the great narrator of death and destruction, who – after the conversation reported above – has engaged in an almost monthly media-transmitted outburst threatening all-out warfare and mass murder,[64] the last of which being the threat of an invasion of The Gambia, has become an example of the outrageous contrast between the invoking of progress as ideological 'sweet talk' and the corruption, greed and abuse of power that characterises political praxis. In other words, he has come to typify the political summoning of the narrative and symbolism of progress to gain power and the subsequent pursuit of the politics of the belly (Bayart 1993). Kumba Yala is seen as the incarnation of 'sweet mouth and dirty belly', full of empty promises and dishonest politics.

The concepts of a sweet mouth and a dirty belly are central concerns for my informants as they seek to forge relationships, unearth social possibilities and increase their life chances. They are seen to be the general characteristics of the terrain my informants seek to navigate.

Sweet Mouth

> *What do you have to do to be a sweet mouth?*
> If you talk sweetly ... If you want something and you talk sweetly and you succeed in getting it you have a sweet mouth.
> *Can anyone have a sweet mouth?*
> Yes.
> *Can children have a sweet mouth?*
> Yes, but ... if a child has a sweet mouth it is not the same thing. You can have a sweet mouth if you like to eat ... If you like things that are delicious, a lot, but it is not the same.

> *So who has a sweet mouth, in the other sense of the word?*
> What?
> *Who can have a sweet mouth?*
> Someone who is clever. Someone who knows how to convince people.

Thus *sabi boca*, sweet mouth, is, in itself, not a negative term. In its broadest sense it characterises the verbal manipulation of people towards personal gain. 'Sweet mouth is when someone speaks deliciously because he wants something in his hand,' Arno said, continuing that men could be sweet mouths when wanting a woman, but that afterwards the woman would remember that this one is only sweet mouth, that is, he promises a lot that he does not live up to. In a non-political context sweet mouth is closely related to *dubriagem*, to tactics. It is the act of a *dubriadur*, of getting what you need without having or requiring the power to enforce your will.

In a political context, however, the concept gains a whole array of negative connotations as it primarily describes the empty promise of wanting to work towards progress. Sweet mouth is the first step towards the politics of consumption as it is closely related to rhetoric qua its proximity to deception and lying. It is, as rhetoric, the manipulation of the interface between truth and fiction within a perceived sphere of possibility. Politically 'sweet mouth' is a manipulation of imaginaries, of what is seen as possible or desirable, and as with political rhetoric it gains its impetus from being deemed possible; the 'sweet mouthness' of evoking progress, as such, shows the two sides of progress as both fact and lack, that is, an objective process in the world, as well as one that Guinea-Bissau somehow fails to partake in. But we can pinpoint the arena in which sweet mouth becomes thoroughly negative and that is when it is connected to 'dirty belly'.

Dirty Belly

That the concept of sweet mouth is similar to the concept of rhetoric becomes even further emphasised by its relation to its twin, *suso barriga*, 'dirty belly'. Dirty belly, when evoked within the context of politics, signifies greed or, more specifically, the act of not sharing or distributing resources along the prescribed relations and obligations. The relationship between the two concepts is primarily one in which a sweet mouth is seen as the means to misappropriating resources: that is, as the means to a dirty belly.

However, as with sweet mouth, the meaning of dirty belly extends further than the sphere of politics, and this time even beyond Guinea-Bissau itself. As Bayart shows:

The terminology of the politics of the belly is not confined to Cameroon. Nigerians talk of 'sharing the national cake'. In East Africa, a faction is called 'Kula' ('eating' in Swahili). When an observer was concerned by the 'appetite' of Guinea's ministers, the head of government replied, 'Let them get on with stuffing themselves. They'll have time to think about it afterwards.' (Bayart 1993: xviii)

In Bayart's analysis 'the politics of the belly' refers to the individual appropriation of resources, and applies to the process of accumulation, the construction of spaces for social mobilisation becoming an aspect of the strategy of demarcating ones own political space. The politics of the belly is thus the politics of intimate liaisons, of corpulence (as a sign of power), nepotism and the location of concrete or invisible forces (ibid.).

In Bissau all the above meanings are embedded within the concept, but dirty belly is not only a phenomenon that occurs within the political context of the state. It refers not only to the enrichment of the patrimonial pinnacle but also to a disregard for the norms of redistribution. The concept is used to designate the act of a mother who hides food from her extended family in order to feed it to her own children better; when friends actively try to deny each other a given resource; or, in general, when resources are not distributed along the socially prescribed channels or networks. Used outside the realm of state politics, dirty belly seems to span the entire length of the distribution and allocation of resources, from the economy of affection and obligation to that of patrimonialism, as I presume it also is in Cameroon if one looks a bit deeper. Having a dirty belly can thus be applied to those who only look after their own interests and those of their immediate connections without attending to their community obligations. Accordingly, it is seen as an overt act of individualism within a collective system, emphasising both the importance of sharing and the perceived selfishness of politicians.

However, whereas sweet mouth and dirty belly are seen as an unacceptable and socially punishable praxis within near or primary social relationships, they seem to be expected – although still negatively evaluated – within bureaucracies or state structures. As Vitór told me when talking about Guinean politicians and the state of affairs under the current president: 'It's sweet mouth. It is only sweet mouth. Here every politician says that he wants to build the land, to take Guinea-Bissau forwards, but it is just sweet mouth, it is only because they want to sit comfortably, so that they can eat.' 'To eat' is the process leading to dirty belly, and the interrelationship is that of making empty promises about progress while in reality pursuing political power as a means of personal gain and enrichment. In the sphere of politics sweet mouth is intimately tied to dirty belly via the concept of 'eating,' or rather 'devouring', implying the consumption of others' resources; thus people are seen as 'eating' money in Bissau when they are using or accumulating money that does not belong to them, that is supposed to be spent for the public good or in a differently socially prescribed manner in the given relationship.

Eating Your Way from 'Sweet' to 'Dirty'

Despite the negative evaluation of the process leading from a sweet mouth to a dirty belly, it is perceived as the general characteristic of Guineans in positions of power: it epitomises the Guinean political process, the persistent, damaging flow of Guinean politics impeding societal progress,[65] as exemplified in one of my conversations with Septimo at the Parliament of the Poor:

> *How do you see the future, will things get better or worse? What do you think?*
> The politicians they say we will do this and this for the people, but it is just sweet mouth, sweet mouth but dirty belly ... Politicians in this country have only dirty belly, only! Like this we will not go forward ... This country has no future, only misery.[66]

Septimo was generally a pessimist. When the crowd at the Parliament were trying to predict if and when there was going to be trouble again he foresaw troubles soonest and seemed chronically depressed 'at living in shit', as he called it. The Parliament of the Poor, being, amongst other things, a site of political discussions usually spilling messily into argument, would often be engaged in debates about what some politician had said and what promises were being made, but, no matter what the promise, Septimo's contribution would normally be *'sabi boca, sabi boca so'*, meaning 'rhetoric, just rhetoric'. One of the most remarkable aspects of the conceptual duality of sweet mouth and dirty belly is, as such, the general perception of the phrase as a valid and dominant political comment in relation to almost any political discussions concerning the state of the country.

Fish, Hyenas, Blacks and the Politics of Greed

Moving from a sweet mouth to a dirty belly is, in other words, seen as inevitable when Guineans get close to positions of power. Or, as Vitór said, when we were talking about the present political turmoil and the country's present and former presidents:

> They are all fish from the same net[67] ... you say fish from the same net, you see? If I throw[68] Nino from power and put Kumba Yala it is the same thing,

you see. If I throw Kumba Yala from power and I put Helder Vaz, it is the same thing; they are all fish from the same net.

Sabi boca and *suso barriga* are thus such ingrained aspects of Guinean politics that they come to constitute the broad strokes of the anticipated future political scenario, just as they are seen to define the general characteristics of the political past, personified by a procession of politicians who have led the country towards steeper decline. In fact, sweet mouths and dirty bellies are seen as at the heart of 'political man'. 'Keep your eyes on the boss so he doesn't sell the country. If we are distracted he will sell the country' was the refrain of the biggest hit song in Guinea-Bissau in 2001, its popularity pointing towards the perceived magnitude of the problem.

The inseparability of power, greed and selfishness implied in the move from *sabi boca* to *suso barriga* is also readily found in popular sayings and proverbs. 'Better a hyena who is full than one who is hungry'[69] is a popular, critical comment on the changes of government within the last few years. The hyena signifies political agents focused on greed, selfishness and brute power and constantly transgressing the norms of redistribution of resources. When I asked Vitór what people meant by it, he said: 'If a person is full he will not each as much', that is, one who is already wealthy is not likely to be as corrupt as the person who is poor. The proverb is a direct comment on the government of Kumba Yala, who was, in the eyes of my interlocutors, supposedly both poor and a drunk before he entered power by way of *sabi boca* and tribal votes, and therefore is seen as stealing with abandon, being excessively hungry for wealth. Or, as Jorge replied when, having been gone for a year, I asked what changes there had been since I left:

> Me, I have not seen any changes yet – not anything – only eat, eat money. Here, there is nothing only eat-eat money and lie-lie.[70] For a long time there has been nothing [here]. This country, truth is not here. Now we are waiting to see if Cadoco will win [the PAIGC election]. Someone poor must not rule here. In all of Africa, poor people cannot rule, it must be someone who is full ... We are tired, really tired.[71]

The poor person referred to here is Kumba Yala. Cadoco, on the other hand, is an example of the hyena who is full. Being a local, wealthy entrepreneur, he is expected to be accustomed to wealth and have the necessary economic foundation not to clean out the state coffer. 'This is the problem,' my informant Dario said, 'the people in power were poor, they ate it all ... Better if Cadoco has power, he will only eat a little.'[72]

Intrinsic Corrosion

However, where the quotes indicate that the temptations of political power are seen as harder to resist for a person who is not used to wealth, they also indicate that they will all steal, that 'eating' towards a dirty belly is an unavoidable fact of Guinean politics. The metaphors of both fish and hyena point our attention to the fact that people expect politicians to have dirty bellies. Moreover not only greed but also destruction and violence are seen as immanent traits of the Guinean subject that become actualised on entering a political context. Africa's prolonged economic, political and social instability is thus directly related to a perceived African – or black – political modality, as can be seen in the following conversation I had with Jaimé:

> *Why do you think that there is so much war in Guinea-Bissau?*
> A black is just a black.
> *A black is just a black ... What is this?*
> You know? A black is just a black. Maybe it is better if the whites build the land, you see? Blacks only want for themselves.

What the quote further shows is a racialisation of political ineptitude. People make sense of the trouble within Guinean society not by inscribing problematic events or processes in teleology but by incorporating and localising them in bodies through analogy and introspection. It is an interpretative movement from the retrospective to the introspective, whereby destructive politics are positioned in the agent rather than in the society or the regional or global. As the social body is no longer seen to be moving independently towards a goal, but is rather seen as having lost its directionality, politics has become removed from ideology and subsequently personalised. As such, the present societal dysfunctionality is positioned in the bodies of the country's citizens as destructive agents: they are the corporal manifestations of aggression and corruption. And so, local regression and destruction become identified as the primary 'social' boundary separating rich societies from poor, peaceful from war-prone and stable from unstable – yet what turns a black into 'just a black' is politics.

Preto i preto so, a black is just a black, is thus a crystallisation or condensation of a discourse on 'black politics' so prevalent that it no longer needs to be unpacked, but can instead be contained in a single tautological maxim (Gilliam 1998, 2004). It is a discursive phrase related to an idea of Guinean, and African, politics so deeply embedded in a context of persistent localised decline that it has come to characterise the flow of postcolonial Guinean politics. The dictatorships, brutality and corruption are seen as part of the process of Guinean becoming and being, ingrained simultaneously in the subject and in the general movement of the Guinean society; as Fransisco once said: 'A black is just a black because it is inside ... Here and here [he touches the skin on his arm and forehead]. Like whites are just whites ... You are born with it, naturally.'[73]

Extrospection: Colour Lines and Geno-globality

I was hanging out with Carlos, a bright young man who before I had left Bissau had spoken of completing secondary school when things got a bit better, his studies having been interrupted by the war. When I came back, I wanted to hear how he was getting on, and one of the first things I asked was if he had started school again. He replied:

> No! They set the price too high, 15,700 FCFA. I have not got that, so I just said [to myself] Leave it. Maybe if they lower the prices ... But they are not even paying the teachers, so they are on strike. People have paid 15,700 but the schools are closed. Africa! (*Africa pa!*)
> *Africa! Why Africa!?*
> No ... it is not all of Africa ... South Africa is almost Europe, and Morocco and Capo Verde are part of the European Union.
> *No they are not.*
> But White Africa.[74] It is almost like Europe ... Tunisia, Libya.
> *Why is there a difference?*
> Because they do not want war, they do not steal.[75] They want to build the land, that is why.

Carlos's quote is an example of an interpretative process whereby Guinean-defined blackness is exploded into the world. It is an expansion of the negative understanding of blackness in relation to Guinean society and to the political situation and movements in Africa in general. Africa, in this manner, becomes an imagined (racial) community (see Anderson 1993; Brigs 1994: 57–59) of shared societal experience and predicament, of a common life and societal situation of war-proneness, corruption and decay qua the specific qualities of bodies. The demarcation between black and white Africa separates negative from positive societal formations and behaviour. In other words, next to, and even in the middle of, areas of guarded and fenced-off richness and plenty there exist enclaves of blackness characterised by decay and destruction (see Delaney 2000), which through the global dissemination of information, are visible from Guinea-Bissau. The overlapping of colour and socio-economic standing thus becomes guidelines in the construction of an understanding of the inability of blacks to prosper, even in systems where others do.[76]

Hence, what we see, through paying attention to the meaning and dominance of the proverb *preto i preto so*, is a discursive phrase that is directly related to a social imaginary in which is embodied a biologised, internal enemy against whom society cannot defend itself as it is the very matter upon which it is built (see Shanklin 1998). As Septimo remarked when I asked him how he saw the present situation of his country:

> Guinea-Bissau changes from shit to shit. Before a war shit after a war shit ... It is because we are black, even if you are born in Europe or America, it does not matter, you still do the same things [as a black], still only misbehaviour.[77] It is the same mentality.
> *But why do all blacks have the same mentality?*
> Because they are black.
> *But are they born with this mentality?*
> Yes, it is because they are black. Black! [he touches his arm, to show me his colour].

Blacks are seen as the destructive agents even in what is normally defined as *terra brancu*, the land of the whites.[78] In other words, as 'racialised' societal dysfunctionality, 'blackness' follows the people rather than the continental plates, and is not confinable to specific locations, but has instead become global in scope, moving us from Afro-pessimism to 'Negro'-pessimism: that is, no longer pertaining to sub-Saharan Africa as a geographical location but to 'blacks' as a perceived socio-racial category. The global overlap between pigmentation and poverty, due to transatlantic slavery, exploitation, unequal distribution of wealth and migration, is coalesced into an immanence of negative social traits. Furthermore, the constant flow of bad news related to war, corruption and the African continent, along with the knowledge of 'black' slums, crime, drugs and poverty in Europe and North and South America stands in dire contrast to portrayals of societal wealth and tranquillity in these same places, which are invariably 'white' expressions. The only 'black' expressions of wealth are marred by their connection to extreme corruption, *sabi boca* and *suso barriga*, all validating the notion of the uncivilised 'black' in contrast to 'white' progress. 'A black is just a black' is thus built and builds on a knowledge and understanding of the global disadvantage of peoples of colour, on contra-identification, supporting the presumption of the societal dysfunctionality of blacks, located in the very grain of the personae, in their skin, in their head and in their *gines*, as I heard it called in Bissau, as well as in the world as they see it. Negative blackness, however, does not build on a specific knowledge of genetics. It might build on a notion that there exists a dominant line of explanation which links pathological states to generic bodily causes. What it primarily builds on is an understanding of not genetics but of genus and genesis, which etymologically refer to not only 'creation', 'generation' and 'coming into being' but also to 'race' and 'kind'. In other words, my interlocutors are not informed by knowledge of the specifics of theories of biomedical genetics but by knowledge of the possible explanation of social difference and acts via ingrained bodily determinants. It is an idea of the embodied genesis of social acts and societal states coupled with a general knowledge of the incredibly sad socio-economic and racial make-up of the world.

Geno-global Identities

What we are seeing in the present Bissau is thus the internalisation of societal dysfunctionality, via a process of racialisation,[79] as well as an externalisation of blackness via a process of contra-identification. Reference to blackness in a political context tells a story of 'nano-societal' dysfunctionality, of destruction and dysfunctionality being engrained in every part of the continuum from the smallest grain of the individual body to that of the largest entity, society itself. It is, moreover, seen as inescapable. People cannot escape their blackness. So, despite my personal view that the global overlap between pigmentation and poverty is contingent upon the history of rampant, porous capitalism, Septimo and more or less all of my other informants see it instead as proof of the societal ineptitude that is somehow ingrained in their bodies.

However, what looks like the reinstatement of a colonial, social Darwinist understanding of racial difference may, in fact, be an exceptionally contemporary phenomenon, because negative blackness is not just drawn from social Darwinist racism but also built on a perception of differences amongst people in a global perspective, enhanced by both the speed and spread of global communication processes and an increasing localisation of societal, social and individual traits and, not least, pathologies, within bodies and genes. So, although not having a specific knowledge of genetics, but only knowledge of the increasing dominance of social explanations that work through embodiment, I believe the Guinean construction of negative blackness to be a sign of what is an increasingly dominant ordering of the world and process of identity formation. Negative blackness is an example of how our identities, through the dual influence of genetics and globality within our current version of modernity, are simultaneously imploded into the body by way of introspection and exploded into the world by way of extrospection.

Negative blackness thus points our attention to and draws its interpretative dominance from an increasing interpretative mutuality between the largest and the smallest of our constituent matter, making it logically consistent to locate global difference in physical difference. The absurd global correlation between levels of wealth and pigmentation comes, in this perspective, to testify to the apparent validity of race as a generator of socio-economic differentiation. In other words, the growing knowledge we have of each other's lives combined with an increasing awareness of the interpretative dominance of seeing the cause of behaviour as located in the grain of bodies has made it possible to construct an explanation of the global social position of blacks by way of which, for example, Septimo is able to locate the present decay of the Guinean society simultaneously in the world and in his body.

Yet, as said, I do not believe that this interpretative process is mimesis, but instead that the dialectics of orientation points to a primary aspect of current identity formation that reaches beyond Guinea-Bissau,[80] as it is related to the two dominant processes affecting our horizons in our current version of modernity, namely genetics and globalisation. What we are witnessing (excuse the neologism) is a contemporary identity formation, a 'geno-global' production of identity, as the simultaneousness of movement in the construction of identities implodes social processes and formations into race/genes and explodes the socially determining aspects of our race/genes into the world. It is this simultaneous process of locating 'blackness', as a genetic principle as well as in its global socio-economic manifestation, that makes possible my interlocutors' negatively perceived historical constitution and dire future prospects.

Prospects: Bringing Histories into the Future

From a prospective point of view my informants do not have many possibilities to envision a positive future for Guinea-Bissau or themselves. Yet their perspectives on the movement of their social terrain have shown us that they clearly have a prospect – although not a positive one – *preto i preto so*, a black is just a black, being the discursive phrase that hints at its dominance. At the present conjuncture, the prospective possibility within my interlocutors' social imaginary is one of continuing decline, conflict and instability. Yet, in order to demonstrate this, I need, almost in conclusion, to make a theoretical detour: to go on a brief excursion into the field of narratives so as to show the way that the retrospective, introspective and extrospective merge to form future scenarios.

From Post to Pre Facto

'Trouble is the engine of narrative,' Jerome Bruner has stated (1996: 99). Bruner is not alone in his observation, as various authors have noted the close relationship between troublesome events and narrative.[81] Equally, the link between traumatic experiences and the construction and narration of histories in the shape of both individual and collective narratives has been noted by Bradd Shore in his book *Culture in Mind*:

> The role of narrative in meaning construction becomes especially clear following anomalous or otherwise disturbing events. An earthquake strikes, a group of people witness a shooting, a baseball player makes an 'impossible' catch to save a game, or an umpire makes an incomprehensible call to lose one. Any such unexpected event is, for normal people, relatively indigestible until it is processed by talk into a palatable form. Following such disturbing events, people generally become talkative. They tell and retell the story until the events are gradually domesticated into one or more coherent and shared narratives that circulate among the community of sufferers. The meanings are emergent in the narrative process. (Shore 1996: 58)

However, I believe we need to take the relationship between narratives and violence further than the purely retrospective, as narratives play an equally important part in our prospective endeavours because they come to inform our action by drawing the past into the future (Bruner 1987: 32). Taking narratives into the future implies that we should boost our awareness of the prospective or projective aspects of narrative. The stories we tell are not only important in relation to how we can interpret change as experienced but also for how we anticipate change and construct modes of action pertaining to the imagined future. Our narrative constructions are directly related to our social or political imaginaries (ibid.). The narrative drawing of a trajectory from past to future not only touches upon the political past and present but also on the future, as the way we see the past is an 'important element in social creativity because it is part of the information which people use in making decisions which affect the future' (Davis 1992: 25). Thus historical narratives flow into the future as they come to inform the way we act in relation to a given emergent situation, as noted by Schmidt and Schröder:

> violence produces unique experiences that are culturally mediated and stored in society's collective memory. Their representation forms an important resource for the perception and legitimation of future violence ... There exists no more important resource for an ideology of violence than the representation of past violence, of former deaths, former loss and former suffering. (Schröder and Schmidt 2001: 8)

Narratives thus begin to acquire centrality before the fighting starts, that is, before the event as well as after the event. Focusing on the position narrative has before the event thus illuminates how the different narrative temporalities merge to form social imaginaries that are essential to grasp in order to make sense of action. What we see in these situations is the interaction between different temporal aspects of collective narratives bringing history into the future, allowing us to position and give the act meaning before its actualisation.[82] To paraphrase the initial quote by Bruner, we seem thus to have reached a point where we can say that not only does trouble become the engine of narrative but narrative equally becomes the engine of trouble.

A narrative analysis of conflict or violence can, in this manner, tell us a great deal about how people cope with and make sense of violence. But without focusing on the relation between narrative, imaginaries and action they will tell us very little about why people turn to violence in the first place and thus very little about the cultural and social dynamics of war and warfare. Thus it seems essential that we start putting narrative to more use than as a mere tool for *post facto* cognition. Narration, including the narrative construction of history, is an active phenomenon throughout the complete social process of conflict, that is, both *pre* and *post facto*, and the former leads us to the social imaginary, connecting moral principle and interest (Apter 1997: 2–3). Thus, before, during and after conflict, histories create future scenarios: they create prospects.

Importantly, however, history in this perspective does not create charters for action, as some authors would have it (see Malinowski 1971; Feldman 1991; Malkii 1995), but rather the anticipated social movement of a horizon. Thus they do not necessarily create scripts, but invariably possible terrains and terrains of possibilities. History and the social imaginary do not bring about mechanical action, which would be granting too much influence to both stories and their creators, but create perception and interpretation of the oncoming. Working with conflict or warfare it is therefore essential that we look further than merely towards narratives as cognitive tools that enter the stage when a given situation is experienced as troublesome or abnormal, as described in the earlier quote by Shore. Rather, I believe, we should train our gaze on correlation between narratives and the social imaginary, in order to be able to fully work with the complex temporality of plots and narratives.

A Return to Navigation

Being constantly presented with the ruins of what was, as well as with the unpromising prospects of what will be, and having no external powers in which to locate the current or oncoming misery, positive prospects do not come easily for my informants. What we see happening in Guinea-Bissau is an interpretative process by which my informants position and make sense of the instability of their society by locating it in their social becoming, and their social becoming within their bodies, resulting in their imaginary – that which lies beyond their immediate horizons but which they nonetheless act in relation to – itself becoming defined by decline and instability.

As my informants seek to navigate their lives through an unstable social terrain, they do so with an eye towards the immediate and towards the oncoming. What choices one makes in the present are thus related to how one sees ones coming into being in the social terrain, how one is able to see this movement of the social terrain and how one imagines the movement of one's position in it. I spent quite a bit of time asking my informants what could be done to improve things in Bissau. I usually received two responses, the first being an emphasis on the lack of possible change, and the second that the people in power (*no garandis*) should work better. When subsequently asking what would make them work better, the answer was either a shrug of the shoulders, *preto i preto so* (a black is just a black), or *Africa-pa* (Africa!); that is, until the opposition arranged a demonstration in October 2000. A few days before the planned demonstration, I asked Dó if he thought that a lot of people would come, seeing that the political atmosphere in Bissau at this point in time was bad and rapidly deteriorating. He replied with a smile:

> Guineans do not want marches, they just want war. Africans do not want this. They just wait until the situation explodes and then they all go ... Just look at the time during the war ... there were demonstrations,[83] but no one went, no one. But if there is a demonstration against the Arabs or against the Nigerians then everybody will demonstrate to tear their asses apart.

Dó's answer emphasises the perceived lack of non-violent options in African political action, that is, the tendency towards violent action stemming from the perceived inherent destructiveness of Africans. The demonstration was arranged as planned and Dó was right, the attendance could have been greater. Yet what Do did not emphasise is the perceived futility of demonstrations in the context of the fear of retaliation where people do not dare commit themselves to political expression.[84] Politics in Guinea-Bissau is seen as inherently violent and violence as an expected political modality. In this way, my informants see their fields of possibilities as constituted by conflict and its radicalisation into warfare – as the defined past, the felt present and the expected future. In seeking to generate and consolidate social ties in order to enhance one's life chances and escape the social moratorium of youth, conflict engagement can thus be a pragmatic response to a perceived possibility. However, as we shall see, the relationship between agent, terrain, societal movement and navigational possibilities that makes mobilisation into war a salient and pragmatic action is paradoxically also what facilitates demobilisation and reintegration. Within the context of conflict and turmoil, the essentialisation of destruction thus has a positive side to it, which is what I shall now, almost in conclusion, turn my attention to.

Notes

1. The social imaginary is, according to Taylor, different from theory, as it is unlimited and indefinite in nature, carried in images, stories and legends instead of theoretical terms. Furthermore, unlike theories, social imaginaries are shared by large groups rather than by small minorities.
2. Without which the concept merely covers such already theorised concepts as culture and habitus.
3. In reading through the social-scientific work on the subject of 'the imaginary', one becomes struck by the fact that by far the majority of the books and articles in which the concepts of 'the imaginary' or 'imagination' figure in the title in fact do not deal with the concept at all. In relation to the number of times it has figured in the title of social-scientific articles, dissertations and books, 'the imaginary' or 'imagination' seems to be an empty addition, serving to direct our attention to a non-defined possibility of orientation or to that which is not real, i.e. the fictitious or fantastic.
4. Nordstrom, in an enlightening book, also makes use of the imaginary to gain a meaningful perspective on violence, warfare and prospects by using the concept to show how Mozambicans creatively rebuild their world and identities after conflict (Nordstrom 1997). The imaginary is effective in processes of 'self-creation' and 'world-building', as it mediates between the given and the possible (ibid.: 202, Chapter 7, nn. 1–2).
5. Fantasy, being an emancipation from the limits of the world, is, as I see it, in direct contrast to the social imaginary, as the latter pertains to possible changes or movements of the world. There is no exact future world as such but an anticipation and expectation of the movement of the terrain and a world in constant unfolding.
6. The social imaginary is a space of possibilities rather than a defined scenario or a project of action (see Schutz and Luckmann 1995: 22–23, 26), towards a specific telos. There is no 'goal orientation' in the social imaginary but only agents tentatively plotting trajectories and seeking to actualise tactics and strategy. The social imaginary is thus not a fixity, like a temporal prolongation of the present or stable field, but a constantly changing, configured and reconfigured space of possibility.
7. The debate on historical factuality is in itself controversial, as it is integrally tied to legitimations of political projects and allocations of authority. In relation to Western historiography, this authorlessness is highly institutionalised (Tonkin 1995). We presume to be writing objective history via the scientific method. Since the Enlightenment, the official construction of history has been seen as a process whereby *res gestae* (the act) becomes *res factae* (the fact) and via the historiograph-

ical methodology, surpasses *res factae* (fiction). Writing history can in this perspective be defined as an interpretative and yet objective event, objectivity again arising out of the understanding of historiographic praxis as essentially authorless, the historical facts being somehow ingrained in events, waiting to be found and interpretatively related to other such 'facts' (Feldman 1991: 229). The institutionalised, academic historiographical methodology is in this perspective what guarantees the avoidance of polemic history and yet if we look at the writing of collective histories they are often, despite their academic armour, clearly directed towards and put to social use. Being tied closely to the Enlightenment, the dominant Western historiographical tradition is intricately related to a belief in progress, state and nation and Western collective histories have been constructed predominantly from the point of view of nations looking out towards their role in the history of civilisations and inwards towards the history of the amalgamation of difference or that of dominant 'ethnic' groups (e)merging as nations. The institutionalisation of historiography has meant that collective histories that were not written with the nation as their primary point of departure have constituted opposing interpretations to that of the 'dominant' historical representation of nations and have often been portrayed as being in conflict with the historiographical demands defined and institutionalised by the state. These histories are, first of all, often constructed in the margins of – or outside – the institutions defined by the state to be the loci of interpretative legitimacy, as well as often making use of historical 'data' that are not deemed factual, or ultimately creating relations between unrelated entities, making them teleological historical interpretations or myth, both concepts indicating falsity. From an anthropological point of view the way people use histories to demarcate communities and lay claim to resources is however far more interesting than 'objective factuality', which, taking the last decade of epistemological development into consideration, is in itself equally interesting to deconstruct but difficult to assert. As such, the difference between academically generated collective histories and myth lies not in the interpreters objective stance or view, but in its political position and the evidentialily of its underlying teleology, that is, the obviousness with which the interpretation is directed towards present problems (Vigh 1998: 67).

8. Collective histories are thus inseparable from the very worldly needs they serve as both representational and cognitive vessels, and must therefore be studied in relation to the context of their construction and actualisation. This is an especially important field of analysis within political anthropology since histories repeatedly show themselves as having potential for peace or for destruction.
9. *Darna* and *cansa*.
10. The people I have spoken with in Bissau have not lost faith in the story of progress in itself, but rather in their own ability to grab onto it. Progress is, for my informants, still desirable and still factual, but equally something you have to move in order to get into contact with.
11. Collective histories as moving space, kinetic topoi, rather than the singular *pathic topos* proposed by de Certeau (1984), serve as the larger social frame in which individuals are able to inscribe their own temporal existence into collective temporal existences. In this manner our perceived collective movement through time comes to constitute the temporal dimension of our social horizon; that is, our historical narrative of who we are and where we came from comes to define our social terrain and our position in it. What Popper (1972) describes as holistic confusion in his perspective on scientific historicism thus presents itself, when focusing on constructions of meaning, as a necessary interpretative tool which enables us to see the social entity as more than the units that constitute it.

12. There is in itself no teleology in Darwinist evolution, as it has no end goal but rather defines the result of a complex adaptive relationship between multiple entities. Yet the upward movement in organic evolution, that is, the progression from prokaryotes through nucleated eukaryotes, to humans (Mayr 1992: 134), has been related to the diversity in human appearance, societies and differences within social organisation and thus been infused with teleology (in its most narcissistic guise), as the social Darwinists in the West have placed themselves at the evolutionary pinnacle. By creating an analogy between the apparent increasing complexity of organic evolution and a movement towards increasing complexity societal evolution, the West was able to place itself at the top of a global hegemonic structuration with innate natural forces as their legitimation. We should, however, note that Spencer and Tylor's evolutionistic theories were prior to Darwin's work on the origin of the species. Evolutionism gained momentum from Darwinism rather than vice versa.
13. See also G. Balandier (1970: 46), P. Mendy (1998) and, not least, M. Jackson (1998), who, in a wonderful book, shows us that the idea of a colonialism as a civilising mission has been historically related to 'pigmented ineptitude' as it is rooted in Christian religious narratives and understandings in West Africa.
14. Césaire was a Caribbean author and poet. Born in 1913 in Martinique, he left for Paris in 1931, eventually earning a degree from the Sorbonne. He subsequently became politically active within the Communist Party, went back to Martinique and worked simultaneously as author and politician till 1993, when he retired from politics. Césaire wrote numerous collections of poetry, novels and plays. His work was to influence Fanon and Senghor, and much of his writing is centred on racial subjugation and inequality, as expressed in the excerpt below:

    my negritude is not a stone
    nor a deafness flung against the clamour of the day
    my negritude is not a white speck of dead water
    on the dead eye of the earth
    my negritude is neither tower nor cathedral
    it plunges into the red flesh of the soil
    it plunges into the blazing flesh of the sky
    my negritude riddles with holes
    the dense affliction of its worthy patience.

15. Including Fanon and Sartre. Although Fanon was obviously inspired by Negritude, and not least Césaire, he nonetheless differs in significant ways, being less interested in the specific category of 'African'. As a nationalist, he advocated the cause of the colonised (his term) in Algeria, rather than advocating for Negritude. In this perspective, Fanon was more focused on social rather than cultural matters and more focused on nation than continent.
16. Leopold Senghor was born in 1906 outside Dakar. When Senegal, in an attempt to liberate itself from French colonial rule, joined with the Sudanese Republic to form the Federation of Mali, Senghor was appointed President of the Federal Assembly. However, when Senegal separated from the Federation, in August 1960, he was elected the first President of Senegal, a seat that he held until 1980. Senghor died in France on 20 December 2001.
17. Negritude was, according to Senghor, inspired by the Afro-American 'Negro-Renascense' [sic] of the early twentieth century set in motion by W.E.B. Du Bois, building on the positive identity and racial traits of the 'Negro', in contrast to the negative traits then dominant in American society (Vaillant 1990).
18. Similar to what Balandier calls 'counter-acculturation' (see Balandier 1970).
19. Ironically, the concepts used and the actual historical interpretations created are almost identical to those used by their colonisers. Negritude was not anti-racist as

such but worked through a concept of reified race, defined by the Negritudinists as the essence of the African, such as the sensuous, natural and intuitive (Senghor 1972: 63–64). These were inverse valorisations of the Eurocentric perspective, used in constituting a counterweight to the negative description of African history and the negative positioning of Africans in the history of civilisation.

20. The difference being between one history encompassing all or many independent histories, each with its own worth.
21. Partido Africano da Independência da Guiné e Cabo Verde (PAIGC), Frente de Libertação de Moçambique (FRELIMO) and Movimento Popular da Libertação de Angola (MPLA).
22. A hierarchisation that Fanon, according to McCulloch, saw as the prime characteristic of European culture (McCulloch 1983: 80).
23. There is a degree of correspondence between the first and second wave of liberation movements and the move from African socialism to Afro-Marxism. The difference between them mainly lies in their degree of dogmatism. Where African socialism was popular 'socialism' that saw contextualisation of the Marxist ideology as a strength, the Afro-Marxists were more dogmatically 'scientific socialist' (Keller 1987: 1–15). However, both the African socialists and the Afro-Marxists were attuned to local conditions. Cabral, classified an Afro-Marxist by most, was himself aware of the fact that the theory of historical materialism had been generated in a different sociocultural context and could not be simply transferred (see Lopes and Rudebeck 1988); also, he did not actively denounce religion and was more nationalistically than internationally orientated.
24. Essentially the same process as that of the anchoring of European civilisation in ancient Greece.
25. Cabral touches upon the subject of culture but mainly by reference to social structure, and he generally interchanges the two terms (see Cabral 1974).
26. As did, for example, Fanon. The main difference between Fanon and the Negritudinists (as well as many of the African second-generation liberation writers) was his opposition to the focus on 'African' culture within the context of liberation, seeing it instead as a question of emancipating and strengthening national culture. Fanon is, as such, a supporter of the peculiar – but populated – category of 'nationalist Marxists'.
27. In a similar focus, both Fanon and Sartre are quite harsh in their critique of the Negritudinists for not being more focused on the future struggle of the masses but rather dwelling on a mummified idea of African civilisations. I shall abstain here from entering into a general critique of Negritude, first, because I wish to focus my attention on how 'Negritude' has entered and influenced the understanding of societal change, rather than on its historical factuality or theoretical flaws, and secondly, because the more contemporary critique of the Negritudinists as being essentialists and biological determinists with a focus on bio-politics (see Barber 2001 for a further discussion) is far removed from my current aim of trying to see them in their contexts, rather than critiquing them from the safe distance of a different paradigm.
28. But not necessarily utilitarian in motive.
29. A narrative of which capitalism and communism alike are exemplary expressions.
30. On the contrary, one of the attractions of the Marxist ideology for the liberation theorists can very well have been that this specific idea of progress defines societies along a very different scale of evolutionary hierarchisation than that of the predominant social Darwinism.
31. However, when Cabral emphasises horizontal social structure and the amalgamation of different tribes, he seems to be talking about a specific part of the Guinean population, namely the Senegambians, who share a number of features especially in language and cultural praxis (Lyon 1980: 158). In other major ethnic groups,

such as the Fula, the Mandinga and the Mandjako, we see distinct social structures that are anything but horizontal; moreover, even within the Senegambian group social structures vary greatly. Cabral seems, as such, to be equating the specific social structure of the Balantas (non-hierarchical, acephalous) with a generic Guinean social structure. The considerable time spent by Cabral in Balanta territory and with the PAIGC army, composed largely of Balantas, during the rural-based liberation war seems to add weight to this point, but it is difficult to postulate a generic, underlying social structure for all of the peoples of Guinea-Bissau taking the differences in culture and political organisation into consideration.

32. The liberation war was a 'people's war' although most of its support initially came from the radical urban petite bourgeoisie, and later on from the peasantry. As the liberation struggle progressed, Cabral consciously changed tactics and opted for revolutionising the peasantry rather than the proletariat, and we could thus be justified in calling it a 'peasants' war'; however, recreating the horizontal social structure of the past in the future meant shedding any remnants of the Portuguese social structure, which is why the petite bourgeoisie, if they really wanted to become part of the real struggle, would have to rid themselves of the negative sociocultural influence of the Portuguese through 'class suicide' (Cabral 1972).

33. From a focus on processes of becoming, the idea of *Formação Militante* is an interesting one. It literally means Military Formation, but *formação* also refers to the act of formation, that is, making someone militant.

34. The changes within the strategic influence of Africa after the end of the cold war scenario, the global demonisation of Marxism and the diminishing possibilities of attracting foreign aid to Bissau.

35. For a further discussion of teleology and finalism, see Mayr (1992).

36. See Monteiro et al. (1996) or Aguilar and Stenman (1997) for thorough and, respectively, negative and positive evaluations of the consequences of the ten years of Structural adjustment programmes in Guinea-Bissau.

37. I am well aware that many aspects of the Guinean politic praxis can be seen to have counteracted the free flow of people, goods and capital, the point being, as we shall see later, that so are my informants.

38. In itself, the conceptual divide between rich and poor countries is seemingly innocent, yet there is from within a capitalist perspective on societal movement a clearly dominant evolutionistic idea of progress, with the first step being the move from economic systems of '*naturalia*' to monetary systems, and thereafter from agrarian societies to the industrial, to societies of knowledge and so on.

39. www.reliefweb.int/w/rwb.nsf/s/78FFA42278C3502985256CBE00731248 p:2.

40. The demise of Marxism and the official embracing of capitalism and structural adjustment programmes did not seem to end in redistribution of resources or cure the economic ills of Guinean society. There is ample evidence that societal and economic changes focused on free trade by disentangling the state from the market economy have been effective only at the level of local markets and small trade, as the major revenues from oil, fishing rights, logging and so on are still directed to and controlled by the state elite (see Monteiro et al. 1996). Consequently the introduction of 'capitalism' has not changed the negative effects of PAIGC 'Marxism', that is, the enrichment of the few at the expense of the many.

41. The retrenchment of the public sector in relation to jobs and pensions has been one of the major factors in the mobilisation of the *antigo combatentes*, the heroes of the liberation war in reaction to their declining social status and position.

42. Roughly speaking those who were over twenty years of age.

43. *Fidjus di Tjong*, that is, proper Guineans.

44. That is, repair/improve it.

45. *Kansa*.

46. *Leba kansera pa Africa*.

47. *Mindjor na tempo di Tugas.*
48. Bissau is the Balanta word for Papel. As the Bissau area used to be Papel heartland it seems more likely that the city was named after its inhabitants.
49. Pureness is often used to emphasise indigenousness commonly heard when *homi garandis* (old men) talk about the past, as they refer to contemporary Creole as being more Portuguese (*portugesada*) and lighter (*lebi*) than the deeper (*fundu*), heavier (*pisado*) or purer (*puru*) Creole of the past.
50. I presume it is his way of being able to talk about the current problems in Bissau at all.
51. *Kila i propri-propri fidju di tjong, puru-puru.*
52. *Ate a gos ... Suso Barriga so.*
53. *Bu ten ku matil.*
54. *Fedi.*
55. A cafe in the centre of Bissau that has a generator and thus is able to run the television and show football games.
56. Apparently at the Presidença, or Presidency.
57. Rocket-propelled grenades.
58. Although not necessarily related in cause, this has sadly not changed; sporadic gunfire is still frequent.
59. *Pa* in this case being a suffix used to indicate emphasis, similar to *de, tok* and *nan* as well as to different suffixes specific to certain adjectives, for example, *branku fandang* (really white), *burmeljo wak* (really red), *suso putc* (really dirty) and so on.
60. The problematic aspect of the idea of a mutual space of resonance is that the social context surrounding experience to a large degree shapes it. In other words, although I was able to gain an insight into my informants' lives, due to the shared fears in being in the midst of a war in which the social dynamics were out of my (or anyone else's) control, the fact that I, as a foreigner, had a possibility of escape and a life and life-chances outside of Guinea-Bissau means that my engagement with and experience of the war were of a different order from those of my informants.
61. That is, first, that Asumané Mané was able to draw on the support of the veterans of the liberation war (*antigo combatentes*) by referring to the 'lack of respect' accorded to him when he was blamed for the disappearance of arms sold to the Diola rebels in Casamance, as well as to the indifference shown by the president and government towards the living standards of the army and the war veterans. secondly, that Asumané Mané did not respect the authority of the government seeking to control promotions within the military. Thirdly, in relation to the brutal killing of Asumané Mané, who was regarded as a respectable man worthy of a dignified death.
62. *Manda.*
63. *Terra branku.*
64. In one of these speeches towards the end of 2001, a period of alleged coups, he concluded by threatening that an eventual war would be so bloody that 'the monkeys would have to come in from the jungle to inhabit the city'.
65. The negative evaluation of the praxis can be seen precisely in the move from authority to power. People who practise 'dirty belly' will be powerful because of the accumulation of money from bribes (which have to be paid for entry into state services). In Bissau money seems not only to be able to buy you immunity from the penal system, but just as easily to buy punishment for others, deserved or undeserved. However, the accumulation of economic capital via these processes will not buy legitimacy, so power acquired by the process of sweet mouth and dirty belly yields little authority.
66. *Kansera.*

67. *Tudo e pis di memo cambua.* A *cambua* is a long, shallow net used to fence off an area of the river so as to drive the fish towards a controlled opening.
68. *Tira.*
69. *Mindjor um Lobo ki farta di ki tene fome.*
70. *Kudme-kume dinhiero e konta-konta mentida so.*
71. *Anos no nervo, no nervo mal.*
72. It must be added that the reason many of my Aguenta informants support Cadoco is that he has been one of the few to hire Aguentas in the post-war period, and because he was an associate of the ex-President Nino Vieira.
73. *Bu padido nan – pa naturesa.*
74. *Africa brancu.*
75. *Furta.* The word means to steal, but in the current context works as a metaphor for corruption, implying stealing from the state; it is also used to signify cheating, as in adultery or in cards.
76. It would at this point be tempting, because of the simplistic ease of the line of explanation, to describe the current racialisation of destruction and decline either as a manipulated re-emergence of a scheme of evolutionary differentiation, or a process of mystification. However, myths of race and racial inadequacies cannot simply be 'imposed' or 'implanted' as Smedley, for example, would have us believe (Smedley 1998: 694–95). Agents are (evidently) not unreflective discursive vessels that pick up on whatever possibilities of syntax are left over or given to them by the creative work of (stronger) others. Furthermore, if we take as our point of departure the position that acts (physical or discursive), as well as non-acts, are inseparable from the situation and context they are articulated in, then emergence becomes the necessary point of departure. This, however, is not to say that social and cultural phenomena are not historically contingent – they most definitely are – but rather that events are always crystallisations of a multitude of overlapping, intersecting and emerging processes that cannot be undone or copied as they are simply too complex.
77. *Rendja malkriadesa; malkriadesa* signifies bad behaviour, but to *rendja malkriadesa* is to look for trouble or incite aggressive behaviour.
78. An understanding equal to that of the xenophobic elements in Denmark, as perceived racial difference becomes indicative of different folk mentalities making Arabs immanently misogynist, blacks immanently violent and the Inuit immanently alcoholic, posing a problem because of the postcolonial inversion of the movement of people between countries of the former colonisers and the colonised (see Balibar and Wallerstein 1991).
79. The process of constructing relationships, social praxis or groups by interpreting them within a racial discourse (Briggs 2001: 669). See also Omi and Winant (1986), Miles (1993) and Barot and Bird (2001).
80. And which is equally evident in the contemporary constructions of white supremacist identities and right wing culturalism that has swept Europe since the 1990s.
81. See, for example, the work of Price (1987), Farmer (1994) and Mattingly (1994) on illness and narrative; Werbner (1991) and Malkki (1995) on conflict and narratives and Agger and Jensen (1990) on trauma and narrative.
82. It is, in fact, a general phenomenon, which is not only related to violence but again seems to pertain to all acts that are not routine.
83. *Marcha.*
84. The conflict of November 2000 took place a few weeks later, in which nearly all of the opposition politicians who participated were jailed without trial and several were hospitalised after allegedly having received severe beatings.

PART V

IN APPEASEMENT?

Chapter 9

RECATEGORISING MEN AS CHILDREN

BOTTOM-UP RECONCILIATION

'I know many Aguentas,' Joel said, 'many, many Aguentas'. He seemed pleased at having found out that he could be of assistance, though I had expected he would be, being a Papel from Bissau. Nearly all the Papels I met during my fieldwork had relatives who fought on the government side of the war, making the major battles of the war tragedies for the Papel community as their kin were slaughtered on the battlefield. 'My cousin was Aguenta,' Joel continued, 'the one that lives over there, in Tjong de Papel,[1] he went to Conakry and all, but last assault he was hit in the foot.' 'How is he now?' I asked. 'Does he have problems or what?' Joel replied: 'No, now he is okay, he has a normal life. There is nothing [no animosity] there.[2] The Aguentas were not guilty, they did not know anything, they were just children.'

I was later to meet and interview Joel's cousin; he was thirty-four! It seemed rather a high age for a child.

Although this book has touched upon some general aspects of the lives of youth in Bissau, of their possibilities of engaging in the world and of their possible identity formations while inhabiting a prolonged period of decline and conflict, it has mainly been focused on the Aguentas: a short-lived, socially diversified and unstable military group that can best be described as a 'community of experience', whose members share the same military background, the same experience of being *carne di bazooka*, 'bazooka meat' or cannon fodder and of trying to survive the ordeals of combat. Yet the Aguentas equally share the same post-war ordeal of being in a socially marginal and vulnerable position, of being losers and perpetrators of war crimes, and, not least, the same position and role within a unique process of reconciliation.

Perpetrators and Persecution

We have seen that entering the war on the government side was never judged positively by the majority of the Bissauian population. Although the Aguentas might have been supported within the Papel community, most seem to have been aware of the fact that they were not fighting what was seen as a popular cause.[3] The Aguentas were, however, to strengthen their unpopularity even further by committing an array of human rights violations during the war. We would thus be justified in expecting that the social reintegration of the Aguentas, vanquished and on the run, would not be easy. Yet the actual reconciliation process has been much smoother than what could have been expected.

Abuse and Atrocities

Before going any further, it should be clarified that I do not wish to overlook or underestimate the hatred and animosity that actually does exist towards the Aguentas, which is not only related to the fact that they fought on the losing side of the war but also caused by their frequently unpleasant behaviour towards the civilian population during it. Despite there being very little actual documentation of abuse or civil-rights violations by the Aguentas, Bissau was, when I first came to the city, busy with rumours of who was Aguenta and who was not and what crimes they had committed. In fact, nearly all Aguentas themselves admit that they did things they were not proud of, yet most emphasise that they were done under orders. The non-Aguenta population, however, emphasised that the actions of the Aguentas were particularly bad when they were on leave or out of uniform. A good part of the atrocities committed can probably be related to the fact that they were traumatised by their war experiences and the heavy casualties they suffered. Yet it also seems that a large part of the abuse was committed in response to the 'empowerment' they gained by being soldiers, showing off their uniforms and power in the process of *ronka*, as boasting is called in Creole.

People were and are thus upset with my informants because of the abuse they committed. Yet, despite this, the Aguentas seem currently to be in the process of being reincorporated into Guinean society and Bissau has not seen the type or scale of persecution that has followed in the wake of changes in the fortunes of war elsewhere. In fact, despite having suffered an incredible amount of verbal abuse, there have not been many physical persecutions, a fact that can be explained by a number of factors.

First of all, there was a series of communiqués over the Radio de Junta, after the *ultimo assalto*, in which the Junta Militar made it clear that they did not condone any persecution of the Aguentas, and that the Aguentas should instead turn themselves in at the barracks in QG. Afraid of being tricked, very few of my informants actually did so, but the communiqué most probably eased the tension and anger there were towards the Aguentas at the end of the war.

Secondly, the very routinisation of conflict as context has entailed an understanding of periodic outbreaks of fighting as unavoidable, endemic to Guinean society and the Guinean subject, which is made clear in the dominance of the comment '*preto i preto so*' in relation to abuse, violence and warfare. Thus there is greater tolerance towards and understanding of events that lead people to take up arms in order to navigate the unstable Guinean terrain. In fact, as outbreaks of fighting in Bissau are not seen to be ideological or interpreted as clashes between radically opposed Others, the violence of warfare has become accepted as a social modality that is related to a specific societal situation. There is a high awareness of the situationality of action in Guinea-Bissau, pointing our attention to the shared understanding of the situation and acts of war, which seems to limit the aggressiveness of the relations between the warring parties after the end of the fighting. In other words, while *guerra di hermonia*, the 'brotherly war', points us towards the existence of opponents rather than enemies, situationality is the consequence of the specific understanding of the terrain, agents and acts of war: people are generally able to situate the acts of war and restrict them to the situation of war, because they know and understand the reasons and motives for the others' war engagement.

The third reason for the relatively low number of persecutions may be found, I believe, in a specific process of reconciliation, which, just like the above interpretative process of situationality, stems from the shared space of the war as a *guerra di hermonia* and results in those who lost the war being socially reintegrated rather than ostracised. In Guinea-Bissau this seems to be attempted through 'generational recategorisation,' a process whereby young men and youth are constructed as children.

Turning Men into Children

However, moving too quickly towards the process of reconciliation might seem to paint too pretty a picture of harmony in the relationship between the Aguentas and the general population, overlooking the fact that my informants are still in a difficult situation. The Aguentas are still engaged in a reconciliatory process rather than having completed it.

Being an Aguenta in the Bissau of today is not easy as they still constitute a marginalised group within Guinean society. Except for the few who succeeded in rejoining the army during or after the conflict between Asumané Mané and Kumba Yala in November 2000 and those in the Guinea Conakrian army, all of my informants are currently struggling to make ends meet while constantly having their endeavours obstructed because of their past. The Aguentas are not viewed with favour in Bissau and, besides having to cope with the traumas of war, they are also on the receiving end of ample verbal abuse and social sanctions, such as having difficulties in getting and holding jobs when people come to know of their military background. Yet despite a small number of punishment beatings and executions of Aguentas in the aftermath of the war in 1999, the abuse that the Aguentas are the victims of is normally not extreme or physical but takes the form of verbal insults, be it from opposed troops or from the civilian population, resembling the 'meta-hostility' of a teasing relationship; or it is expressed through the manipulation of social categories as in calling or treating them as children – evident in the case of Joel's cousin, Adilson, with which I introduced the present chapter.

A Child at Thirty-four

The intriguing thing about the introductory quote, is of course, that the category of child will normally not be able to encompass a man of thirty-four in Guinea-Bissau, or elsewhere. From a chronological perspective, the categorisation seems absurd, yet the very key to making sense of Adilson's ascribed 'childness' lies in the difference between chronological and generational or social age. Recategorising and scolding the Aguentas as children is a symbolic manipulation premised upon generational dynamics (see Fortes 1984).

The recategorisation of the Aguentas as children is made possible by the fact that they are seen as the weaker party on the government side. There is generally in Bissau an understanding of the lack of life chances and ambivalent agentive position of youth, as well as of their marginal position within both the economy of affection and obligation, patrimonial networks and the predicament of the social moratorium of youth. There exists, in other words, a general knowledge of their position in the terrain as well as of their navigational possibilities within the terrain. Equally, the recategorisation itself works through a manipulation of generational categories and dynamics.[4] In other words, although it is not chronologically possible to be a man of thirty-four years of age and moved into the social category of child, it is possible to be in the category of youth and subsequently redefined as a child. The paradox of being thirty-four and called a child is thus integrally tied to the social moratorium of youth and becomes softened if we look at the recategorisation with a generational rather than a chronological perspective. As decline continues, the chronological span between people defined as youth is currently being expanded due to the lack of possibilities of upward social mobility, the absurdity lying not so much in the fact that a man of thirty-four can be recategorised as a child (a mere consequence) but rather in the fact that he is generally positioned in the category of youth. In fact, as decline continues, the very category of youth seems increasingly to designate a social position rather than a generational category, and seems likely to change in meaning, becoming presumably internally hierarchised in relation to the increasing differences within the category.

Recategorisation at Work

Whatever the case, being defined or treated as a child, relegated to the very bottom of the pecking order, is not pleasant for a young man, whatever his age. Yet it not only has a very tangible edge to it in relation to the lack of status the position of 'child' grants the Aguentas, but it also has an ironic edge to it as most of my informants joined the Aguentas for the very possibility of rising in social status, to escape the social moratorium of youth and become an *adulto completto*, a full adult. Yet the recategorisation also has a pleasant side to it, as it follows the logic of the perceived responsibilities and abilities embedded in the different generational categories. The recategorisation of the Aguentas from youth to children thus reveals the defining difference between youth and childhood in Guinea-Bissau, namely, one's knowledge of the social world and the degree to which one is responsible for one's acts. Following on the heels of the humiliation of being treated as a child is thus a relative acquittal of responsibility for one's (mis)deeds.

Rather than being symbolic violence, the definition of the Aguentas as children is symbolic creativity; by placing the emphasis of the Aguentas' deeds during the war on the aspect of guilt and the taking of responsibility, and then shifting both guilt and responsibility, a process of social reconstruction is enabled. '*E ka tene kulpa eraba mininos so*', 'they were not to blame because they were only children', is thus one of the most commonly heard answers when asking people what they think of the Aguentas, pointing our attention towards both generational recategorisation and the existence of a community-generated reconciliation process, as it gives the socially ostracised a point of entry into a process of re-socialisation, a possibility to re-enter society. Thus, generational categories are manipulated and agents redefined so as to enable the social reintegration of marginalised subjects, giving them a second chance – through what is potentially almost a process of absolution.

This describing of the Aguentas as children thus renders them harmless while relieving them of control over their actions during the war. It follows a logic of the non-socialised child, who, not knowing social rules and consequences, cannot be held accountable for its actions and should not be held responsible for its misdeeds. Asking a young woman of twenty years of age why she referred to the Aguentas as children, seeing that it did not fit her own definition of the category of child, she said: 'They are without responsibility[5] because they think like children. They do not know anything. When someone says go there, they go.'

The Unknowing Child

'Not knowing anything' is in this situation not to be confused with lack of intelligence. Children are unknowing, without full knowledge of the social world – of social rules, norms and expectations – but they are not seen as without intellect, the ability to understand. Banter with reference to intelligence thus refers to more than the incompetence of poor social navigation. Rather it is an ascription of a general lack of social knowledge, a defining ascription as it is seen as an essential trait of childhood and thus a prerequisite for being able to be defined as a child at all. The Aguentas-as-children are thus defined by being characterised by a general lack of social knowledge of which the faulty readings of terrains, faulty action in relation to terrains and faulty plotting of trajectories are the most salient manifestations; yet the identificatory and reconciliatory aspects of being generally unknowing are profound, as the unknowing can be taught and a 'child' can be (re)socialised.

In Bissau, as elsewhere, a child is seen as an emergent social being bound in a formative relation to its surrounding world. It is not yet entity but still process, which means that it can be (re)shaped and (re)positioned within the social terrain and, not least, that its actions are caused by ignorance rather than ill will.[6] Being recategorised as a child thus works through a similar logic to that of being acquitted through 'temporary insanity', though in this case there is talk of a logic of 'temporary inanity'. The categorical classification of Aguentas as children and the emphasis on their unfinished character in terms of social knowing becomes, in this point of view, a means of reconciliation though it denies them socio-political agency until they are seen to know better.

By ascribing the Aguentas to the category of child, a category that is defined by a lack of social awareness and knowledge, the Aguentas can thus become socially reincorporated into civilian Guinean society starting as children and being symbolically resocialised before being redefined. Furthermore the recategorisation of the Aguentas as children is, as said, a common one and its general acceptance can be seen in the fact that many of my Aguenta interlocutors will define themselves in such a manner, with the emphasis being exactly on the lack of responsibility, or in Vitór's words, shortly before the war in 2000: 'There is reconciliation. It exists for the people of low rank, you see. That is to say, people that do not have rank, people like us. We went. We do not have rank. We are children. There is reconciliation on that behalf. The Junta do not think anything of us.'

The fact that it is the people 'who do not have rank' who are classified as children and who thus experience reconciliation points our attention to the generational recategorisation only being possible for the combatants who were youth, that is, to the combatants who have not yet been able to position themselves as social entities in the social terrain, demarcating themselves as adults and thus engaging in war from a strategic rather than a tactical point of departure. What we see is that a group that is stigmatised because of its wartime activities is being socially sanctioned through abuse and banter at the same time as the individuals constituting it are reintegrated into society and relieved of guilt by being classified as children. By criticising the group of Aguentas, but categorically holding the individuals of the group free of guilt, the Aguentas are able to re-enter society, without having their deeds of war dragging messily after them. To put it another way: the verbal abuse of the group facilitates the social purification of the individual.

Insults and Silence: Just Desserts

The generational recategorisation is in itself a strange phenomenon to witness, yet what probably strikes the outsider most, as it so clearly shows the power relationship embedded in the process, is the silence. I have seen Aguentas being insulted by peers for what seemed like ages, accepting it in silence, with only a momentary apologetic smile. One particular instance of insults carried on for so long that I finally reacted and said: 'Leave him alone, someone has to lose in war.' My reaction was met by a friend taking my hand saying: 'They are only teasing him, just teasing.' However, it was obviously not a pleasant situation for the one being teased, as he left as soon as the group had lost interest in him. Yet, for the social sanitation to be effective the Aguentas are, in the process of their redefinition, forced into silence; they do not have the status to object, cannot argue their case and must accept being told off like children in order to be able to be symbolically placed in the category at all. In Carlos's description of the abuse he receives:

He [a peer] could say: 'You are stupid, why did you not go to the Junta, you were with the government, you were Aguenta.' If it is someone who is angry then you could have problems ... if you are talking to me, and you know that I was Aguenta, and if you talk to me and you talk badly about me, I will not talk [back] to you.

So silence is a part of the process of resocialisation as it symbolises powerlessness and acceptance of the position and of the social process. Carlos, whom I quoted above, is built like a brick wall, he is a keen wrestler and regularly wins fights and prises;[7] he is most certainly not a person that you would make the target of your banter if you thought he could get angry, but the fact is that he gets a lot of abuse, which he accepts silently. In other words, were it not for the social reintegration and repositioning made possible by the reclassification, I am quite sure that Carlos would not have been the target of the abuse, precisely because he would not have accepted it peaceably. Although there are many problems in the social reintegration of Aguentas, as they are still stigmatised and marginalised despite the war being almost five years gone, the process of recategorisation functions effectively as a bottom-up reconciliation. Yet recategorisation does not stand alone as a reconciliatory mechanism but is supported by pragmatic perspective on mobilisation, as much of the banter that the Aguentas are the targets of testifies to.

Being a Poor Dubriadur

As shown, suffering insults and verbal abuse in silence is part of the strain of being an Aguenta in the Bissau of today. The verbal abuse of the Aguentas is categorised as teasing, and is highly negotiated and regulated with clear limits demarcating when the 'snatch' becomes a 'bite', to use a Batesonian differentiation; nevertheless, the amount of verbal abuse that the Aguentas suffer in silence is large. It is directed mainly towards faulty tactics, as well as the ever popular '*Aguenta di merda*',[8] which is obviously being purely derogatory, though most frequently people just yell 'Aguenta, Aguenta' loudly enough for others to hear, testifying to the fact that the ascription of the identity is a socially recognised stigma.

In situations of direct dialogue, however, what is most commonly emphasised is lack of knowledge: that is, pointing out the stupidity of the Aguentas for becoming Aguentas in the first place. Yet, if we turn our attention away from the aspect of 'lack of knowledge' to that of faulty tactics we no longer see the Aguentas as children but as youth misjudging the movement of the shifting terrain, in effect, stressing the symbolic character of the recategorisation as the Aguentas are moved in and out of the category at will. Yet from a perspective of *dubriagem*, being an Aguenta is truly a sign of failed tactics in terms of affiliation with the wrong side,[9] not the engagement with warfare in itself. In this perspective, joining the Aguentas was not the move of a good *dubriadur*, but is related to poor navigation of the immediate and the oncoming. As Adilson revealed when I asked what sort of abuse he would get:

> People will say: 'You are stupid, what did you look for there?' And you see, the Junta had lots of young people. Why? Because they were against the president, this is why people talk badly to you if they know [that you were an Aguenta]. And that is why I say: I am not Aguenta. If people do not know, they do not know.

Thus Adilson, as an Aguenta, is insulted for choosing to support the losing side of the war, with the phrase *ke ku bu bai buska la*, 'what did you look for there?', being a direct reference to the flawed navigation of entering war without harvesting gain. Most significantly, Adilson is teased for choosing bad tactics. Stupidity as an insult has in this perspective nothing to do with general intellectual abilities but is related to a poor reading of the terrain of war and the hopeless navigation implied in ending up as an Aguenta. This again seems to emphasise the entering into warfare as tactical praxis, with a restricted presence of ideology.

So, although it seems clear that the verbal abuse directed at the Aguentas contains a degree of social sanctioning, it is significant that the Aguentas are generally accused of making a bad choice in their engagement in war rather than being seen as bad people: that is, they are not typified or essentialised. The term Aguenta is equivalent to being stupid, *burro*, someone void of social intelligence, *ki ka tene kabeça*, or someone who, like a child, does not know better, *ki ka sibi nada*. Yet the bantering is directed towards the praxis of reading and navigating terrains, and there are numerous factors differentiating acceptable from excessive abuse and banter, the transgression of which carries with it an accepted retaliation. When I asked Vitór, my much-quoted key informant and field assistant, about the types of abuse he would receive, he seemed not to be able to stop, listing situations and quoting conversations ad infinitum. As I became indignant on his behalf, I asked:

> *But do you not get angry if someone insults you on the street?*
> Me? If you pass me ... For example. I pass you today and you insult me and tomorrow I pass you and you insult me ...
> *You will get angry?*

No, I will really get irritated, I will be angry[10] and I will react. Quickly. But others they can feel free. If they call me: 'Aguenta, you are Aguenta,' I will say: 'Yes, cool, how are you?'

Although the above quote, containing two ridiculously leading questions, is a textbook example of how not to conduct ethnographic research, anger or emotionality being guaranteed to ruin methodological praxis, it nonetheless indicates that both recategorisation and bantering are in themselves related to specific underlying negotiations and regulations; it would seem that the Aguentas have become part of a socially defined relationship by which they have been socially repositioned. Equally we see that whereas the verbal abuse often seems to paint a negative picture of the Aguentas, it is followed by reference to the situationality of action or by recategorising the Aguenta as a child. Having already illuminated the process of generational recategorisation I shall now turn towards the third aspect accounting for the lack of persecution after the war, namely that of situationalism.

Situationality and the Brotherly War Revisited

Besides generational recategorisation, the replies one most often hears in relation to the aspects of responsibility for crimes committed during warfare and hatred for those who committed them are *'guerra i suma'*, 'war is like this', or *'guerra kaba'*, 'the war is over'. Insubstantial and superficial as these sentiments may seem, they reiterate that acts of warfare are seen as situated in the field of war they emerged from. In other words, whereas generational recategorisation allowed my informants to be reintegrated through a symbolic process of resocialisation, situationality works, like the pragmatics of the banter, towards reconciliation by placing the act as emergent from within a situation rather than the agent. However, this does not imply that violence is external to the agent, but rather an understanding of the possibility of violence as embedded in all agents (or, as seen in the former chapter, in all blacks), with the situation determining whether violence becomes dominant as a social modality. Just as the discourse of blackness is situated, so are the acts of blackness, which can be seen in the following quote from a conversation I had with Dó after I had found out that he knew one of my informants during the war. I asked Dó what he specifically knew about him and he answered:

> We knew him because he lived close to us, over there [he points to a house on the opposite side of the street]. I was angry with him during the war because he beat up one of my friends. We were at a disco – you know the

discos were open during the war? – and Seku was there in uniform and with a gun. He was very aggressive and as we started to walk for the door he began beating my friend with a metal truncheon. I wanted to intervene but I could not do so because of the uniform. He beat my friend badly. I met him again [on the street] the days after the last attack, and I was still angry with him and you know that not all the Aguentas were caught, so I pointed him out and started calling 'Aguenta, Aguenta, Aguenta'. He ran.
So how do you feel towards him now?
Nothing ... The war is over.

Guerra kaba, the war is over, in this perspective succeeds in confining the abusive act to the situation of the war positioning the negative relationship between Seku and Dó as emergent within the situation of war. The situationalism of *guerra kaba* thus provides closure by emphasising the context which makes violence relevant as a social modality rather than ascribing it to the personal characteristics or inner nature of the individual Aguenta as perpetrator. The acts committed during the war do not easily spill over into peacetime.

Situationalism and Reconciliation

Yet there are also counter-processes to the recategorisation and situationality so prevalent in general social attitudes. The Guinean courts, for instance, have been working overtime, passing sentence on one leading insurgent after another, localising guilt within the person on trial. In other words, it would seem, as already said, that the situationality and recategorisation only apply to those who navigate the terrain of war tactically rather than strategically, those who *dubria* to survive rather than those who generate war as a means to *suso barriga*, dirty belly, in order to become fat at the expense of others. Yet even this distinction has a certain relativity to it, as the outrage over the killing of Asumané Mané in November 2000, felt even by those fighting against him as seen in Mbuli's case in the initial chapter of the book, seems to indicate that he should have been left to get on with his life after having lost the war. In fact the stiltedness of the judicial process in relation to the aftermath of wars or coups seems almost ritualistic, being representations rather than deep process, and tuned more to buzzwords of the international society and donor countries, such as 'peace and reconciliation committees' and tribunals of war, than to what the population want. And perhaps smartly so, as the community-generated reconciliation process is not high-profile or all that politically correct if seen from a Western perspective.

In fact, situationalism is, from a Western perspective, a controversial view on warfare, as it runs contrary to most attempts at creating stable post war societies and 'cultures of accountability' via war tribunals and the punishment of the guilty. It goes against our European understanding of individual responsibility for our acts and even the shape and understanding of our interpersonal relationships. The difference in perspective can be explained by the perceived differences in the constitution of the agent and the terrain he has to navigate. This relationship between agent and terrain has, as said, ensured that, within the conflictual process in Guinea-Bissau, there has not been a construction of a radical Other seen as endowed with radically different understanding, interpretations,[11] plans or motives. Without radical Others, ethnic, religious or ideological, who can be seen as having different motives or being guided by different aspirations from those of the rest of the agents engaged in warfare, it becomes difficult to essentialise and typify the opposed troops, which is needed before one can decontextualise and subsequently personalise violent acts. Furthermore, and paradoxically, the fact that Guinean society and the Guinean subject, via the processes of retrospection, introspection and extrospection, are seen as having a potential for violence means that acts of violence are generally confined to the situations they are committed in rather than seen as specific to the agents of violence. The perceived situationality of warfare, amongst the people I have spoken to, Aguentas or not, hinders the carrying of hatred from a war situation into a situation of peace, and thereby – in a reconciliatory perspective – facilitates the reconstitution of a non-conflictual public sphere of interaction between Guineans.

Going Full Circle: Situating War

The understanding of acts of war as situated thus takes us back to the initial theoretical points of departure listed in the introductory chapter of this book, that is, that acts of violence and conflict must be analytically situated rather than essentialised and should be seen as socially rather than psychologically emergent. Yet, whereas in the introductory chapter this was stated as a theoretical point, the Guineans go a step further, in effect, showing that theory can be praxis.

By emphasising situationality in making sense of the crimes and deeds of war, the Guineans are able to grant a vulnerable and marginalised group the possibility of recreating their lives as complete social beings, making it possible for my informants to start afresh without having their misdeeds, committed in a situation of war, following them into other spheres of life. Generational recategorisation and situationalism allow my informants to get on with their lives after the war has ended, through awareness and understanding of the social process that leads young men into war. In other words because of a common awareness of the difficult situation of youth confined to a social moratorium and the understanding of the war as fought between agents trying to navigate very difficult, constantly shifting terrain, the deeds of warfare that are committed by soldiers – rather than the people in charge – can be located in the situation that is seen to produce them.

However, situationalism also works on a different level: the retrospective historicising, the introspective essentialisation and the extrospective localisation of violence in the body of 'blacks' makes it possible for my informants to see conflict and violence as a political modality. Whereas we in a European tradition have an understanding of violence as something that characterises a minority of our citizens – making us able to see it as an essence within some (who are ethnically, religiously or psychologically defined) and enabling us to incarcerate them as socially deviant – my informants see it as something inherent in them all, relating the violent act to the situation that spurs it rather than the person who commits it.

The conceptual variables that underlie the understanding of deeds of war as situated thereby lead us through all the different aspects dealt with during the course of this book: from social position, to social confinement, to social navigation, to the common understanding of the instability of the terrain and identification with decline and conflict. Taken together, all of the above aspects go to show that, although appeasement seemingly comes easily to the Guineans, so too does warfare and remobilisation, as destruction and decay are seen as coloured and inherent.

Brighter Futures?

Am I painting too bleak a picture? I wish the answer were an unequivocal 'yes'. Yet, when looking at Guinea-Bissau from the perspective of youth, life chances and factional conflict, the de- and remobilisation of young men seems far from over. In evidence of this, we have since the end of the civil war in 1999 seen a process of instability and conflict in which some Aguentas have been politically realigned and remobilised. Many of the Aguentas I know have thus either repositioned themselves within the Guinean socio-political terrain or re-engaged in military activity.[12] Taking the hardness of life and the constant political tension into consideration, it furthermore seems likely that these conflicting factions and patrimonial networks will once again become militarised.

Furthermore, the government of Kumba Yala, in which so many placed their hopes for a more prosperous Guinea-Bissau after the war, was equally to inscribe itself into the long line of *sabi boca* and *suso barriga* that has come to characterise Guinean political life. Instead of working towards democracy, prosperity and respect for human rights, Yala's government succeeded in concentrating power in the hands of one ethnic group, the Balantas;[13] in increasing the production of religious divides between the Muslim and Christian/animist parts of the population; in being rampantly corrupt and wreaking havoc within state finances;[14] and in creating an increasingly repressive state system showing diminishing respect for even the most basic human rights. As a result, Yala' government fell victim to yet another coup d'état, leaving the political and social make up of Guinean society polarised in the extreme and constantly on the verge of collapse, bearing the brunt of constant socio-political instability, and the number of coups, coup attempts, purges, bouts of gunfire and undefined fighting of the last few years (Mork 2003).[15]

Yet, in the shadow of conflict, poverty and negative self-identity there is with the last two elections in 2005 also a beginning optimism. The most recent coup in 2003, the subsequent installation of an effective interim government, under President Henrique Rosa, and the democratic election of Prime Minister Cadogo's government in 2004 appear to have been able to restore calm and, at least temporarily, create a milieu in which stability seems possible.

The End of the Parliament of the Poor

When I came back to Bissau in the autumn of 2003, the 'Parliament of the Poor' had disintegrated. Due to unusually heavy rains the roof of Yvette's house had collapsed and the 'the parliament' had dispersed. 'The Parliament broke,' they said, referring to it in the past tense, yet most of the Parliamentarians were present and seemed to be doing the same as always: sitting on a (new) wall, debating the political situation, trying to make sense of political change and to anticipate movements and possibilities. Despite the change of location, it was, in other words, status quo for the *collegason*, as they did not have more money than usual or better possibilities. Yet something had changed; for the first time they seemed genuinely optimistic, stating that now things might move forwards, though agreeing that it probably would not. The reason behind the optimism was the new government, which, besides being seen as favourably minded towards the Aguentas,[16] was actually putting an effort into getting the country back on its feet. When I asked why they thought that this government might actually change things, Piné answered, 'He is not like the others. He is not black, he is coloured.'[17]

For my informants, soiled politics seems a pigmented fact of life.

Notes

1. A suburb of Bissau.
2. *I ka ta ten nada la.*
3. A fact that is, in itself, evident in the discredited use of the discourse of ethnicity, in the attempt to attract Papels to sign up and the common use of the name Aguenta as a stigma.
4. In itself bearing testimony to the plasticity of the generational concept.
5. *É ka tene kulpa.*
6. This innocence and freedom from responsibility seem to be applicable to every manner of transgression of social norms, even including homicide. As a *collega* told me: 'If a child kills someone, it is not as bad as if an adult does, because he more has maturity. A child does not know anything.'
7. The indigenous type of wrestling is referred to as *luta traditional*.
8. I.e. 'shit Aguenta'.
9. The exact Creole phrasing is *kai na dubria*. *Kai* meaning to fall, it implies that the slippery terrain you are seeking to navigate got the best of you.
10. *Abrucido.*
11. Although it can be said to be on its way, with the growing emphasis on ethnicity within the political arena.
12. The Aguentas have also been able to use their relations with the neighbouring state of Guinea Conakry – forged during the civil war in 1999 as the majority of them were trained at the barracks in Kindia and two battalions from the Guinea Conakrian army fought (and lost) together with the Aguentas on the *Governo* side of the war – to re-enter military service. According to my information, the Aguentas have been welcomed into the Conakrian army and there are numerous reports of their participation in the conflict areas of the subregion. (http://www.geocities.com/CapitolHill/Parliament/1007/6246.html [15 May 1999]; http://www.geocities.com/CapitolHill/Parliament/1007/6409.html [31 August 1999]; http://www.peacelink.it/afrinews/38_issue/p10.html [24 *Marts* 2003].
13. The *Gazeta de Noticias*, a Bissau-based newspaper, called this a *Balantização*, that is, a Balantafication, of the country, with the Balantas currently being in control of the government, the state apparatus, the armed forces and the judicial system, and largely having gained this control at the expense of Muslim positions of power (*Gazeta de Noticias* 11 December 2000). The war between the government of Kumba Yala and the Junta Militar thus saw a consolidation of not only an ethnic divide but also a religious one, as the majority of the Junta troops and officers were reportedly Muslim (Fula, Mandinga, Beafata) and the large majority of the government troops were Christians (Balantas, Papel). This divide was and remains at the core of the very conflict in question as a struggle over Muslim or Christian control of the military
14. Per capita GDP fell from $238.0 in 1997 to $161.6 in 2001, alongside a more than 100 per cent increase of expenditure on public administration and an equally massive increase in central government expenditure on wages and salaries (IMF Country Report, July 2002). Eighty per cent of the state revenues disappear before they reach the public coffers (*Diario de Noticias* 19 November 2001), and there is an increase from FCFA 24 million to FCFA 41.5 million in government – not public – expenditure (IMF Country Report, July 2002).
15. Panafrican News Service 05 Marts, 2001; UN Integrated Regional Information Network 06 December 2002.
16. The current Prime Minister, Carlos Cadogo, was one of the only people to employ Aguentas after the war in 1999.
17. *I um algin di cor.*

Chapter 10

CLOSURE

He blocked the pavement. 'You can't walk here,' he yelled. 'You can't walk here. Fulas, Mandingas, Brankus,[1] you cannot walk here. Only Balantas can walk here. Only Balantas.' His arms were spread out, protecting the bit of pavement especially reserved for Balanta feet. Though frail and old, his madness scared me a bit. Yet, as he stood there, frenzied, bombarding people with political comment, discursive phrases out of context, his pavement apartheid was clearly a critical comment on the recent political and military dominance of the Balantas: on the fact that they, during Yala's short stay in power, had gained control over the judicial apparatus, the army and the state revenue; that the political situation had been getting more and more tense; that the freedom of press had been more and more restricted; that more and more dissidents have been jailed without trial, and, indirectly, that the mad – too distant from both reality and power to pose a threat – are left as the only ones able to publicly criticise the political state of affairs.

Commencing a Closure

After an attempt on his life, the opposition leader and political critic Carlos Schwartz blamed the government for the assassination attempt. Explaining what had happened to the Portuguese news agency Lusa, he said: 'This can only be the work of the same people that have systematically killed Guineans recently ... [who] imprison journalists and close down radios,' going on to state that the regime seeks to instil a 'climate of fear and intimidation' ahead of the coming elections.[2] Although Mr Schwartz – as an opposition politician – has a vested interest in portraying the current government as negatively as possible, one can hardly disagree: in relation to the sphere of politics, a climate of fear did and does indeed exist in Bissau. *Gos, bu ka ta osa papir*, 'Now, you do not dare speak,' people say, and the fear of articulating one's opinion, if unfavourable to the present President, stretches from opposition politicians to 'the man on the street'. As a closure, my aim within this chapter is to sum up the analytical and theoretical arguments of the book and to turn my thoughts to the political situation, and the socio-political environment through which my informants continue to navigate.

The Analytical Trajectory

My line of argument has had its point of departure in the realisation that the Aguentas were not fighting against an enemy but for a possibility. Their battle was not so much against an Other as for a process of social becoming and improvement of their life chances. Locating my analysis in social possibilities and life chances led to an illumination of the constitution of the Aguenta militia in relation to the general context of decline, conflict and factional struggle that characterises Guinean society.

Youth as Social Navigators

In the first part of the book, I thus sought to shed light on the general characteristics of the Guinean political process, on the specificities of the relationship between the opposed parties within the Guinean civil war, and on the specific praxis and understanding of the war as a *guerra di hermonia*, a brotherly war. Turning my attention towards this representation and praxis of conflict as fraternal, between opponents rather than enemies, I was able to show how the mobilisation of the Aguentas was related to a collective understanding of the possibility of action of youth within the Guinean socio-political environment. Through demonstrating that the generational position of youth has become a social moratorium, defined by the lack of ability of youth to realise their social becoming, I was able to illuminate the relationship between warfare and social possibilities for youth in Guinea-Bissau.

Social Navigation

In the second part of the book I documented how my interlocutors seek to make the best of their lives despite the confinement of the social moratorium and a bare minimum of life chances. The political space and possibilities that are available to young Bissauian men are characterised by decline, conflict and occasional warfare, yet rather than being crushed by the situation, they are able to navigate it, keeping their focus on possibilities for improving their life chances within a shifting terrain. I sought in this part of the book to illuminate their praxis and conceptualisation of the choices and experiences of actual mobilisation through the Guinean term *dubriagem*.

Through focusing on *dubriagem* I demonstrated how the Aguentas, by navigating the terrain of war, sought to construct a path through a socio-political environment in constant disfiguration and reconfiguration. *Dubriagem* was the tactics and praxis of agents seeking to make the best of societal turmoil beyond their control. It was the attempted construction, plotting and actualisation of a social trajectory, not on a defined and demarcated stable ground, but in a moving and fluctuating socio-political environment. *Dubriagem*, as tactics, is action attuned to social change: a conceptualisation of action which I have translated into 'social navigation', that is, the complex political praxis of moving towards a goal while at the same time being moved by a socio-political environment. It is praxis as motion within motion.

The Social Terrain

In plotting and actualising action we navigate not only the immediate but also the imaginary. We act simultaneously in relation to current needs, opportunities, and obstacles to our defined telos, and in relation to our understanding of the movement of the waters that lie between where we are and where we wish to go. In other words, we act in relation to that which has been, which is and which we anticipate will be. The third part of the book therefore turned towards these different temporalities, their intersection and their amalgamation into a social imaginary.

I sought in this part of the book, to show how my interlocutors see their lives as embedded in a terrain in which decline, conflict and hardship are interpreted and experienced as historical constants, in which uncertainty has come to define an important part of the Guinean everyday. Instability and decline have as a consequence come to be seen as the defining aspect of the Guinean movement through time, and have become the lenses through which my interlocutors make sense of the past, their present position and possibilities and anticipate the future. As Vitór, quoted earlier, put it, the socio-political situation in Bissau has come to resemble the rainy season: 'It darkens, and then everything falls down. Then it darkens again and ...'.

I thus showed that in Bissau the retrospective, introspective and extrospective have merged to form a picture of dire prospects. In fact, the dominance of decline and conflict has been so massive that they have consequently become interpretatively imploded into the body of Guineans as well as exploded into the world. The result is that destructive politics have come to be seen as an essential trait of the Guinean political subject: of his/her past constitution, present predicament and future expectations, ingrained in the body of the Guinean political subject and manifest in the socio-political shape of the world and the global differences between colour and wealth: a twofold process I have termed and analysed as a geno-global identity construction.

Appeasement?

Finally, I brought the different threads of the book together to provide the necessary empirical and analytical background for illuminating the process of appeasement and social reincorporation of the Aguentas.

There seems to be a mutual understanding between the conflicting parties in Guinea-Bissau of the hardness of life in the country and of the contextual character of decline and conflict which serves to create a situationalist understanding of mobilisation and conflict engagement that greatly facilitates social reintegration as well as minimising hatred. The notion of differentiated generational responsibility and culpability and the recategorisation of the Aguentas afford them, as perpetrators, a second chance of social becoming. The Aguenta as child is freed from intention, being unknowing and punished through varieties of verbal abuse, which, though harsh, are at least not fatal, a process which was aided by a generally situationalist understanding of violence enacted in war. Yet there are also the darker aspects of this process. As situationalism comes to facilitate reconciliation by placing the emphasis on the situation that generated the act rather than the agent that performed it, it equally comes to constitute political violence as a social modality rather than a normative transgression.

Theoretical Closure

Throughout the book I have given primacy to a perspective on social becoming and the theory of social navigation. Social navigation is central to my frame of reference as it provides a way of understanding the Aguentas that has heuristic value in relation to both the logic and the seeming illogic of their socio-political perspective and praxis. Via the concept of *dubriagem*, I have attempted to build the idea of navigation into a perspective that is capable of taking into account the complexity of socio-political motives and relations involved in the act of engaging in warfare. The strength of the concept of social navigation is that, as an analytical perspective, it is able to encompass 'instability' and movement in our understanding of action while building on an awareness of both individual will and social forces. In a larger perspective the concept of social navigation thus contributes to the ongoing theoretical debate concerning the relationship between 'agency' and 'structure' and illuminates a part of the dialectic relationship, which has been overlooked by the existing theories on the subject, namely that we act within constantly shifting environments and across shifting terrains.

Steering a Course or Drifting Astray

In an inspiring book, Jackson quotes George Bernard Shaw saying: 'to be in hell is to drift ... to be in heaven is to steer' (Jackson 1998: 19). The quote echoes a similar distinction drawn by Hastrup, between merely staying afloat and steering a course as different social modes of being in the world (1990: 49) and can equally be related to Habermas's description of identity crisis as caused by 'steering problems' (1992: 4). With the concept of navigation we become aware that we are all, continuously, both steering and drifting, both moving expediently along a course and being moved by the course of events; being simultaneously afloat, adrift and in control is a fundamental condition of social being, as we seek to steer our lives through social environments set in motion by a myriad individual and collective acts, forces and consequences beyond our control. Social navigation, as an analytical optic, enables us simultaneously to see how agents seek to move within the social terrain and are moved by the social terrain, and thus places our focus on the intersection of agency and structure. As a general concept, it adds to our understanding of the way in which we seek to control our lives in and through constantly shifting social terrains.

Reading and Navigating Terrains

Social navigation thus grants us a perspective on human action that incorporates temporality and change as prime features of plotting trajectories and praxis. As we seek to overcome immediate problems and constraints we do so with an understanding of what has been and with an eye to what is to come. We simultaneously act and react in relation to our current position within a social terrain, in response to existing constraints and possibilities, as well as in relation to our perception of the future terrain. In order to move towards where we wish to go, we sometimes take detours, sometimes refrain from acting, and sometimes engage in apparently illogical acts, shaped in anticipation of what is to come. Social-scientific analysis most often either centres on illuminating the change of social terrains in a diachronic perspective or the acts of agents in a synchronic perspective; however, the concept of social navigation forces us see a more complex relationship between agents and their social terrain, as it directs our analysis both towards the temporal and the spatial aspects of praxis towards the complex intermorphological process of moving within a shifting terrain that simultaneously moves the agent.

So, although we always seek to navigate our lives in the most expedient manner, we do so well knowing that we do not always control the direction of our movement, as we are embedded in larger social bodies and movements that move us as we seek to move within them. We thus sometimes find ourselves caught in storms, being moved forcefully by circumstances beyond our control; we sometimes slowly drift through windless passages without possibility of movement, and at times we run aground. We obviously seek to move safely along the trajectory we planned and anticipated, yet due to the movement of the social terrain we often have to reorient ourselves and redirect our course as we go (see Ingold 2000).

What we have seen in the case of the Aguentas is a group of agents whose social possibilities are limited in the extreme and yet who constantly attempt to navigate the social terrain they are positioned in, through relating their social position to their social possibilities and the immediate to the imagined. From forging patrimonial ties, entering the Aguenta militia, to letting oneself be the uncomplaining brunt of post-war banter,[3] what we have seen are attempts at navigating lives through shifting and volatile socio-political circumstances.

Demobilising to Remobilise

Finally, the focus on social navigation has shown us that it does not make sense to divide peace, conflict and warfare into discrete and structurally different social processes. The Aguentas seek to navigate the general social terrain as it oscillates between peace, conflict and (at times) warfare, with hardness of life and decline being seen as the stable elements of their social terrain.

Empirically the book has sought to demonstrate that, if we wish to shed light on conflict and warfare, we should do so seeing them not as distinct provinces of human action but as integral parts of social processes. An analysis of conflict engagement should, as Richards (1996) has shown us, take its point of departure in the social, political and discursive environment that the fighting forces are part of. Following Richards's example, one of the empirical aims of this book has been to account for the socio-political position and possibilities that underlie my informants' mobilisation in order for us to deepen our understanding of youth in conflict. The reason our knowledge of this group is restricted has, of course, to do with the dangers of investigating conflict environments. Being stuck in Bissau during the outburst of fighting in November 2000 gave me a chance to see the dynamics of mobilisation, and, although an unpleasant experience, it was an ethnographically valuable one, providing me with a possibility of gaining an insight not only into reconciliation and demobilisation but also into 'conflictualisation' and remobilisation. It helped me to see the way in which young, urban males through conflict engagement seek to balance social death and violent life chances. I hope that the book and the insight gained will contribute to the nuancing of perspectives on youth in war.

Notes

1. Whites.
2. http://www.lusa.pt/show_doc.asp?op=show&search%5Fid=%7B055CC0F5%2DB100%2D4273%2D9F1C%2D1AA4F411B857%7D&page=1&from=simple&fafavname=&id=SIR-4863279 [31 March 2003. Notícia: SIR-4863279]
3. In itself showing how voluntary servitude can be navigational praxis.

BIBLIOGRAPHY

Abdullah, I. 1997. 'Bush Path to Destruction: the Origin and Character of the Revolutionary United Front (RUF/SL)', *Africa Development* 22(3–4): 45–76.

Agger, I. and S.B. Jensen. 1990. 'Testimony as Ritual and Evidence in Psychotherapy for Political Refugees', *Journal of Traumatic Stress* 3(1): 115–30.

Aguilar, R. and Å. Stenman. 1997. 'Guinea-Bissau: from Structural Adjustment to Economic Reform', *Africa Spectrum* 32(1): 71–98.

―――― 2001. 'Guinea-Bissau: a Rocky Road to Reform and Stability', in M. Lundahl (ed.), *From Crisis to Growth in Africa?*, Florence Kentucky: Routledge.

Aho, J.A. 1999 [1994]. *This Thing of Darkness: a Sociology of the Enemy*, Seattle: University of Washington Press.

Aimé, N. 1999a. 'Observações e Constatações Feitas Durante a Visita aos ex-Aguentas no Centro da Liga Guineensedos direitos Humanos em Quinhamel', unpublished manuscript, Bissau: Rädda Barnen.

―――― 1999b. 'Estudo sobre Criancas Afectadas pelo Conflicto Armardo na Guiné Bissau', unpublished manuscript, Bissau: Rädda Barnen/UNICEF.

Allen, C. 1999. 'Warfare, Endemic Violence and State Collapse in Africa', *Review of African Political Economy* 26(81): 367–84.

Amnesty International. 1999. *Guinea-Bissau: Human Rights in War and Peace*. Amnesty International Report, 30 July 1999 at http://web.amnesty.org

Anderson, B. 1993 [1983]. *Imagined Communities: Reflections on the Origin and Spread of Nationalism*, London: Verso.

Andrén, U. 1998. 'Situationen i Guinea-Bissau – en indledande rapport', unpublished manuscript, Promemoria: Swedish Embassy in Guinea-Bissau.

Apter, D.E. 1997. 'Political Violence in Analytical Perspective', in D.E. Apter (ed.), *The Legitimization of Violence*, New York: New York University Press.

Armitage, J. and P. Virilio. 1999. 'From Modernism to Hypermodernism and Beyond: an Interview with Paul Virilio', *Theory, Culture and Society* 16(5–6): 25–56.

Balandier, G. 1970 [1955]. *Political Anthropology*, London: Penguin Press.
Balibar, E. and I. Wallerstein. 1991. *Race, Nation, Class: Ambiguous Identities*, London: Verso.
Bangura, Y. 1997. 'Understanding the Political and Cultural Dynamics of the Sierra Leone War: a Critique of Paul Richards's Fighting for the Rain Forest', *Africa Development* 22(3–4): 117–48.
Banton, M. 1977. *The Idea of Race*, Boulder: Westview Press.
Barber, M.D. 2001. 'Sartre, Phenomenology and the Subjective Approach to Race and Ethnicity in Black Orpheus', *Philosophy and Social Criticism* 27(3): 91–104.
Barbosa, L.N. de H. 1995. 'The Brazilian *Jeitinho:* an Exercise in National Identity', in D.J. Hess and R.A. DaMatta (eds), *The Brazilian Puzzle: Culture on the Borderland of the Western World*, New York: Columbia University Press.
Barot, R. and J. Bird. 2001. 'Racialization: the Genealogy and Critique of a Concept', *Ethnic and Racial Studies* 24(4): 601–18.
Barth, Fredrik. 1959. 'Segmentary Opposition and the Theory of Games: a Study of Pathan Organization', *Journal of the Royal Anthropological Institute* 89: 5–21.
_____ 1969. *Ethnic Groups and Boundaries: the Social Organisation of Cultural Difference*, Bergen: Universitetsforlaget.
_____ 1981. *Features of a Person in Swat: Collected Essays on Pathans*, London: Routledge.
Bateson, G. 1972. *Steps to an Ecology of Mind*, New York: Ballantine Books.
Bauman, Z. 1992. 'Survival as a Social Construct', *Theory, Culture and Society* 9(1): 1–36.
Bayart, J.-F. 1993 *The State in Africa: the Politics of the Belly*, London: Longman.
_____ 2000. 'Africa in the World: a History of Extraversion', *African Affairs* 99(395): 217–68.
Bayart, J.-F., S. Ellis and B. Hibou. 1999. 'From Kleptocracy to the Felonious State?', in J.-F. Bayart, S. Ellis, and B. Hibou (eds), *The Criminalization of the State in Africa*, Oxford: James Currey.
Beck, U., W. Bonns and C. Lau. 2003. 'The Theory of Reflexive Modernization: Problematic, Hypotheses and Research Programme', *Theory, Culture and Society* 20(2): 1–33.
Benedict, R. 1989 [1947]. *The Chrysanthemum and the Sword: Patterns of Japanese Culture*, Boston: Houghton Mifflin Company.
Berger, P.L. and T. Luckmann. 1967 [1966]. *The Social Construction of Reality: a Treatise in the Sociology of Knowledge*, New York: Anchor Books.
Bevir, M. 1999. 'Foucault and Critique: Deploying Agency against Autonomy', *Political Theory* 27(1): 65–84.
Beyerchen, A. 1992. 'Clausewitz, Nonlinearity, and the Unpredictability of War', *International Security* 17(3): 59–90.
Bhabha, H.K. 1994. *The Location of Culture*, London: Routledge.
Blake, J.W. 1942. *The Europeans in West Africa, 1450–1560: Documents to Illustrate the Nature and Scope of Portuguese Enterprises in West Africa, the Abortive Attempt of the Castillians to Create an Empire There, and the Early English Voyages to Barbary and Guinea*, London: Hakluyt Society.
Bourdieu, P. 1984. *Distinction: a Social Critique of the Judgement of Taste*, London: Routledge.

_____ 1986 [1983]. 'The Forms of Capital', in J.G. Richardson (ed.), *A Handbook of Theory and Research for the Sociology of Education*, Westport: Greenwood Press.
_____ 1988. 'Den Biografiske Illusion', *Kontext* 52: 39–44.
_____ 1989. 'Social Space and Symbolic Power', *Sociological Theory* 7(1): 723–44.
_____ 1992 [1977]. *Outline of a Theory of Practice*, Cambridge: Cambridge University Press.
_____ 1994 [1991]. *Language and Symbolic Power*, Cambridge: Polity Press
_____ 1998. *Practical Reason: on the Theory of Action*, Cambridge: Polity Press.
_____ 1998. *Acts of Resistance: Against the New Myths of our Time*, Cambridge: Polity Press.
Bourdieu, P. and L.J.D. Wacquant. 2001. *Refleksiv Sociologi: Mål og Midler*, Copenhagen: Hans Reitzel.
Boudon, R. 1998. 'Limitations of Rational Choice Theory', *American Journal of Sociology* 104(3): 817–28.
Briggs, C. 2001. 'Modernity, Cultural Reasoning, and the Institutionalization of Social Inequality: Racializing Death in a Venezuelan Cholera Epidemic', *Comparative Studies in Society and History* 43(4): 665–770.
Bruner, J. 1987. 'Life as Narrative', *Social Research* 54(1): 11–32.
_____ 1996. *The Culture of Education*, Cambridge, Massachusetts: Harvard University Press.
Bucholtz, M. 2002. 'Youth and Cultural Practice', *Annual Review of Anthropology* 31: 525–52.
Cabral, A. 1972. *Revolution i Guinea*, Copenhagen: Demos.
_____ 1973 [1970]. *Return to the Source: Selected Speeches*, New York: Monthly Review.
_____ 1974. *Kulturens Rolle i Uafhængighedskampen*, Aarhus: De Portugisiske Desertørers Komite.
_____ 1980. *Unity and Struggle: Speeches and Writings*, London: Heinemann.
Cairns, E. 1995. *Children and Political Violence*, Oxford: Blackwell.
Castoriadis, C. 1997 [1987]. *The Imaginary Institution of Society*, Cambridge: Polity Press.
Chabal, P. 1983. 'Party, State, and Socialism in Guinea-Bissau', *Canadian Journal of African Studies* 17(2): 189–210.
_____ 1996. 'The African Crisis: Context and Interpretation', in R.P. Werbner and T.O. Ranger (eds), *Postcolonial Identities in Africa*. London: Zed Books.
_____ 2002. 'Part 1. Lusophone Africa in Historical and Comparative Perspective', in P. Chabal (ed.), *A History of Postcolonial Lusophone Africa*, London: Hurst.
Chabal, P. and J.-P. Daloz. 1999. *Africa Works: Disorder as Political Instrument*, Oxford: James Currey.
Clausewitz, C.M. von. 1997 [1976]. *On War*, Ware: Wordsworth.
Cohen, A. 1969. *Custom and Politics in Urban Africa*, London: Routledge.
Cole, J. 2004. 'Fresh Contact in Tamatave, Madagascar: Sex, Money, and Intergenerational Transformation', *American Ethnologist* 31(4): 573–88.
Collier, P. 2000. 'Doing Well out of War: an Economic Perspective', in M. Berdal and D. Malone (eds), *Greed and Grievance: Economic Agendas in Civil Wars*, Boulder, Colorado: Lynne Rienner Publishers.

Comaroff, J.L. and J. Comaroff. 1999. 'Occult Economies and the Violence of Abstraction: Notes from the South African Postcolony', *American Ethnologist* 26(2): 279–303.

Crapanzano, V. 2004. *Imaginative Horizons: an Essay in Literary-philosophical Anthropology*, Chicago: University of Chicago Press.

Crowder, M. 1978. *Colonial West Africa*, London: Frank Cass.

Dahrendorf, R. 1979. *Life Chances: Approaches to Social and Political Theory*, Chicago: University of Chicago Press.

_____ 1988. *The Modern Social Conflict: an Essay on the Politics of Liberty*, London: Weidenfeld & Nicolson.

Daniel, E.V. 1996. *Charred Lullabies: Chapters in an Anthropography of Violence*, Princeton: Princeton University Press.

Davis, J. 1992. 'History and the People without Europe', in K. Hastrup (ed.), *Other Histories*, London: Routledge.

Deas, M. 1997. 'Violent Exchanges: Reflexions on Political Violence in Colombia', in D. Apter (ed.), *The Legitimization of Violence*, New York: New York University Press.

de Boeck, F. and A. Honwana. 2000. 'Faire et Défaire la société: enfants, jeunes et politique en Afrique', *Politique Africaine* 80: 5–11.

de Certeau, M. 1988 [1984]. *The Practice of Everyday Life*, Berkeley: University of California Press.

Delaney, D. 2002. 'The Space that Race Makes', *Professional Geographer* 54(1): 6–14.

Deleuze, G. and F. Guattari. 2002 [1987]. *A Thousand Plateaus: Capitalism and Schizophrenia*, London: Continuum.

Douglas, M. 1987. *How Institutions Think*, London: Routledge.

Duffield, M. 1998. 'Post-Modern Conflict: Warlords, Post-adjustment States and Private Protection', *Civil Wars* 1(1): 65–102.

_____ 2001. *Global Governance and the New Wars: the Merging of Development and Security*, London: Zed Books.

Dunn, K. 2000. 'Tales from the Dark Side: Africa's Challenge to International Relations Theory', *Journal of Third World Studies* 17(1): 61–90.

Durham, D. 2000. 'Youth and the Social Imagination in Africa: Introduction to Parts 1 and 2', *Anthropological Quarterly* 73(3): 113–20.

Einarsdóttir, J. 2000. *'Tired of Weeping': Child Death and Mourning among Papel Mothers in Guinea-Bissau*, Ph.D. dissertation, Stockholm: Stockholm Studies in Social Anthropology.

Eisenstadt, S.N. 1964 [1956]. *From Generation to Generation: Age Groups and Social Structure*, New York: Free Press.

Eisenstadt, S.N. and L. Roniger. 1981. 'The Study of Patron–Client Relations and Recent Development in Sociological Theory', in S.N. Eisenstadt and R. Lemarchand (eds), *Political Clientelism, Patronage and Development*, London: Sage.

Enzensberger, H.M. 1994. *Civil War*, London: Granada Books.

Estroff, S.E. 1993. 'Identity, Disability, and Schitzophrenia: the Problem of Chronicity', in S. Lindenbaum and M. Lock (eds), *Knowledge, Power and Practice: the Anthropology of Medicine and Everyday Life*, Berkeley: University of California Press.

Evans, K. and A. Furlong. 1997. 'Metaphors of Youth Transition, Niches, Pathways, Trajectories or Navigations', in J. Bynner, L. Chisholm and A. Furlong (eds), *Youth, Citizenship and Social Change in a European Context*, Aldershot: Ashgate.

Evans-Pritchard, E.E. 1965 [1940]. *The Nuer: a Description of the Modes of Livelihood and Political Institutions of a Nilotic People*, Oxford: Clarendon Press.

Fallers, L. 1956. *Bantu Bureaucracy: a Century of Political Evolution among the Basago of Uganda*, Chicago: University of Chicago Press.

Fanon, F. 1990 [1965]. *The Wretched of the Earth*, London: Penguin.

Farmer, P. 1994. 'Aids-Talk and the Constitution of Cultural Models', *Social Science and Medicine* 38(6): 801–9.

Feldman, A. 1991. *Formations of Violence: the Narrative of the Body and Political Terror in Northern Ireland*, Chicago: University of Chicago Press.

Ferguson, J. 1999. *Expectations of Modernity: Myths and Meanings of Urban Life on the Zambian Copperbelt*, Berkeley: University of California Press.

Flanding, M.K. 2002. *A Study of War Experiences, Continuity and Dis-Continuity in Guinea-Bissau, West Africa*. Specialerække 251, Copenhagen: Institut for Antropologi, University of Copenhagen.

Forrest, J.B. 1987. 'Guinea-Bissau since Independence: a Decade of Power Struggles', *The Journal of Modern African Studies* 25(1): 95–116.

―――― 1992. *Guinea-Bissau. Power, Conflict, and Renewal in a West African Nation*, Boulder: Westview Press.

―――― 2002. 'Guinea-Bissau', in P. Chabal (ed.), *A History of Postcolonial Lusophone Africa*, London: Hurst & Company.

―――― 2003. *Lineages of State Fragility: Rural Civil Society in Guinea Bissau*, Athens: Ohio University Press.

Fortes, M. 1969 [1949]. *The Web of Kinship among the Tellensi: the Second Part of an Analysis of the Social Structure of a Trans Volta Tribe*, London: Oxford University Press.

―――― 1984. 'Age, Generation, and Social Structure', in D.E. Kertzer and J. Kieth (eds), *Age and Anthropological Theory*, London: Ichaca.

Furley, O. 1995. 'Child Soldiers in Africa', in O. Furley (ed.), *Conflict in Africa*, London: I.B. Tauris Publishers.

Gable, E. 1995. 'The Decolonization of Consciousness: Local Sceptics and the Will to be Modern in a West-African Village', *American Ethnologist* 22(2): 242–57.

―――― 2000. 'The Culture Development Club: Youth, Neo-tradition, and the Construction of Society in Guinea-Bissau', *Anthropological Quarterly* 73(4): 195–203.

Galtung, J. 1979. *On Violence in General and Terrorism in Particular*. Chair in Conflict and Peace Reseach. Papers no. 72, Oslo: University of Oslo.

―――― 1990. 'Cultural Violence', *Journal of Peace Research* 27(3): 291–305.

Gaonkar, D.P. 2002. 'Toward New Imaginaries: an Introduction', *Public Culture* 14(1): 1–20.

Geertz, C. 1993 [1973]. *The Interpretation of Cultures*, London: Fontana Press.

Gell, A. 1993. 'How to Read a Map: Remarks on the Practical Logic of Navigation', *Man (N.S.)* 20(2): 271–86.

Gerth, H.H. and C.W. Mills. 1958 [1946]. 'Introduction: the Man and his Work', in H.H. Gerth and C.W. Mills, *From Max Weber: Essays in Sociology*, New York: Oxford University Press.

Giddens, A. 1984. *The Constitution of Society: Outline of the Theory of Structuration*, Cambridge: Polity Press.

Gilliam, L. 1998. *'When Catholics and Protestants Fight': en analyse af konfliktforståelser blandt børn i Belfast*, Københavns Universitet: Specialerække 119, Institut for Antropologi.

―――― 2004. 'Restricted Experiences in a Conflict Society: the Local Lives of Belfast Children', in K.F. Olwig and E. Gulløv (eds), *Children's Places: Cross-Cultural Perspectives*, London: Routledge.

Gluckman, M. 1963. *Order and Rebellion in Tribal Africa*, New York: Free Press of Glencoe.

Green, L. 1994. 'Fear as a Way of Life', *Cultural Anthropology* 9(2): 227–56.

Greverus, I.-M. 1996. 'Anthropological Horizons, the Humanities and Human Practice', in J. van Bremen, V. Godina and J. Platenamp (eds), *Horizons of Understanding: an Anthology of Theoretical Anthropology in Europe*, Leiden: Research School CNWS, Leiden University, pp. 124–37.

Gullestad, M. 1992. *The Art of Social Relations: Essays on Culture, Social Action and Everyday Life in Modern Norway*, Oslo: Scandinavian University Press.

Habermas, J. 1992 [1976]. *Legitimation Crisis*, Cambridge: Polity Press.

Hage, G 2003. '"Comes a Time we are all Enthusiasm": Understanding Palestinian Suicide Bombers in Times of Exighophobia', *Public Culture* 15(1): 65–89.

Harker, R., C. Mahar and C. Wilkes. 1990. *An Introduction to the Work of Pierre Bourdieu – the Practice and Theory*, London: Macmillan.

Hastrup, K. 1990. 'Udvikling eller Historie – Antropologiens Bidrag til en Ny Verden', *Den Ny Verden* 23: 36–54.

―――― 1992. 'Uchronia and the Two Histories of Iceland, 1400–1800', in K. Hastrup, (ed.), *Other Histories*, London: Routledge

Hawthorne, W. 2001. 'Nourishing a Stateless Society during the Slave Trade: the Rise of Balanta Paddy-rice Production in Guinea-Bissau', *Journal of African History* 42(1): 1–24.

Henriksen, T.H. 1977. 'Some Notes on the National Liberation Wars in Angola, Mozambique, and Guinea-Bissau', *Military Affairs* 41(1): 20–37.

Herzfeld, M. 1992. *The Social Production of Indifference: Exploring the Symbolic Roots of Western Bureaucracy*, Oxford: Berg Publishers.

Hinkelammert, F.J. 1993. 'The Crisis of Socialism and the Third World', *Monthly Review: an Independent Socialist Magazine* 45(3): 105–14.

Honwana, A. 2000. 'Innocents ou coupables? Les enfants-soldats comme acteurs Tactiques', *Politique Africaine* 80: 58–79.

Husserl, E. 1964. *Phenomenology of Internal Time-consciousness*, Bloomington: Indiana University Press.

Hydén, G. 1983. *No Shortcuts to Progress*, London: Heinemann Educational.

Ingold, T. 2000. 'To Journey Along a Way of Life: Maps, Wayfinding and Navigation', in *The Perception of the Environment: Essays in Livelihood, Dwelling and Skill*, London: Routledge.

Jackson, M. 1998. *Minima Ethnographica: Intersubjectivity and the Anthropological Subject*, Chicago: University of Chicago Press.

_____ 2002. *The Politics of Storytelling: Violence, Transgression, and Intersubjectivity*, Copenhagen: Museum Tusculanum.

Jespersen, S.B. 2002. *In Search of Recognition: a Study of War Veterans in Guinea-Bissau*. Specialerække 171, Copenhagen: Institute of Anthropology, University of Copenhagen.

Johnson-Hanks, J. 2002. 'On the Limits of Life-Stages in Ethnography: Towards a Theory of Vital Conjunctures', *American Anthropologists* 104(3): 865–80.

Jones, G. and C. Wallace. 1992. *Youth, Family and Citizenship*, Buckingham: Open University Press.

Kaldor, M. 1999. *New & Old Wars: Organised Violence in a Global Era*, Cambridge: Polity Press.

Kalyvas, S. N. 2001. '"New" and "Old" Civil Wars: a Valid Distinction?', *World Politics* 54(1): 99–118.

Kapferer B. 1976. 'Introduction: Transactional Models Reconsidered', in B. Kapferer (ed.), *Transaction and Meaning: Directions in the Anthropology of Exchange and Symbolic Behavior*, Philadelphia: Institute for the Study of Human Issues.

Kaplan, R.D. 1996. *The Ends of the Earth: a Journey at the Dawn of the 21th Century*, New York: Random House.

Keller, E.J. 1987. 'Afro-Marxist Regimes', in E.J. Keller and D.S. Rothchild (eds), *Afro-Marxist Regimes: Ideology and Public Policy*, Boulder: L. Rienner Publishers.

Kelman, H.C. and L.V. Hamilton. 1989. *Crimes of Obedience: Toward a Social Psychology of Authority and Responsibility*, New Haven: Yale University Press.

Kemedjio, C. 1998. 'When the Detour Leads Home: the Urgency of Memory and the Liberation Imperative from Aimé Césaire to Franz Fanon', *Research in African Literature* 29(3): 191–202.

Kleinman, A. and J. Kleinman. 1997. 'The Appeal of Experience: the Dismay of Images: Cultural Appropriations of Suffering in our Times', in A. Kleinman, V. Das and M. Lock (eds), *Social Suffering*, Berkeley: University of California Press.

Kleinman, A., V. Das and M. Lock. 1997. 'Introduction', in A. Kleinman, V. Dasand M. Lock (eds), *Social Suffering*, Berkeley: University of California Press.

Koselleck, R. 2004. *Futures Past: on the Semantics of Historical Time*, New York: Columbia University Press.

Kovsted, J. and F. Tarp. 1999. *Guinea-Bissau. War, Reconstruction and Reform*. Working Papers 168, Helsinki: UNU World Institute for Development Economics Research.

Krohn-Hansen, C. 1994. 'The Anthropology of Violent Interaction', *Journal of Anthropological Research* 50(4): 367–81.

Laclau, E. 1990. *New Reflections on the Revolution of our Time*, London: Verso.

Lambert, M.C. 1993. 'From Citizenship to Negritude – "Making a Difference" in Elite Ideologies of Colonized Francophone West Africa', *Comparative Studies in Society and History* 35(2): 239.

Leidner, R. 1993. *Fast Food, Fast Talk: Service Work and the Routinization of Everyday Life*, Berkeley: University of California Press.

Liga Guineense dos Direitos Humanos. 1999. 'Programa de Reinserção Social dos Joven Militares "Aguentas"', unpublished manuscript, Bissau: Liga Guineense dos Direitos Humanos.
Linde, C. 1993. *Life Stories: The Creation of Coherence*, Oxford: Oxford University Press.
Lindquist, M. 1996. 'Times of Crisis', *Studia Ethnologica Upsaliensia* 17.
Lobban, R. and J. Forrest. 1988. *Historical Dictionary of the Republics of Guinea-Bissau and Cape Verde*, Metuchen: Scarecrow Press.
Löfgren, O. 1990. 'The Danger of Knowing What You Are Looking For: on Routinising Research', *Ethnologia Scandinavica* 20: 3–15.
Lopes, C. and L. Rudebeck. 1988. *The Socialist Ideal in Africa*. Research Report no. 81. Uppsala: Scandinavian Institute of African Studies.
Lourenço-Lindell, I. 1996. 'How do the Urban Poor Stay Alive? Modes of Food-Provisioning in an Squatter Settlement in Bissau', *African Urban Quarterly* 11(2): 163–68.
———— 2002. *Walking the Tight Rope: Informal Livelihoods and Social Networks in a West African City*. Ph.D. dissertation, Stockholm: Almqvist & Wiksell International.
Luttwak, E. 1972. *A Dictionary of Modern War*, London: Allen Lane.
Lutz, C. 1999. 'Ethnography at the War Century's End', *Journal of Contemporary Ethnography* 28(6): 610–19.
Lyon, J.M. 1980. 'Marxism and Ethno-nationalism in Guinea-Bissau, 1956–76', *Ethnic and Racial Studies* 3(2): 156–68.
Lyotard, J.-F. 1991. *Phenomenology*, New York: University New York Press.
Mabogunje, A.L. 1971. 'The Land and Peoples of West Africa', in J.F.A. Ajayi and M. Crowder (eds), *History of West Africa*, London: Longman.
Malinowski, B. 1971 [1926]. *Myth in Primitive Psychology*, Westport: Negro University Press.
Malkki, L. 1992. 'National Geographic: the Rooting of Peoples and the Territorialization of National Identity among Scholars and Refugees', *Cultural Anthropology* 7(1): 24–44.
———— 1995. *Purity and Exile: Violence, Memory and National Cosmology among Hutu Refugees in Tanzania*, Chicago: University of Chicago Press.
Mannheim, K. 1952. *Essays on the Sociology of Knowledge*, London: Routledge.
Mark, P. 1999. 'The Evolution of "Portuguese" Identity: Luso Africans on the Upper Guinean Coast from the Sixteenth to the Nineteenth Century', *Journal of African History* 40: 173–91.
———— 2002. *Portuguese Style and Luso-African Identity*, Bloomington: Indiana University Press.
Massumi, B. 1997. 'Deleuze, Guattari, and the Philosophy of Expression', *Canadian Review of Comparative Literature* 24(3): 745–82.
Mattingly, C. 1994. 'The Concept of Terapeutic "Emplotment"', *Social Science and Medicine* 38(6): 811–22.
Mayer, A. 1966. 'The Significance of Quasi-Groups in the Study of Complex Societies', in M. Banton (ed.), *The Social Anthropology of Complex Societies*, London: Tavistock.
Mayr, E. 1992. 'The Idea of Teleology', *Journal of The History of Ideas* 53(1): 117–35.
Mbembe, A. 1995. 'Figures of the Subject in Times of Crisis', *Public Culture* 7(2): 323–52.

_____ 2003. 'Necropolitics', *Public Culture* 15(1): 11–40.
McCulloch, J. 1983. *In the Twilight of Revolution: the Political Theory of Amilcar Cabral*, London: Routledge
Mead, M. 1969 [1928]. *Coming of Age in Samoa: a Study of Adolescence and Sex in Primitive Societies*, Harmondsworth: Penguin Books.
Meillassoux, C. 1981 [1978]. *Maidens, Meal and Money: Capitalism and the Domestic Community*, Cambridge: Cambridge University Press.
Mendy, P.K. 1999. 'Guinea Bissau: State Decay and Factional Struggles 1973–1998', *Sapem*, May.
_____ 2003. 'Portugal's Civilizing Mission in Colonial Guinea-Bissau: Rhetoric or Reality?', *International Journal of African Historical Studies* 36(1): 35–53.
Merton, R.K. 1968 [1949]. *Social Theory and Social Structure*. New York: Free Press.
Mertz, E. 2002. 'The Perfidy of the Gaze and the Pain of Uncertainty', in C.J. Greenhouse, E. Mertz and K.B. Warren (eds), *Ethnography in Unstable Places: Everyday Lives in the Context of Dramatic Social Change*, Durham: Duke University Press.
Miles, R. 1993. *'Racism after 'Race Relations'*, London: Routledge.
Mitchell, Clyde J. 1969. 'The Concept and Use of Social Networks', in J.C. Mitchell (ed.), *Social Networks in Urban Situations: Analyses of Personal Relationships in Central African Towns*, Manchester: Manchester University Press.
Monteiro, A. et al. 1996. *O Programa de Ajustamento Estrutural na Guiné-Bissau: análise dos efeitos socio-economicos*, Bissau: INEP.
Mork, N.P. 2003. *Guinea-Bissau Profile*, World of Information: Walden Publishing.
Murdoch, I. 1970. *A Fairly Honourable Defeat*, London: Chatto & Windus.
Nordstrom, C. 1997. *A Different Kind of War Story*, Philadelphia: University of Pennsylvania Press.
_____ 1999. 'Visible Wars and Invisible Girls, Shadow Industries and the Politics of Not-Knowing', *International Feminist Journal of Politics* 1(1): 14–33.
_____ 2001. 'Carita's War', *Development* 44(3): 30–35.
Nordstrom, C. and A.C.G.M Robben. 1995. 'Introduction: the Anthropology and Ethnography of Violence and Socio-political Conflict', in C. Nordstrom, C. and A.C.G.M Robben (eds), *Fieldwork under Fire: Contemporary Studies of Violence and Survival*, Berkeley: University of California Press.
O'Brien, D.B.C. 1996. 'A Lost Generation? Youth, Identity and State Decay in West Africa', in R.P. Werbner and T. Ranger (eds), *Postcolonial Identities in Africa*, London: Zed Books.
Okumo, W. 2001. 'Afro-Pessimism and African Leadership', *The Perspective*, 5 April.
Olwig, K. F. 2000. *Generations in the Making: the Role of Children*. Unpub. Manus. Paper presented at the 6th Biennial EASA Conference, Krakow.
Olwig, K.F. and E. Gulløv. 2004. 'Towards an Anthropology of Children and Place', in K.F. Olwig and E. Gulløv (eds), *Children's Places: Cross-cultural Perspectives*, London: Routledge.
Omi, M. and H. Winant. 1986. *Social Formation in the United States: from the 1960s to the 1980s*, New York: Routledge.

Parsons, T. 1966. *The Social System*, Glencoe: Free Press.
Peters, K. and P. Richards. 1998. '"Why we Fight": Voices of Youth Combatants in Sierra Leone', *Africa* 68(2): 183–210.
Pink, S. 2001. 'Sunglasses, Suitcases, and other Symbols: Creativity and Indirect Communication in Festive and Everyday Performance', in J. Hendry and C.W. Watson (eds), *An Anthropology of Indirect Communication*, London: Routledge.
Popper, K. 1972. *The Poverty of Historicism*, London: Routledge.
Price, L. 1987. 'Ecuadorian Illness Stories: Cultural Knowledge in Natural Discourse', in D. Holland and N. Quinn (eds), *Cultural Models in Language and Thought*, Cambridge: Cambridge University Press.
Reed-Danahay, D. 1996. *Education and Identity in Rural France*, Cambridge: Cambridge University Press.
Richards, P. 1995. 'Rebellion in Liberia and Sierra Leone: a Crisis of Youth?', in O. Furley (ed.), *Conflict in Africa*, London: Tauris Academic Publishers.
_____ 1996. *Fighting for the Rain Forest: War, Youth and Resources in Sierra Leone*, Portsmouth, New Hampshire: Heinemann.
Riches, D. 1986. 'The Phenomenon of Violence', in D. Riches (ed.), *The Anthropology of Violence*, Oxford: Basil Blackwell.
Ricoeur, P. 1991. *From Text to Action*, London: Athlone.
Rieff, D. 1998. 'In Defence of Afro-Pessimism', *World Policy Journal* 15(4) 10–22.
Rudebeck, L. 1992. 'Politics and Structural Adjustment in a West-African Village', in L. Rudebeck (ed.), *When Democracy Makes Sense: Studies in the Democratic Potential of Third World Movements*, Uppsalsa: AKUT.
_____ 2000. 'Hur Kan Demokrati Konsolideres? Et Fallstudie av Guniea-Bissau 1998–2000', unpublished manuscript.
Sahlins, M. 1974. *Stone Age Economies*, London: Tavistock Publications.
Schafer, R. 1992. *Retelling a Life: Narration and Dikalogue in Psychoanalysis*, New York: Basic Books.
Schmidt, B.E. and I.W. Schröder. 2001. 'Introduction: Violent Imaginaries and Violent Practices', in B.E. Schmidt and I.W. Schröder (eds), *Anthropology of Violence and Conflict*, London: Routledge.
Schutz, A. 1996 [1973]. *Collected Papers*, The Hague: Nijhoff.
Schutz, A. and T. Luckmann. 1995 [1989]. *The Structures of the Life-world*, Evanston: Northwestern University Press.
Scott, J.C. 1998. *Seeing Like a State: How Certain Schemes to Improve the Human Condition have Failed*, New Haven: Yale University Press.
Seekings, J. 1996. 'The Lost Generation: South Africa's Youth Problem in the Early-1990s', *Transformations* 29: 103–25.
Senghor, L. S. 1972. *Mod en ny Civilisation*, Copenhagen: Munksgaard.
Shanklin, E. 1998. 'The Profession of the Color Blind: Socio-cultural Anthropology and Racism in the 21st Century', *American Anthropologist* 100(3): 669–79.
Shore, B. 1996. *Culture in Mind: Cognition, Culture, and the Problem of Meaning*, New York: Oxford University Press.
Smedley, A. 1998. '"Race"and the Construction of Human Identity', *American Anthropologist* 100(3): 690–702.

Taussig, M. 1992. *The Nervous System*, New York: Routledge.
Taylor, C. 2002. 'Modern Social Imaginaries', *Public Culture* 14(1): 91–124.
_____ 2004. *Modern Social Imaginaries*, Durham: Duke University Press.
Tilly, C. 1978. *From Mobilisation to Revolution*, Reading: Addison-Wesley.
Tin, Hjalte. 1997. *A Typology of Civil Wars*. Working papers, DUPI, Copenhagen: Danish Institute of International Affairs.
Tonkin, E. 1995. *Narrating our Pasts: the Social Construction of Oral History*, Cambridge: Cambridge University Press.
Turner, V. 1967. *The Forest of Symbols: Aspects of Ndembu Ritual*, Ithaca: New York.
Twain, M. 1963 [1896]. *Life on the Mississippi*, New York: Bantam Books.
Utas, M. 2003. *Sweet Battlefields: Youth and the Liberian Civil War*, Uppsala: Uppsala University Dissertations in Cultural Anthropology.
Vaillant, J.G. 1990. *Black, French, and African: a Life of Léopold Sédar Senghor*, Cambridge, Massachusetts: Harvard University Press.
Vigh, H.E. 1998. *'They are Trying to Destroy our Culture': en analyse af konfliktnarrativer blandt paramilitære protestanter i Nordirland*, Københavns Universitet: Specialerække 127, Institut for Antropologi.
_____ 2002 [2004]. 'Introduktion til Voldens Antropologi: fra erfaring til fællesskab', *Tidskrift Antropologi* 46: 3–15.
_____ 2003. 'Navigating Terrains of War: Youth and Soldiering in Bissau', Ph.D. Dissertation, Department of Anthropology, University of Copenhagen.
Virilio, P. 2001. *Hastighed og Politik*, Frederiksberg: Introite! Publishers.
Waage, T. 2002. *'Chez Nous On se Debrouille'. Om å Håndtere Uforutsigtbarhet: fortellinger fra syv ungdomsmiljøer I den polyetniske byen Ngaoundéré I Nord-Kamerun*. Afhandling for graden Doctor Rerum Politicarum, Institutt for Socialantropologi, Universitetet i Tromsø
Weber, M. 1965 [1947]. *The Theory of Social and Economic Organization*, New York: The Free Press.
_____ 1982 [1971]. *Makt og Byråkrati: essays om politikk og klasse, samfunnsforskning og verdier*, Oslo: Gyldendal.
Werbner, R. 1991. *Tears of the Dead: the Social Biography of an African Family*, Edinburgh: Edinburgh University Press.
Whyte, S.R. 1997. *Questioning Misfortune: the Pragmatics of Uncertainty in Eastern Uganda*, Cambridge: Cambridge University Press.
Wikan, U. 1992. 'Beyond the Words: the Power of Ressonance', *American Ethnologist* 19(3): 460–82.
Willmott, L. 1997. 'Introduction', in C.M. v. Clausewitz, *On War*, Ware: Wordsworth.
Wolf, E. 1966. 'Kinship, Friendship, and Patron-Client Relations in Complex Societies', in M. Banton (ed.), *The Social Anthropology of Complex Societies*, London: Tavistock.
Wulff, H. 1994. 'Ungdomskultur I Sverige', *FUS-rapport* 6: 127–141, Stokholm: Brutus Östlings Bokförlag Symposion.
_____ 1995. 'Introduction. Introducing Youth Culture in its own Right: the State of the Art and New Possibilities', in V. Amit-Talai and H. Wulff (eds), *Youth Cultures: a Cross-cultural Perspective*, London: Routledge.

INDEX

A
Abdullah, Ibrahim, 11
abjection, 186
action, 147, 150–55, 156, 158, 159, 164, 175, 189, 206–9
    situated, 13, 14, 28, 30, 80–81, 82, 173, 221, 228
    strategic, 29, 129, 134, 135, 162
    tactical, 123, 124, 126, 129, 136–39, 167 *see also* dubriagem
action set, 107n. 34.
African socialism, 180, 180n. 23.
Afro-Marxism, 180, 180n. 23.
Afro-pessimism, 190, 203
age
    group, 17n. 13., 146, 146n. 9.
    social, 89, 222
Agger, Inger and Søren B. Jensen, 148n. 12., 206n
Aguilar, Renato and Åsa Stenman, 44
Allen, Charles, 104
Aho, James, 75, 79, 83
Anderson, Benedict, 19, 66, 76, 93, 202
Andrén, Ulla, 46n. 27., 48n. 37., 49nn. 42, 46., 50, 57
anomie, 96, 99, 103, 184, 186, 187
    critique of, 100n. 23.
Apter, David, 179, 207
Armitage, John
    and Paul Virilio, 165

B
Balandier, George, 177n. 13., 179n. 18.
the Balanta, 40, 42n. 13., 70, 181, 182n. 31., 232, 232n. 13.

Balibar, Etienne and Immanuel Wallerstein, 203n
Bangura, Yusuf, 11, 106, 109
Banton, Michael, 177
Barber, Michael D., 181n. 27.
Barbosa, Livia, 129
Barot, Rohit and John Bird, 204n
Barth, Fredrik, 53, 164–65
Bateson, Gregory, 130, 226
Bauman, Zygmunt, 94, 94n. 9.
Bayart, Jean-François, 4, 27, 30, 110n. 41., 143, 196, 197, 198
    on generation, 97,
    on patrimonialism, 108, 110, 111, 112, 121, 122
    the Beafata, 40
becoming, *see* social becoming
Benedict, Ruth, 166, 166n. 45.
Berdal, Mats and David M. Malone, 28
Berger, Peter L.,
    and Thomas Luckmann, 154, 167n. 48.
Bevir, Mark, 160
Bhabha, Homi K., 152
Bird, John
    and Rohit Barot, 204n
Blackness, 194, 195, 196, 202, 203, 204
Boudon, Raymond, 30
de Boeck, Philip
    and Alcinda Honwana, 11
Bourdieu, Pierre, 11, 12, 24, 134, 143, 174, 188
    on capital, 29, 164
    critique of, 165n. 40.
    economism and, 29n

on field, 80, 164n. 34, 35., 165, 165n. 39.
games and, 164
on habitus, 154, 164n. 37.
on heterodoxy, 150
and Loïc Waquant, 164
strategy and rules, 135, 164nn. 34, 35.
on violence, 23
Briggs, Charles, 195, 202, 204n
Bruner, Jerome, 206
Bucholtz, Mary, 92
Budjugu, 40, 40n. 13.

C

Cabral, Amilcar, 43, 180, 180n. 25., 181, 182, 182n. 31., 187, 190
Cairns, Ed, 119, 120n. 7.
capital, 164
capitalism, 69, 183, 184, 185n. 40., 187
Castoriadis, Cornelius, 31n. 38., 173
Césairé, Aime, 177n. 13., 178
Chabal, Patrick, 8n, 43, 45, 177, 187
and Jean-Pascal Daloz, 8n, 95, 96
charter, 207
chronicity, 105
Clausewitz, Carl M. von, 66, 66nn., 132,
Cohen, Abner, 124
Cole, Jennifer, 92
collegason, 17n. 13., 19, 98, 146–48, 147n. 10., 195 *see also* mandjuandade
Collier, Paul, 28
Comaroff, Jean
and John Comaroff, 97
Comaroff, John
and Jean Comaroff, 97
communism, 183
community of experience, 19–20, 19n. 17., 20n. 19., 20, 93n. 3.
Crapanzano, Vincent, 31
crisis, 81, 117, 159–60, 166, 182
agency and, 159–64
chronicity and, 105, 150–52, 152n. 18., 163
definition of, 189
everyday, 155–58, 158n, 169–69

D

Dahrendorf, Ralf, 5, 14, 110
Daloz, Jean-Pascal
and Patrick Chabal, 8n, 95, 96
Daniel, Valentine E., 26, 176
Davis, John, 206

Deas, Malcolm, 64, 157
de Certeau, Michel, 131, 132, 133, 134, 134n. 28., 176n. 11.
Delaney, David, 202
Deleuze, Gilles and Felix Guattari, 18, 131, 134
Demobilisation, 209
Diola, 40, 40n. 3.
discursive phrase, 120, 201, 203
Douglas, Mary, 110
dubriagem, 128, 129–30, 197
Duffield, Mark, 27, 190
Dunn, Kevin, 111
Durham, Deborah, 90, 92, 136

E

economism, 29
economy of affection, 54, 104, 105, 106–7, 194, 198, 222
critique of, 54n. 55., 104n. 29.
Einarsdóttir, Jónína, 3n
Eisenstadt, Sahmuel N., 105n. 32., 164n. 9.
enemy, 64–69, 70, 77, 235
ideology and, 66, 69n. 6.
Other and, 65, 81–84,
as opponent, 71–75, 79, 80, 83, 221
Enzensberger, Hans M., 28
Estroff, Sue, 105, 152
ethnicity, 52–55
hatred and, 53–54
homeland and, 51, 51n. 49., 51n. 51.
politics and 52–54, 124
Evans, Karen
and Andrew Furlong, 14n. 7.
Evans-Pritchard, Edward E., 124
event, 13, 14, 27, 28 148, 158, 163, 175n. 7., 179, 194, 201
narrative and, 206–8
war and, 81, 82, 148–50
everyday, 22, 155–58, 158n, 162, 163, 167, 186, 189
definition of, 158n.
extrospection, 174, 175, 202–5, 230, 236

F

factions, 45, 110, 119, 121
Fanon, Frantz, 177n. 13, 178, 179, 180nn. 22, 26., 181n. 27., 190
Farmer, Paul, 206n
Feldman, Allen, 175n. 7, 207
Ferguson, James, 104, 146, 152, 185, 186, 190

field, 12, 80, 128, 154, 158–166
  critique of, 164–65, 165n. 39., 168
  strategy and tactics, 128, 132–35
Flanding, Malene, 143n. 2.
FLING, 43, 43n. 16.
Forrest Joshua, B, 15n. 11., 40, 41, 42, 46, 47
  and Richard Lobban, 15n. 11., 40, 43
Fortes, Meyer, 50, 76, 98, 98n. 16., 100n. 22., 124, 222
FRELIMO, 180, 180n. 21.
Fula, 40, 40n. 3., 40n. 8., 41n. 11., 182n. 31.
fundamentalism, 69n. 7.
Furley, Oliver, 50n
Furlong, Andrew
  and Karen Evans, 14n. 7.

G
Gable, Eric, 15, 97, 104, 146n. 9.
Galtung, Johan, 23
game theory, 164–66, 164n. 36.
  critique of, 165
Geertz, Clifford, 67n. 4., 68,
Gell, Alfred, 13
generation, 19n. 18., 92–100, 104, 222, 223
  anomie and, 103
  definition of, 93nn. 4, 5.
  the lost, 105
  violence and, 91–92
genetics, 203, 204, 205
geno-globality, 202, 204–5
Giddens, Anthony, 166, 166n. 4., 176
Gilliam, Laura, 120, 120n. 6, 7., 201
globalisation 204, 205
Gluckman, Max, 69–70
Green, Linda, 148n. 11., 153n. 23.
Guattari, Felix
  and Gilles Deleuze, 18, 131, 134
Gullestad. Marianne, 158n
Gulløv, Eva
  and Karen F. Olwig, 92

H
Habermas, Jürgen, 159–60, 238
Habit, 155, 163, 151n, 155n
  contra routine, 154n
habitus, 12, 154, 164n. 37., 174n. 2.
habituation, 154–55, 163
Hage, Ghassan, 103
Hastrup, Kirsten, 152n. 17., 186, 238
Hawthorne, Walter, 40, 41
Henriksen, Thomas K., 3n. 17.

Hertzfelt, Michael, 109
Hinkelammert, Franz J., 109, 185
history, 175, 175nn, 176nn
Honwana, Alcinda, 11, 13, 92
  and Philip de Boeck, 11
horizon, 13, 15, 18, 22, 23, 30–32, 92, 93, 138, 139, 162, 166, 166n. 45., 173, 175, 176n. 11.
  definition of, 31n. 39., 174–75
  prospects and, 207
Husserl, Edmund, 31n. 38., 174
Hyden, Göran, 54n. 55., 104

I
ideology, 67, 67n. 4., 69–70, 79, 83, 121
  Cabralian, 44
  discursive phrase and, 120–22, 121n. 9.
  enemy and, 67–68
  lack of, , 28, 59, 71, 78, 117, 227
  Marxist, 45
  narrative and, 59
  social Darwinst, 44
  war and, 66, 67, 69, 80
illusio, 174
imagination, 163 *see also* social imaginary
  versus the fictive, 31n
Ingold, Tim, 11, 14, 239
  on navigation, 121, 131n. 27.
introspection, 174, 175, 192–202, 230, 236

J
Jackson, Michael, 11, 13, 159, 177n. 13., 190, 238
  on violence, 23, 30
Jensen, Søren B. and Inger Agger, 148n. 12., 206n
Johnson–Hanks, Jennifer, 13
Jones, Gill and Claire Wallace, 96

K
Kaldor, Mary, 27, 28, 68, 91
Kalyvas, Stathis, 28, 29, 91
Kapferer, Bruce, 162
Keller, Edmond J., 180, 180n. 23.
Kemedjio, Cilas, 178, 180
Kleinman, Arthur, 27
  and Joan Kleinman, 91
Koselleck, Reinhart, 30, 31
Kovsted, Jens and Finn Tarp, 46, 47
Krohn-Hansen, Christian, 23

L

Laclau, Ernesto, 167n. 48.
Lambert, Michael C., 178
life chances, 7, 11, 11n. 1., 14–15, 90,
    93–95, 99, 102, 104, 110, 112,
    125, 127, 134, 137, 138, 144, 160,
    192, 196, 208, 222, 231, 235
    affluence and, 93–96
    definition of, 14
    modernity and, 14n. 9.
    war and, 83
    violent, 240
life stage, 105n. 32.
life story, 148–49
    foreground and background, 149
Linde, Charlotte, 148n. 12.
Lindquist, Mats, 189
Lobban, Richard
    and Joshua B. Forrest, 15n. 11., 40
Löfgren, Orvar, 158n
Lopes, Carlos
    and Lars Rudebeck, 180n. 23.
Lorenço-Lindell, Ilda, 17n. 12., 185
Luckmann, Thomas
    and Alfred Schutz, 31, 92, 154, 156
    and Peter L. Berger, 154, 167n. 48.
Lutz, Cathrine, 25, 90
Lyon, Judson M., 46, 182n. 31.
Lyotard, Jean-François, 167n. 48.

M

Mabougunje, Akin, 40
Malinowski, Bronislaw, 207
Malkki, Liisa, 18n. 16., 176, 206n, 207
Malone, David M.
    and Mats Berdal, 28
the Mandinga, 40, 40n. 3., 40n. 8.,
    182n. 31.
the Mandjako, 182n. 31.
mandjuandade, 17, *see also* collegason
Mannheim, Karl, 19, 19n, 92, 93
Mark, Peter, 41
martyrs, 64, 65, 65n, 69
Marxism, 67, 181n. 30., 182, 185n. 40.,
    186, 187
    Cabralian, 178, 180–82
Massumi, Brian, 188
Mattingly, Ceryl, 206n
Mayer, Ernst, 45, 177n. 12., 183n. 35.
Mbembe, Achille, 28, 149, 150, 168,
    173, 186
    critique of, 149n. 14.
McCulloch, Jock, 180, 180n. 22.
Mendy, Peter C., 177n. 13., 182
Meillassoux, Claude, 100n. 22.

Merton, Robert K., 100
Mertz, Elizabeth, 13
methodology, 21–23, 157–58, 194
the MFDC, 26n, 46, 47, 48, 70, 73
Miles, Robert, 204n
the MING, 45n. 22
Mitchell, Clyde J., 107n. 34.
mobilisation, 12, 28, 51, 56, 122, 118,
    126–27, 137–38, 137n. 39., 209,
    231
    ethnicity and, 53, 118
    multi-causal, 117–120
modality, 30, 76
    political, 189, 201, 208
    social, 221, 228, 229
the MPLA, 180, 180n. 21.
Murdoch, Iris, 160
mythico-history, 176
mystification
    critique of, 67n. 5.

N

the Nalu, 40
narrative, 69n. 6., 205, 206, 207
    eschatological, 68
    mythical, 68
    teleological, 65, 67, 68
negritude, 176–81, 177n. 13., 178n.
    17., 180n. 26., 181n. 27., 195
networks, 13, 17–18, 97, 99, 102–3,
    119, 122, 124, 126, 129, 136, 137,
    145, 146, 167. 169, 195 *see also*
    patrimonialism
    ethnicity and, 54, 55
    family, 52
    as Rhizome, 18 n. 15., 110, 111,
Nordstrom, Carolyn, 17n. 14., 174
normality, 149, 149n. 13.

O

O'Brien, Donald C., 105, 136
Okumo, Wafula, 1990
Olwig, Karen F., 92
    and Eva Gulløv, 92
Omi, Michael
    and Howard Winant, 204n

P

the PAIGC, 43, 43n. 16., 180n. 21.
patrimonialism, 106, 194, 198, 231
    definition of, 107
    ethnicity and, 121, 122, 124
    networks and, 48, 83n. 19.,
    105–16, 105n. 32., 118, 121, 122,
    124–26, 136–37, 145, 145n. 46.,
    167, 183, 222, 231

the Papel, 15n. 11, 20n. 22., 40, 42n.
  13., 55, 89n, 220
the PIDE, 44n. 18.
Peters, Krijn
  and Paul Richards, 4
plot, 13, 127, 130, 131, 139, 155, 159,
  163, 166, 169, 179, 207, 224, 236,
  238
Popper, Karl, 176n. 11.
praxis, 11, 17, 18, 22, 23, 28, 154, 186,
  195, 196, 227, 238, 239
  agency and, 158–61
  ethno-political, 53
  the everyday and, 158n
  the social imaginary and, 174
  social navigation and, 12, 13, 14,
    129–37
  youth and, 19, 20, 109
Price, Laurie, 206n
prospection, 174, 175, 205–7, 236
protention, 174

R
racialisation, 201, 202n. 76., 203, 204
reflexivity, 166n. 45
reconciliation, 219
retrospection, 174, 175–92, 201, 206,
  230, 236
Richards, Paul, 4, 1, 27, 28, 108, 239
  barbarism, 25–26, 92
  and Krijn Peters, 4
Riches, David, 23
Ricoeur, Paul, 167n. 48
routinisation, 148, 148n, 149, 150–55,
  163, 153n. 21, 23., 174, 189, 192,
  221
  discourse and, 151
  narrative and, 151
  everyday and, 152
  praxis and, 151
  reflexive, 166–68, 166n. 46.
Rudebeck, Lars, 44n. 19, 46
  and Lopes, 180n. 23.
Rønsbo, Henrik, 24n. 26.

S
Sahlins, Marshall, 109
Sartre, Jean-Paul, 181n. 27.
Schafer, Roy, 148n. 12.
Schmidt, Bettina
  and Ingo W. Schröder, 25, 206
  imaginaries and, 179
  on war, 25n. 29.
Schröder, Ingo W.
  and Bettina Schmidt, 25, 206
  imaginaries and, 179
  on war, 25n. 29.
Schutz, Alfred, 31, 31n. 38.
  and Thomas Luckmann, 31, 92,
    154, 156
Scott, James, 14, 129, 130
sedimentation, 163, 164n. 37., 167,
  167n. 48.
Seekings, Jeremy, 105
Senghor, Leopold, , 178, 178n. 16., 179,
  180
the Serer, 40
Shanklin, Eugenia, 203
Shore, Brad, 164n. 36, 206, 207
situationality, 81, 82, 83, 221, 227,
  229, 230
social becoming, 11–12, 11n. 3., 18n.
  15., 32, 40, 92–104, 100n. 22.,
  109, 111–12, 118, 128, 136, 138,
  144, 152, 160–2, 173, 175, 177,
  208, 235, 237
  history and, 175–77
social Darwinism, 177–78, 181n. 30.,
  184, 191, 204
  development and, 184
  evolutionism and, 177, 177n. 12.
social death, 103–4, 240
social imaginary, 148, 174, 174nn. 1–
  3., 175, 183, 197, 205, 206,
  207–9, 236
  action and, 207
  broken, 187, 188
  habitus and, 174n. 2.
social navigation, 32, 89, 107, 110,
  117, 118, 135, 136, 138, 139, 143,
  144, 147, 149, 154, 159, 173–
  74, 222, 231, 237–9
  definition, 11–15, 128–34, 131n.
    27., 163–66
  failed, 224, 227
  networks and, 109
  plot and, 13
  space and, 104–6
social suffering, 24, 160
  critique of, 24n. 27., 94n. 9.
social terrain, 11, 12, 23, 30–1, 133,
  138
  of action
  domain and, 133
  environment and, 12, 14
  fields and, 163
  routinisation and, 151
  space, 126, 132, 133, 134, 153, 163,
    166, 194
  of commonality, 19

moving, 134, 176n. 11.
of possibility, 30, 70, 93, 94, 96, 134, 174n. 6.
political, 90, 106, 110, 111, 198
smooth, 136, 134n. 28.
social, 19, 90, 92, 95, 105, 105n. 33., 135–37, 146, 164, 176
speed, 13, 153n. 19, 165, 169, 204
Stenman, Åsa
    and Renato Aguilar, 44
strategy, 10, 132–37, 158

T
tactics, 10, 14, 132–37, 158, 226, 227, 236
Tarp, Finn
    and Jens Kovsted, 46, 47
Taussig, Michael, 23, 153, 157
Taylor, Charles, 174,
teleology, 13n. 6, 177n. 12., 183
telos, 13n. 6, 162, 163, 174n. 6., 176
terror, 25
Tilly, Charles, 153
Tin, Hjalte, 26
Tonkin, Elizabeth, 175n. 7.
Turner, Victor, 92

U
the urban-rural continuum, 20, 51
Utas, Mats, 11, 17n. 14.

V
Vaillant, Janet G., 178
Vigh, Henrik, 8, 11, 69n. 6., 92, 175n. 7.
    on violence, 24
violence, 23–24, 24n. 27., 25, 25n. 29., 26, 27, 28, 29, 30, 30n. 36., 118, 120, 138, 159, 160
    as background, 157, 189
    immanence and, 195, 201
    military hierarchy and, 90
    modality and, 30, 228–31, 237
    narrative and, 205–8
    state and, 111
Virilio, Paul, 165
    and John Armitage, 165

W
Waage, Trond, 129
Wallace, Claire
    and Gill Jones, 96
Wallerstein, Immanuel
    and Etienne Balibar, 203n

war, 25–29, 131, 132, 133, 138
    brotherhood and, 71, 76
    identity politics and, 68
    kinship and, 77, 77n
    old and new, 27–29, 68–70, 138
    and forms of violence, 90–91
    small, 25–26
Weber, Max, 111, 152, 153, 153nn. 20, 21.
Werbner, Richard, 19, 206n
Wikan, Unni, 192, 194n. 60.
Willmott, Louis, 66
Winant, Howard
    and Michael Omi, 204n
Whyte, Susan Reynolds, 11
Wulff, Helena, 92, 95

Y
youth, 11, 90–112
    crisis of, 108n. 37.
    cultural moratorium of, 95
    negative reciprocity and, 109
    social moratorium of, 95–112, 135, 147, 160–62, 185, 194, 208, 222, 223, 235
    urban, 17n. 12., 18, 22
    war and, 11, 12, 25–29

www.ingramcontent.com/pod-product-compliance
Lightning Source LLC
Chambersburg PA
CBHW071226080526
44587CB00013BA/1515